SUSANNA DE VRIES is an art historian and lectures for the Continuing Education Department of the University of Queensland. Born in London, she studied art history, literature and history at the Sorbonne in Paris and the University of Madrid.

An Australian citizen since 1975, Susanna has been the recipient of a Churchill Fellowship to study Renaissance art in Italy and has written extensively on European and Australian art and history and on the history of women. She was made a Member of the Order of Australia in 1996 'for services to art and literature'. In 2001 she was awarded a Tyrone Guthrie Fellowship to write in Ireland by the Literature Board of the Australia Council. Her biography of Joice NanKivell Loch, *Blue Ribbons, Bitter Bread: The Life of Joice NanKivell Loch, Australia's Most Decorated Woman*, won the Sligo Non-Fiction prize and was shortlisted for the Queensland Premier's Non-Fiction award.

Susanna is the author of the following books, several of which have won awards: *Historic Brisbane*; *Historic Sydney: The Founding of Australia*; *Pioneer Women, Pioneer Land*; *The Impressionists Revealed*; *Conrad Martens on the 'Beagle' and in Australia*; *Ethel Carrick Fox: Travels and Triumphs of a Post-Impressionist*; *Strength of Spirit: Australian Women 1788–1888*; *Strength of Purpose: Australian Women of Achievement 1888–1950*; (co-author) *Raising Girls and Parenting Girls*; *Blue Ribbons, Bitter Bread: The Life of Joice NanKivell Loch, Australia's Most Decorated Woman*; *The Complete Book of Great Australian Women*; and *Heroic Australian Women in War*. She is currently working on her next book, a biography of Daisy Bates.

GREAT PIONEER
WOMEN OF THE OUTBACK

SUSANNA DE VRIES

HarperCollins*Publishers*

HarperCollins_Publishers_

First published in 2005 by HarperCollins_Publishers_ Pty Limited
ABN 36 009 913 517
A member of the HarperCollins_Publishers_ (Australia) Pty Limited Group
www.harpercollins.com.au

HarperCollins_Publishers_
25 Ryde Road, Pymble, Sydney, NSW 2073, Australia
31 View Road, Glenfield, Auckland 10, New Zealand
77–85 Fulham Palace Road, London W6 8JB, United Kingdom
2 Bloor Street East, 20th Floor, Toronto M4W 1A8, Canada
10 East 53rd Street, New York, NY 10022, USA

National Library of Australia Cataloguing-in-Publication data:

De Vries, Susanna.
    Great pioneer women of the outback.
    Includes index.
    ISBN 0 7322 7663 2.
    1. Women pioneers - Australia - Biography. 2. Pioneers -
    Australia - Biography. I. Title.
994.0922

Cover pictures from left to right: Catherine Langloh Parker, Jeannie Gunn, Myrtle Rose White
Unless otherwise stated, all photographs are from private collections
Maps by Jake de Vries © Pirgos Press
Author picture © Jake de Vries
Cover by Gayna Murphy, Greendot Design
Internal design by Louise McGeachie
Index by Kerry Biram
Typeset in 12/15.5pt Bembo by Helen Beard, ECJ Australia Pty Ltd
Printed and bound in Australia by Griffin Press on 79gsm Bulky Paperback White

6 5 4 3   05 06 07 08

To Dame Elisabeth Murdoch, whose life of outstanding generosity to worthy causes that have touched her heart is an inspiration to all Australian women today.

And in memory of all those women who, like Georgiana Molloy, died in the outback giving birth to children but who lack gravestones or memorials and whose names have been forgotten.

ACKNOWLEDGEMENTS

Thanks are due to Judith Stove, the granddaughter of Emma Withnell; Rosalie Kunoth-Monks, granddaughter of Amelia Kunoth, star of the movie *Jedda* and a worker for Aboriginal rights; the descendants of Dolly Bonson in Darwin; Ron Maunsell, son of Evelyn Maunsell; and to the Archives Service of the Northern Territory and the AITSIS (Australian Institute of Aboriginal and Torres Strait Islander Studies) Library for its help with the names of various Aboriginal groups.

I would also like to thank Stuart Traynor, Senior Interpretive Officer with the Northern Territory Department of Primary Industry, Planning and Environment, for information on Atlanta Bradshaw; Rob McDonald, Librarian at the Arid Zone Research Institute, Alice Springs; Graeme Shaughnessy of the Strehlow Research Centre, Alice Springs; Graeme Powell and Valerie Helson of the Manuscripts Department of the National Library of Australia; Gisela Triesch, German translator; my publishers Helen Littleton and Amruta Slee, and all the staff at HarperCollins who have worked on this book.

Special thanks are due to my husband, Jake de Vries, who read through the manuscript and suggested amendments, scanned old photographs and drew the maps which are such a help in a book of this nature. And, of course, not forgetting my loyal literary agent, Selwa Anthony, whose encouragement and support throughout the publication of this series of five books has been phenomenal. Special thanks go to Terry Underwood, a great contemporary woman of the outback.

Susanna de Vries

Permission to quote from Hector Holthouse's *S'pose I Die*, courtesy Sybil Holthouse. Every effort has been made to contact copyright holders of quoted extracts. The author apologises for those cases where it has been impossible to obtain permission, and invites copyright holders to contact her care of HarperCollins.

CONTENTS

ℓℓ ℓℓ ℓℓ

Terry Underwood is the author of the best-selling autobiographies *In the Middle of Nowhere* and *Riveren, My Home, Our Country*. She and her husband run Riveren, a successful Northern Territory cattle station, 600 kilometres south-west of Katherine.

FOREWORD

by Terry Underwood

A s a modern pioneer woman, I followed my man to the back
of beyond. It was 1963 and I was an eighteen-year-old
trainee nurse at St Vincent's Hospital, Sydney, when I nursed the
patient who broke his back to meet me. After a five-year courtship
by correspondence, the strapping young stockman from way up
north and his city nurse were married in St Mary's Cathedral in
Sydney. We took to the road in a red Bedford truck, loaded with
six tea chests of wedding presents, and drove for days — and days
and days — to our new home, a bough shed on the banks of a dry
creekbed. My journey from the big smoke to one of the most
remote locations in the Northern Territory, Australia, the world,
was just the beginning of a lifetime of unimaginable adventure.

How could there have been any signposts for the new bride?
There wasn't a coil of wire, let alone a fence, no building, no herd
of cattle. The nearest hospital and shops were 600 kilometres away.
But knowing that our love would make all things possible, I
remained undaunted by the challenges of building from scratch our
own cattle station in the middle of nowhere, as indeed it was.

How I empathise with my soul mates of yesteryear. The passage
of time has done little to dissipate many of the parallels in our
lives. The 1960s heralded an era when roadtrains were replacing
drovers, but telephones and televisions were just dreams of the

future. My new homeland, the last frontier, was considered still to be no place for a woman, just as it was two centuries ago, when opportunities and incentives lured new settlers to our undeveloped lands.

Everyone knew that 'ladies' did not go outback. But this was also an era when wives were duty-bound to follow their husbands wherever the men went. Hard-working, ambitious husbands reassured their loyal wives that the primitive conditions and services would improve in time.

With limited resources but unlimited determination, pioneer women carved out an existence for their families. Of necessity they adopted the roles of teacher, cook, seamstress, storekeeper, gardener, hostess, nurse and midwife. They worked beside their men to clear land, erect shelters and fences, as well as tend livestock. With strength of spirit and dogged persistence, they battled the scourges of the bush.

As each of the stories in this book unfolds, Susanna de Vries faithfully documents the effects of droughts and sandstorms, cyclones and floods in lands blanketed by isolation. We feel the blazing sun, scorching temperatures and drying winds that burn deep, as we traverse the kilometres of bush and desert travelled by the women in buggies or on horseback.

We marvel at the unwavering stoicism of our women forebears. Reliable doctors, medical supplies and fresh food were scarce. As mothers mourned their dead babies, they prepared to fight another round. Somehow courage, commitment and endurance became the pillars of their survival.

Interwoven throughout these stories is an aching loneliness. It is not coincidental that tender friendships with Aboriginal women were developed in nearly each case here. Women of different languages and cultures embraced the unspoken reality that they needed each other, thereby exchanging skills and information. With conflict on many fronts, while the original inhabitants of Australia and the new settlers adjusted to each other, the women from both worlds demonstrated that they could live in great harmony.

It has been said by some that colonial life was boring, tiring and repellent. In an era when females too often failed to realise their worth, these women stood proud. They learned to appreciate and interpret the vibrant colours and raw beauty of their rugged inhospitable terrains, the purity of the air and the fascinating plant life. What astonishing historians were our pioneer women as they collated, documented and wrote now priceless journals and stories! Perhaps one of the most cherished is the Australian classic, *We of the Never-Never*, by Jeannie Gunn.

Today the ancient land that has claimed my family remains stunningly beautiful, totally demanding, and still treacherous and unforgiving. The Aboriginal families who have lived and worked beside us at Riveren have demonstrated their unique brand of loyalty and friendship. We all remain inextricably linked by our empathy with the land. Inevitable stumblings at mountainous hurdles and at times sheer unadulterated terror have left us counting more thankfully and frequently than ever all of our blessings.

In the midst of worldwide fear and uncertainty, it has never been more important to pay tribute to the endurance of the land and its people. Complex issues continue to confront us, as the wheels of life spin out of control for too many. At a time when bush people feel abandoned and undervalued, the cry 'go west' has become a hoarse whisper. Yet people everywhere reach out for grass-roots reassurance and inspiration.

Over the decades I have been driven by a very real passion and sense of responsibility to showcase who we are and what we do. Wife, mother, cattlewoman, nurse, cook, teacher, gardener, photographer, author and counsellor are amongst the roles I still juggle each day on our now thriving 3000-square-kilometre cattle station. The vagaries of nature continue to haunt and taunt those who provide vital food to the cities. Yet this city convert remains overwhelmed by the majesty of our timeless country, and the dedication and diverse skills of those who live in harmony with their land, livestock and each other.

I applaud and uphold the legacy of our great pioneer women of the outback. They made it possible for others to follow in their footprints. This superb book rightfully acknowledges their contribution to the development of Australia.

Terry Underwood
Riveren, Northern Territory, 2005

INTRODUCTION

The remarkable stories of ten pioneer women whose lives touch our hearts today illustrate the diversity of women's experiences in many different parts of colonial Australia. These brave women made long, hazardous journeys by ship, buckboard, buggy and horseback to reach remote outback stations.

Travel by horseback, buckboard or buggy was uncomfortable. Pioneer women were forced by Victorian prudery to wear long cumbersome skirts and corsets — uncorseted women being deemed of dubious morality and possibly 'loose women'.

Atlanta Bradshaw was injured when she was thrown from a jolting buggy and fell under the horses' hoofs. She managed to save the baby she was nursing by throwing her to the side. Myrtle Rose White's account of days travelling to take a sick child to hospital was so poignant that the Reverend John Flynn would read it out to audiences from whom he was trying to raise money for the new Flying Doctor Service.

Those who began their journey by steamer or sailing ship faced other hazards: seasickness, stormy weather and shipwreck. Emma Withnell not only saw her family's stock and possessions swept overboard in a storm, but was deposited unceremoniously on an unknown beach along the isolated north-west coast of Western Australia after their ship ran aground.

The women featured in this book can be divided into two categories: those who followed husbands whose work took them temporarily to the outback; and those who went there intending to take up land and settle.

Among the first group was Atlanta Bradshaw, wife of the superintendent of the Alice Springs Telegraph Station, a woman with young children to worry about and no doctor for hundreds of miles. Also in this group were Jeannie Gunn, Evelyn Maunsell and Myrtle White, whose husbands were station managers working on other people's properties.

Women who went to the outback with the idea of taking up their own land and settling permanently included Georgiana Molloy, the Bussell sisters, Emma Withnell and Katie Langloh Parker.

In the outback all these resourceful women faced isolation, danger and tragedy — the classic example being Jeannie Gunn whose husband died from malarial dysentery. For Evelyn Maunsell on Mount Mulgrave Station in Queensland, the isolation was complete during the Big Wet, when the area flooded and became a malaria-ridden hell hole. One of the most emotive stories is that of delicately nurtured Evelyn, living in a manager's house which was little more than a tin shed and nearly dying of malaria while miscarrying when her husband was away at a remote corner of the property.

In the nineteenth century and the early years of the twentieth century, scores of outback children died in childbirth. Georgiana Molloy lost a baby nine days after the birth and later lost a precious toddler by drowning. Each birth and childhood illness in the outback was an anxious and dangerous experience.

Injury, disease and the lack of medical facilities were ever-present. Housing was frequently basic. Floors were often just dirt or ant-bed; walls were usually timber lined with newspaper. Primitive kitchens were separate from the main house with an improvised kerosene tin for a sink, and a wood-fired stove — for which women lacking domestic staff had to chop the wood. There was no glass in the windows, just rough wooden shutters, and no screens to avoid malarial mosquitoes. Summer was hellish, not only due to the heat, but because flies swarmed over eyes and mouths and infected food.

Another terror for these women in a predominantly male world was rape: when husbands were away they feared the swagmen who came to their doors asking for a meal in return for work. Some women were raped or murdered by white swagmen or by Aborigines who bore a grudge against Europeans who had shot their relatives or given them flour laced with strychnine. None of the women featured here recorded a rape (perhaps for reasons of delicacy), but they endured some life-threatening episodes.

Men often remarked that the outback was 'no place for a woman'. This was not only for the amount of drinking and trading of Aboriginal girls that went on, but because there were no proper lavatories. Stockmen and station hands urinated and defecated wherever they wanted. Latrines were open pits with a couple of saplings laid across them to act as a seat; or the lid of a 44-gallon drum with a hole cut in it might be placed across the pit. Most 'dinkum dunnies' lacked a door, so there was scant privacy for women. Victorian prudery prevented most pioneer women writing about this in their journals.

By the 1920s and 1930s, some houses or homesteads had the luxury of a 'thunder box' with a wooden seat and a door that locked — plus a few huge spiders and even a snake or two.

A number of these pioneer women went to live in some of the harshest places on earth and watched creeks and waterholes vanish in the Dry. Myrtle White decried the never-ending dust and sand of north-eastern South Australia. Both she and Katie Langloh Parker endured two of the most severe droughts on record and watched their animals starve and die as crows pecked out their eyes.

Amid this life of hardship, it is heartening to learn that many of these pioneer women developed loving, affectionate relationships with some of their station Aborigines. Atlanta Bradshaw, Katie Langloh Parker and Jeannie Gunn informally fostered part-Aboriginal children, usually girls they saw as neglected or orphaned. They may well have been aware that these girls were at risk from stockmen and telegraph linesmen, who bartered alcohol and tobacco with elders for a bit of 'black velvet'. The father of little Bett-Bett (Dolly Cummings) — Jeannie Gunn's Little Black Princess — for example, was a Scottish telegraph linesman, something Jeannie Gunn never revealed in her writings. In far north Queensland, Mary, a girl from the Coleman River tribe married Albert, who worked for Charlie and Evelyn Maunsell on Mount Mulgrave. Albert and Mary were devoted to Evelyn Maunsell and insisted on staying with her and Charlie even after the family left Mount Mulgrave and started up their own dairy farm on the Darling Downs.

The stories of the European women who pioneered the outback are extraordinary and heartbreaking. In several cases the harshness of the outback triumphed. Drought meant that Myrtle White and Katie Langloh Parker walked away from their properties with nothing to show for decades of hard work. Jeannie Gunn left the Elsey Station grieving and depressed after her husband died of malarial dysentery. Although some women hated and feared Aborigines, it is clear from their writings that Jeannie Gunn, Katie Langloh Parker, Atlanta Bradshaw, Evelyn Maunsell and Emma Withnell took a genuine interest in the welfare of the Aboriginal women they employed and their families, when many settlers were either uninterested or actively taking steps to remove Aborigines from their land.

The voices of these women show us an Australia which was very different from the one we inhabit today — just as articles in the *Bulletin* published in the colonial era reflect a totally different ethos about the land, its Aboriginal inhabitants, the British Empire and the role of women from that of today.

These pioneer women (some of whom had been city dwellers) were all intelligent, adaptable and resourceful. They found themselves keeping a pastoral station, ordering stores, nursing dying men and sick children, planting gardens, sometimes feeding hens, pigs and nursing sick lambs, working harder than they could ever have imagined. They coped bravely with a life that few would put up with today.

With stories from many different areas of Australia placed together for the first time, this book forms an important record for anyone seeking an understanding of Australia's complex past and the day-to-day life of outback women.

CHAPTER 1

Georgiana Molloy
1805 – 1843

Frances ('Fanny') Bussell
1806 – 1881

Elizabeth ('Bessie') Bussell
1812 – ?

Charlotte Cookworthy Bussell
1808 – 1899

She was, of course, far too good for him: but as nobody ever minds having what is too good for them, so he was steady . . . in his pursuit of such a blessing.

JANE AUSTEN, *MANSFIELD PARK*, 1814

FARMING FRESH FIELDS

In the summer of 1829 the engagement was announced between Miss Georgiana Kennedy, eldest daughter of the late Mr David Kennedy and Mrs Mary Kennedy, formerly of Crosby Lodge, Cumberland, and Captain Jack Molloy of the 95th Rifle Regiment. The wedding was to take place later that summer in Scotland before the couple departed for Western Australia.[1]

Georgiana Kennedy resembled one of those pretty girls in white muslin dresses who feature in novels like *Emma, Mansfield Park* and *Pride and Prejudice*; they lose their dowries but still manage to marry the handsome hero. The premature death of Georgiana's father in a hunting accident meant her mother had to sell the family home with its beautiful flower garden and park, dismiss the servants and take her children to live in genteel poverty in the midland town of Rugby, where Georgiana's youngest brother, George Kennedy, attended Rugby School.

In that era, girls were intended to be 'the angels of hearth and home' and sacrifice themselves for their brothers and husbands. Selling handsome Crosby Lodge and moving to a smaller, less expensive house ensured that there was enough money to buy Georgiana's eldest brother, David Dalton Kennedy (known as

Dalton to his family) a commission in the prestigious 95th Regiment, and keep her younger brother at school — but there would be no money left to provide dowries for the daughters.

The shock of their father's death and the move from their ancestral home affected the whole Kennedy family. Georgiana's mother's health deteriorated, Georgiana turned to religion for comfort, and her two younger sisters set about finding husbands to support them.

Georgiana was considered the most attractive of the three Kennedy girls. Her portrait shows a magnolia complexion, large intelligent blue-grey eyes under long lashes, and long fair hair which framed her face with ringlets. She was gentle and reflective by nature, and loved poetry, reading and playing the piano.

The Kennedy sisters, like the Bennett sisters in *Pride and Prejudice*, knew that without dowries they were at a disadvantage in finding husbands. Marriage in that era meant that, while a husband gained a wife and housekeeper, a wife gained lifelong security and status, depending on the husband's income and occupation. Marrying an 'eligible man' was one of women's chief preoccupations, and essential when they were denied access to university or the right to careers or even bank accounts.

Unlike her giddy but mercenary younger sister Mary, Georgiana did not think endlessly of ball gowns, cotillions and weddings. Intelligent but pious, Georgiana was happiest when gardening, playing the piano or reading. She enjoyed 'botanising', which entailed pressing specimens of flowers and seeds between the heavy pages of a large album called a *hortus siccus*, or herbarium, finding their Latin names and noting their habitats and characteristics.

Knowing how unhappy Georgiana was with town life and her reduced circumstances in the cramped little house in Rugby with her quarrelsome sisters, Georgiana's best friend, Helen ('Nellie') Dunlop, invited her to spend time with the Dunlop family at Keppoch House, a Georgian mansion in the south-west of Scotland. Helen Dunlop, her sisters Maggie and Mary, and the rest of the family were Presbyterian followers of Edward Irving, an emotional evangelist whose message warned of the nearness of judgement day. Helen was at the time preparing to marry an evangelical clergyman who was also drawn to Irving.

The era following the Napoleonic Wars was one of high unemployment and those with a strong social conscience, like the Dunlops, were moved to do something to help. They saw doing good works in the Lord's name as a way to counter the evils of slum housing, alcoholism and the lack of schools for the children of the poor and unemployed. The Dunlops of Keppoch House embraced evangelical Christianity with fervour. They involved themselves in setting up 'ragged-schools' for the poor, studied the Bible each day, and soon converted Georgiana to their way of thinking, which required a total commitment to the faith.

Georgiana came to believe that God had a plan for her life. She attended church with the Dunlops twice on Sundays and studied a passage from her Bible each day. She was certain God would make 'the right man' cross her path at the appropriate moment.

Georgiana returned to her mother's home in Rugby, where she tried to impose her religious beliefs on her sisters, causing more conflict between them. With her mind in turmoil, Georgiana wrote to Helen, by now married to the Reverend Robert Story and living in the south-east of Scotland, asking if she could come and stay with her again.

Helen wrote back to say she and Robert would be delighted to have her with them at Rosneath Manse. Georgiana travelled north and found Helen happily living in an attractive old stone manse in a picturesque lakeside vicarage on the Rosneath Peninsula. Here in this tranquil place with its magnificent garden, she felt at peace.

Helen Story and her clergyman husband worked together for the good of their parishioners and seemed utterly content in doing so. Georgiana enjoyed helping Helen visit the sick and the elderly, arranging flowers from the garden in the church, teaching the local children at Sunday school — and making periodic visits to her family.

Georgiana had by this time come to the notice of a handsome man with money, Captain Jack Molloy, hero of Waterloo and senior officer in her brother's regiment. Molloy was reputed to have Royal connections by way of being the illegitimate son of Frederick, Duke of York, one of the many dissolute sons of King George III. What is known for sure is that Jack Molloy had been adopted by a raffish former sea captain who had been court-martialled for cowardice and left penniless. Lending credence to the rumour about his real father being the Duke of York was the fact that Jack's fees for the exclusive Harrow private school and Oxford University had reputedly been paid by lawyers acting on behalf of the Royal family. Molloy also bore a striking resemblance to Frederick 'the military Duke', who had supposedly paid for Jack's commission in the exclusive 95th Regiment.[2]

Jack Molloy was tall and broad-shouldered and more than twice Georgiana's age — a strikingly handsome man who looked far younger than his years. His alleged Royal connections meant he had a certain cachet with women, but he had up till now resisted matrimony. As Captain Molloy and Lieutenant Dalton Kennedy were in the same regiment, it seems likely that this is how he came to meet the Kennedy girls. It may be supposed that Georgiana's sisters, Mary and Elizabeth, did their best to arouse the interest of the captain, simpering and fluttering around him, but it was the much quieter but highly intelligent Georgiana who interested the captain as a potential wife, and he maintained a correspondence with her while he was away with his regiment.

Most of the letters between them have been lost, although a letter from Georgiana dated 11 December 1828 shows them on friendly terms, with Georgiana pleased to hear Captain Molloy's regiment was not travelling to Canada as had been generally believed. By the next year, at the age of forty-eight and with further promotion unlikely, Captain Molloy was planning to forsake military life in favour of opportunities as a civilian.

The economic recession of the post-Napoleonic era had seen great interest in emigration among army and naval officers, who realised their chances of promotion were now very restricted. Captain Molloy had been present at a speech on the advantages of the new colony of Western Australia given by fellow officer Captain James Stirling on his visit to England in 1828. Stirling, who had briefly explored the Swan River area, claimed that Western Australia was highly suitable for settlement and promoted the new colony enthusiastically among army and naval officers.

With the prospect of emigrating to a land where there were few single girls, Jack Molloy badly needed an energetic and resourceful wife and companion. Who better than the beautiful, virtuous Miss Georgiana Kennedy?

Molloy was obviously not put off by any attempts Georgiana might have made to convert him to evangelical Christianity. Her letters discussing religion and its importance to her may indeed have made him keener to make her his wife. Like many men who have led a rakish life, Captain Molloy was probably determined to marry a virgin. It is quite likely that one of Georgiana's attractions for the gallant captain was her purity, sincerity and total innocence of the darker side of life.

In July 1829, he wrote to her proposing marriage and outlining his plans for emigration. Georgiana received Molloy's letter at Rosneath. She must have found 'Handsome Jack', as he was known in his regiment, attractive. For middle-class girls of this period options were limited. They could marry or remain that despised entity a 'spinster' or 'old maid'. But she was a prudent, cautious girl, unsure about the rightness of marrying a man who was not an evangelical Christian.

Doubtless Georgiana spent a long time discussing Jack Molloy's proposal of marriage with Helen. One can imagine Georgiana would have prayed a great deal about what course of action to follow and perhaps read and comforted herself with the redemptive passage in the Bible describing the joy God felt over 'a sinner that repenteth'. The more Georgiana prayed, the more she might have reflected that God intended her to marry Jack Molloy, convert him to her brand of evangelical Christianity and save his soul.

Georgiana was now twenty-four; most girls of her background were married by the time they turned twenty-one. She knew she could not continue to stay forever with Helen Story at Rosneath or with the Dunlop family at Keppoch House. And marriage to Captain Molloy and life in warm, sunny Australia must have seemed far more attractive than either remaining at the house in Rugby or becoming a poorly paid governess.

Georgiana must have convinced herself that she was doing God's will by accepting Captain Molloy and making a new life with him in the Antipodes. She wrote to him accepting his offer, then to her mother telling of her decision to marry and explaining that after a quiet wedding at Rosneath she and her husband would sail ten thousand miles and set up a farming enterprise in Western Australia.

It must have been galling for Georgiana's sisters to think that such an eligible bachelor as Captain Molloy had chosen their high-minded sister in preference to them. Elizabeth had only succeeded in attracting the attentions of a humourless clergyman-turned-librarian; she would soon become the wife of boring Mr Besley, a poorly paid curate.

≈ ≈ ≈

Captain Molloy was risking his entire capital in this emigration venture and placed a great deal of trust in Captain Stirling's support of the Swan River settlement scheme. He had no idea that the promoters of the Swan River Association were financially dubious and that the area was nothing like the fertile, productive land Stirling had promised them.

In 1826 Captain Stirling, accompanied by the government botanist and sixteen men, had explored the Swan River region on a brief seventeen-day expedition. After only a cursory examination, Stirling had declared the area ideal for settlement and spent a good deal of energy promoting the region. In producing this over-optimistic version of the truth, Stirling may have been encouraged by his father-in-law, wealthy James Mangles, whose interests in the East India Company gave him reason to wish to see a trading port established on the west coast of Australia.

Stirling had duties that kept him in Australia until 1828. He then returned to Britain to personally take up his campaign for free settlement of the Swan River region — as he saw it, before the French took possession. Although the British Government was disinclined at first to fund another colony, Stirling allied himself with a group of investors who had formed the Swan River Association to 'market' a settlement scheme, and he continued lobbying.

One of the original investors of the Swan River Association was Thomas Peel, a woolly-headed idealist and a distant relative of the distinguished statesman Sir Robert Peel, whose name was used to lend the scheme a veneer of respectability. When his associates pulled out of the scheme, Peel teamed up with a silent financial backer, a dubious ex-convict from Sydney named Solomon Levey, and several others.[3]

The Association proposed a scheme by which it would attract and convey free settlers to the Swan River in return for extensive first-choice grants there to Peel and his silent backer. Only people with a certain amount of capital, stock and equipment would be eligible for the scheme, and settlers would be allocated land according to the capital they brought to the colony.

By the end of 1828 the government was persuaded of the need to claim Western Australia for the Crown. After rejecting Peel's initial proposals, it agreed to grant him 250,000 acres, once he had 400 settlers in the new colony. Stirling received a grant of 100,000 acres and was appointed commander of the colony. Regulations were drawn up describing the terms for grants.

Publication of the generous terms for land caused much interest in emigration. This was fanned by entrepreneurs who saw commercial opportunities in the mass migration of wealthy middle-class people and their belongings. Leaflets were widely distributed, offering investor-settlers hundreds of acres of land 'free of charge', just as long as they bought their livestock and provisions and sailed on ships chartered by the promoter. Indeed, land around the Swan River had 'every attraction that a Country in the State of Nature can possess and [was] highly suitable for settlement ... Emigrants [would] not have to wage hopeless and ruinous war with interminable forests but be given acres of land ... to which they will be heirs forever'.[4]

Stirling left for Western Australia with a detachment of the 63rd Regiment in February 1829, and arrived there in June. By August, the first free settlers had landed in the new colony, quickly followed by more. By September, with most land still not surveyed nor grants allocated, about 200 migrants were camped on the beach at Fremantle trying to feed families, tend stock and salvage belongings.

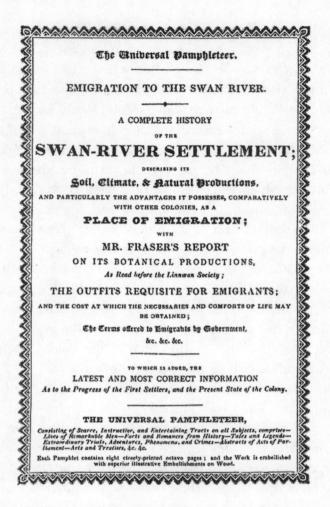

The Universal Pamphleteer.

EMIGRATION TO THE SWAN RIVER.

A COMPLETE HISTORY
OF THE
SWAN-RIVER SETTLEMENT;
DESCRIBING ITS
Soil, Climate, & Natural Productions,
AND PARTICULARLY THE ADVANTAGES IT POSSESSES, COMPARATIVELY
WITH OTHER COLONIES, AS A
PLACE OF EMIGRATION;
WITH
MR. FRASER'S REPORT
ON ITS BOTANICAL PRODUCTIONS,
As Read before the Linnæan Society;
THE OUTFITS REQUISITE FOR EMIGRANTS;
AND THE COST AT WHICH THE NECESSARIES AND COMFORTS OF LIFE MAY
BE OBTAINED;
The Terms offered to Emigrants by Government,
&c. &c. &c.

TO WHICH IS ADDED, THE
LATEST AND MOST CORRECT INFORMATION
As to the Progress of the First Settlers, and the Present State of the Colony.

THE UNIVERSAL PAMPHLETEER,
Consisting of Scarce, Instructive, and Entertaining Tracts on all Subjects, comprising—
Lives of Remarkable Men—Facts and Romances from History—Tales and Legends—
Extraordinary Trials, Adventures, Phenomena, and Crimes—Abstracts of Acts of Par-
liament—Arts and Treatises, &c. &c.
Each Pamphlet contains eight closely-printed octavo pages; and the Work is embellished
with superior illustrative Embellishments on Wood.

Pamphlet setting out the advantages of emigrating to the Swan River settlement.

Around that time in Scotland, Miss Georgiana Kennedy and Captain John Molloy were married at Rosneath by the Reverend Robert Story — on 6 August 1829. At the reception at Rosneath Manse, guests wished the bride and groom good luck and happiness in their new lives as pioneers. Finally, came the sad moment when Georgiana had to say goodbye to Helen Story and Maggie and Mary Dunlop, her dearest friends. Tears flowed as the four young women embraced, knowing they might never see one another again. The colony of Western Australia was ten thousand miles (16,000 kilometres) away.

The newlyweds stopped off at Rugby to see Georgiana's mother, who presented her daughter with seeds of flowers from her garden and bulbs of the tall, white yucca lilies that Georgiana loved.

From Rugby, the couple went to London, where Georgiana went shopping for her new life. She knew that the clothes she took with her to the isolated colony would have to last her for many years. Sensibly, she bought herself plain serviceable dresses which would not show marks and would wash and wear well.

In London, Jack Molloy commissioned a portrait of his new wife. The artist painted her in a low-cut gown, her long blonde hair piled high and falling around her face in fashionable ringlets. This was to be the last time she would ever have her hair styled professionally, although she would not have realised it at the time.

Her adoring husband bought expensive tickets to the opera at Covent Garden and the theatre at Drury Lane. However, the dire poverty Georgiana saw around her in London disturbed her. She was shocked and saddened by the sight of undernourished beggars in the streets, and girls soliciting outside Covent Garden Opera House.

Molloy had already purchased sight unseen two cows, twelve merino sheep, five lambs, twelve pigs, a dozen or so hens and ducks, a dozen fruit trees, two ploughs, two harrows, assorted building tools, horseshoes, and a crate of nails to build their new house and barns. Georgiana now busied herself buying household equipment and supplies. The couple also bought additional provisions for their first months at the Swan River.

Georgiana carefully listed the provisions that were to be loaded in London — whole sides of salt beef and pork, sacks of rice and split peas, twenty-five gallons of vinegar, 600 bottles of wine and 233 gallons of brandy. Jack Molloy was delighted by the capable way his young wife handled their business affairs.

Under the settlement scheme, each settler who sponsored an indentured servant to remain with them for a term of three (or five) years was to receive an additional 200 acres (500 hectares) of land. To receive the maximum land grant possible, and since there were many unemployed men who were happy to volunteer for a chance at a new and better life, Molloy engaged sixteen servants, some married, some single.

For Molloy, who had never handled a plough in his life, the idea of owning hundreds of acres of virgin land seemed an attractive proposition. He had spent a large sum, convinced he would become one of the biggest landowners in the new colony and a man of some importance as the West Australian settlement developed.

Although the Molloys and many other investor-settlers were ready to leave, the departure date of the *Warrior*, the ship that was to transport them was constantly being postponed, as the charterer, Hamilton Semphill, endeavoured to get more passengers for the vessel. With the extended delay and the living in London expensive, the Molloys had to find different accommodation, and they moved to Gosport near Southampton where lodgings were much cheaper. Not only did they need accommodation for themselves and their staff but also barns to store their fruit trees, tools and livestock.

The long delay in sailing also meant that the number of servants engaged by the Molloys dwindled away until the only ones to remain were Captain Molloy's former batman, Elijah Dawson, and his wife, neither of whom had farming experience; Robert Heppingstone and his wife and children; and Staples, an unmarried gardener.

Meanwhile in Gosport, the Molloys met other emigrants, people like themselves, former officers with capital, who were facing redundancy from the army. They, too, were bringing as many servants and animals as possible with them as a way of gaining more land. One of these was Captain Francis Byrne, whose indentured servant George Withnell would become the father-in-law of Emma Withnell (see chapter two).

Finally notice arrived that the ship was to sail and the passengers began loading their possessions. Although Captain Molloy had paid for first-class accommodation, the Molloys were disappointed when they were shown to a dark, cramped cabin underneath the poop deck. This was at least better than steerage class passengers' accommodation, which was located below the deck that held the settlers' horses and cows tethered in their stalls, and hens and roosters clucking away in coops. What no one had foreseen was that excrement and urine from the livestock would drip through the boards to the deck below, causing a terrible reek, while the thud of horses' hoofs drumming on the deck kept many a passenger awake at night.

The *Warrior* sailed on 22 October 1829 with the decks piled high with bales of hay, sacks of dried peas and beans and crates of building materials purchased by the settlers. Initially Georgiana suffered from seasickness, compounded by the fact that she was now in the early stages of pregnancy. The cramped and unsanitary conditions on the ship did little to relieve things, nor did the meals which, even for first-class passengers, were unappetising and in short supply. Semphill had scrimped and loaded insufficient food aboard. In steerage class it was worse; there passengers lived on ship's biscuits and salt beef or pork.

Once she gained her sea legs and ventured out of her cabin, Georgiana made the acquaintance of several families of quality. Among the other passengers was a man Captain Molloy had met six months earlier, a penniless 26-year-old divinity student just down from Oxford. His name was John Garrett Bussell. John had renounced the idea of entering the Anglican Church, but had been unsure of what to do instead. He wanted to marry his sweetheart Sophie Hayward but lacked the capital to do so. Captain Molloy had encouraged John to consider emigrating to Western Australia and given him some leaflets put out by the Swan River Association.

When John's father, the Reverend William Marchant Bussell, died, his widow, Mrs Frances Bussell, had been left with six boys and three girls to raise on a tiny pension. Lack of money meant the Bussell family was forced to move out of their comfortable rectory, and emigration seemed like a suitable solution to their financial problems.

It was agreed that the second boy, William, a medical student, would stay behind in England with his widowed mother and sisters Fanny, Bessie and Mary, and their youngest brother, Lenox, who was only twelve. The other four boys, including John, would emigrate. Once a home was prepared for the family and William had qualified as a doctor, the rest would sail out to Western Australia. It was also agreed that once the Bussell boys were financially secure, John would return to England to marry Sophie Hayward and bring her out to Western Australia.

Aboard the *Warrior,* Molloy made contact with John and his three younger brothers, who were travelling in steerage to save money. He introduced his wife to dark-haired John Bussell and his brothers, nineteen-year-old Charles, sixteen-year-old Alfred and fourteen-year-old Vernon.

Of the four Bussell boys, Charles, who stammered badly, was the most susceptible to feminine charms. He was impressed by the beauty of Mrs Molloy and described her as having 'the air of a lady well born and well bred without having mixed much in the world . . . inclined to the romantic.'[5] He was right: Georgiana's head was still filled with romantic ideas about the joys of pioneering.

The Molloys also met a builder named James Turner, who was a good amateur artist. At the relatively late age of forty-nine (like Jack Molloy), Turner was emigrating with his wife and eight children in search of a better life. Although wealthy, the Turners were of a very different social standing from the Molloys and, despite the awful shipboard conditions, as optimistic as everyone else setting out on the *Warrior.*

Georgiana was excited by the prospect of a new life. She was also very proud of her handsome husband, whom she referred to in a letter to Helen Story as 'dear Molloy'. She was still deeply imbued with a sense of religious mission, sometimes offending her fellow passengers with her efforts to convert them or censure them for impropriety. It soon became apparent that although John Bussell and Georgiana were both religious, they held widely differing views.

Throughout the long and arduous voyage Georgiana insisted that her husband and their servants attended morning and evening prayers. The gallant captain, not known for his religious fervour, seems to have accepted this as the price of a virtuous and dutiful wife.

When finally they arrived at Cape Town, Georgiana and Captain Molloy went ashore so that Georgiana could purchase materials for baby clothes, and Captain Molloy could replace those hens and sheep which had died or been swept overboard in stormy seas.

It was here that the unsuspecting Molloys received their first intimation that the Swan River colony was in trouble.

The British Government had failed to fulfil its promises to the settlers, including Thomas Peel, who had been promised a huge tract of land for his Swan River Association along the southern banks of the Swan River. Instead it had allocated most of the fertile land to those officers and migrants who had arrived earlier in the colony than Peel. Solomon Levey, the official dry goods supplier and hidden promoter of the Swan River Scheme, would never receive his land grant on Cockburn Sound. Unfortunately for Peel's settlers, Levey's ship bearing sacks of flour and other dry goods for members of the Association sank on the way to the Swan River. It was not good news for those coming in their wake.

Georgiana was also advised by friends in Cape Town to have her first child there so she could receive assistance from an experienced doctor or midwife. But her husband was determined that they should continue on to the Swan River, fearing that all good land would be allocated before they arrived. Georgiana agreed with him, something she may have come to regret later.

However, at the time, Georgiana could write to Helen Story from Cape Town, telling her how happy she was in her marriage:

> If [other married friends] are as happy as Jack and I they
> cannot wish for more conjugal affection. Molloy is a dear
> creature and I would not exchange him for ten thousand
> pounds per annum and a mansion in a civilized country.[6]

Further unforeseen delays meant that Georgiana was more than halfway through her pregnancy by the time the *Warrior* eventually sailed from Cape Town bound for the Swan River. On 30 March 1830, five months after leaving England, the *Warrior* arrived at the new colony and anchored off Gage Roads, between the mouth of the Swan River and Rottnest Island.

The following day the ship moved to the area that would eventually become the port of Fremantle. Here the Molloys caught their first sight of what they had been told was a land of milk and honey. They had been expecting a few streets lined with buildings, but all they could see were dense forests reaching down to the water's edge and white sandy beaches stretching away as far as the eye could see. On the beaches were rows of tents surrounded by crates, boxes, furniture and livestock, all jumbled together.

There were no jetties or wharves and no dockworkers to help settlers unload their goods. The arrivals had to load their farm tools, provisions and livestock onto flimsy rafts, and some of their precious cows and hens fell overboard and drowned. The sailors held the settlers to ransom, demanding extra money to carry their belongings ashore from the rafts before throwing the goods higgledy-piggledy on the beach, leaving the settlers to wade ashore as best they could.

The prospect that faced the Molloys and other settlers was described by a young woman named Mary Anne Friend, who accompanied her husband, naval officer, Captain Matthew Friend, to the Swan River in 1830. The Friends had arrived three months before the Molloys with a view to settling but decided not to stay and sailed on to Tasmania. In her journal Mary Anne complained about the blowflies, fleas and mosquitoes at the Swan River. She also noted that polluted water gave the settlers dysentery and that some feared they and their children might eventually starve to death. She wrote that '. . . dread is felt lest there should be a scarcity of provisions. I have never slept in such a miserable place; everything so dirty and such quantities of mosquitoes and fleas'.[7]

An engraved watercolour of the Swan River by Mary Anne Friend shows families camping amid sand dunes with their trunks, grand pianos, bookcases and crates of books, alongside hen coops and tethered calves. It also shows a settler's wife doing her best to cope with the difficulties of cooking over an open fire.

Captain Molloy had been notified that he could select a grant of 12,813 acres based on the considerable sum of money he had outlaid. But this was a hollow promise. The Swan River colony was now in trouble. What little fertile land there was had already been allocated to Captain Stirling's relatives and cronies. Meanwhile hundreds of new settlers were debating whether to go or stay in the hope things would improve. Most of those with money to spare were booking their passage home to Britain.

Engraved watercolour of a camp at the Swan River by Mary Anne Friend (1830).

Some settlers had spent all their money and could no longer continue paying their servants; some of these took to the bottle. Unmarried servant girls, desperate to escape what they feared could be a winter of starvation, had become sailors' molls in the hope of a free passage back to England with their new paramours.

Many of the indentured servants were angry they had been persuaded to travel 16,000 kilometres by sea to face a sandy wilderness. In revenge they did as little as possible for their employers.

For the brief time the Molloys were forced to camp on the beach, Georgiana was excruciatingly uncomfortable. She found their tent hot and stuffy and suffered badly from the heat and infected flea bites. Thousands of fleas lurked in the sand and at night her ankles were black with them. To add to her misery, her stomach was now so swollen she had difficulty walking through the soft sand.

Captain Molloy took careful stock of their situation and how much of his money remained. There was no question of returning. He decided almost immediately that they should make for Perth, the administrative centre of the new colony, where settlers registered before taking up a land grant. With this in mind he paid an exorbitant fee to boatmen to row himself, Georgiana, their servants, and their goods and livestock the twenty-two kilometres upriver to Perth in long boats. Before they even left Fremantle,

Captain Molloy was held to ransom by the greedy boatmen who demanded a premium because the current was so strong.

Yet the journey was a pleasant one — sunlight sparkling on the waters of the river and black swans and pelicans swimming in small bays fringed with reeds. Finally, the Swan widened out into a broad shallow area, and after disembarking the Molloys felt the passage money had been well spent. Perth was a most attractive place. They made their way to St Georges Terrace and asked for Governor Stirling's office. They were directed to a large tent where they learned Captain James Stirling was down south, exploring new land to colonise.

On hearing of Captain Molloy's military credentials and the fact that he had a personal letter of introduction to the Lieutenant Governor, Stirling's staff billeted the Molloys in a series of officers' houses. Mrs Ellen Stirling had remained in Perth, so Georgiana went to leave a calling card on the Governor's wife, as was customary. She found Ellen Stirling to be young, pretty and highly intelligent. The former Miss Ellen Mangles had married James Stirling straight out of the schoolroom and, although quite intrepid, was worried by the situation she now found herself in, like Georgiana expecting her first child in a place with few medical facilities. The two young women discovered they had much in common and had struck up a friendship before Captain Stirling returned from his expedition to the Leschenault and Vasse River estuaries. With his usual optimism, Stirling announced that both areas were suitable for agriculture.

Lieutenant Governor Stirling seemed delighted to meet Captain Molloy. The two men had mutual friends and shared a common background, both being used to command and regarding themselves as aristocrats. Despite the fact that Stirling had made rash promises over land, he was still enthusiastic about the new colony, and Captain Molloy was keen to get whatever advantage he could.

Mrs Stirling told her husband she was impressed with Mrs Molloy's poise and charm under extremely difficult circumstances and this may have been the reason they received a formal invitation to an official reception hosted by the Stirlings.

On the day of the reception, those who had secured invitations

— people with family connections and government posts — unpacked their best clothes from their trunks. The guests assembled in the huge Government tent where refreshments were served. Conversation was polite, stilted and formal. Plans for literary and musical societies, lending libraries and schools were discussed. On a platform draped with the Union Jack, Lieutenant Governor Stirling made a brave but fulsome speech to the new settlers, most of whom knew little or nothing about farming under harsh Australian conditions. He urged those who had not yet taken up their land to sail south to where it was cooler. They would find better land for their crops and livestock there, he said.

Georgiana found Perth beautiful but she suffered badly in the stifling heat. Once she learned the weather would be cooler there, she was keen to go south. Trusting the advice of Stirling, the Molloys, along with the Bussell brothers and James Turner and his family, whom they had remet, prepared to take up land in the south-western corner of the new colony.

Although he had never visited it, Stirling had, on the basis of reports from seal-hunters, sung the praises of the area that he had named Augusta, between Cape Leeuwin and Flinders Bay. All three families would have their main land grant for housing close to the beach between Seine and Flinders Bays and they would be given additional grazing land in the interior.

Since there were no roads to take them south, the settlers agreed to share the costs of chartering a ship. Just like the boatmen on the Swan River, the captain of the transport vessel *Emily Taylor* charged them a highly inflated fare.

By now, due to so many unforeseen expenses, Jack Molloy's funds were dwindling and he feared they would be left penniless. He was very relieved when Governor Stirling appointed him resident magistrate at Augusta for which he would be paid a small but regular salary. James Stirling also agreed to make up the balance of the money owing for the ship's charter from government funds on condition that the ship would transport the government surveyor, Captain Kellam, and a group of British soldiers — and then announced that he would accompany them also.

As soon as the *Emily Taylor* was ready, the Molloys and their servants, the Bussells and Pearce, their indentured servant, the Turner family, a labourer named John Herring, who was paying his own way, and half a dozen soldiers loaded all their goods and livestock aboard the ship. The weather was fine as they sailed down the coast and rounded Cape Leeuwin. They must have felt they were true pioneers, the first white settlers in the largely unknown frontier.

On 2 May 1830 the ship arrived off Flinders Bay. Over the following four days Captain Molloy and the other men made trips from the ship to explore the land. Satisfied, they decided to begin the slow process of disembarking. When Georgiana finally reached shore, she found herself facing a strip of white sandy beach fringed by forests of huge jarrah trees which grew nearly down to the water's edge. Between them was dense undergrowth made up of small shrubs, groundcovers and creepers. For Georgiana, the prospect of giving birth to her first child at such a remote spot with no medical help or midwife on hand must have been a nightmare.

Satisfied or not, having come so far and spent so much money to get to Flinders Bay, the pioneers had little choice but to unload their goods. Once again they pitched their tents on the beach.

Stirling, possibly embarrassed that his enthusiastic reports on the suitability of the Swan River area had caused the settlers to take up hundreds of acres of infertile land, immediately made each of the pioneer families their small land grant at Augusta so they could start building. He allotted James Turner twenty acres; Captain Molloy fifteen acres, the Bussell brothers ten acres and John Herring likewise. Stirling promised that further acreage would become available once the surveying was completed. His promise meant that the indentured servants thought only of breaking their indentures and trying to obtain land of their own.

Before sailing back to Perth, Stirling left Captain Kellam in charge of the survey, which would take over a year to complete, together with a few soldiers commanded by Lieutenant Richard Dawson. Surrounded by vast jarrah forest, the settlers were now completely on their own. To make matters worse the winter rains started to pour down.

The men set about cutting down the jarrah trees to clear the land. It took six men three days of hard work to cut down a single tree, as the timber was so hard. Then they had to grub out the stumps before their primitive ploughs could work the land and prepare it for planting. The settlers had believed such magnificent trees must mean the soil was fertile but this also turned out to be a fallacy.

Heavily pregnant Georgiana confined herself to the area on shore near their tent. In the intervals when the rain ceased, she attempted to stew the wild fowl her husband and their servant Elijah Dawson had shot; the only vegetables available in this wilderness were the split peas they had brought with them in sacks from England.

Once her labour pains came on, Georgiana lay in her leaky tent on the small strip of sandy beach with an umbrella over her bed to keep the rain off her. With no doctor or midwife to help, on 24 May 1830, after twelve hours of agonising labour, Georgiana's first child was born. The only assistance Georgiana received was from Ann Dawson, who probably knew little about midwifery, but was at least able to cut the umbilical cord.

The Molloys named their much-wanted baby Elizabeth Mary after both of Georgiana's sisters. The baby was weak, had difficulty breastfeeding and kept bringing up her food. There was no doctor to consult, and no remedies offered to help the baby keep down her mother's milk.

Despite Georgiana's loving care, nine days after her birth, Elizabeth died, causing intense grief to both of her parents. That evening they buried their baby girl in a tiny plot. Georgiana scattered wild flowers over the grave. Leaving the tiny corpse in the damp soil was the hardest thing poor Georgiana had ever done.

The horror of burying her first child under such harsh circumstances scarred Georgiana

Tents for Travellers & Emigrants

BENJAMIN EDGINGTON,
Marquee, Tent, Rickcloth & Flag Manufacturer

Georgiana Molloy would have given birth to her first child in a tent like this on the beach at Augusta.

deeply. She struggled to find religious meaning and comfort in the tragedy. Possibly she regretted continuing with her husband to Augusta instead of remaining in Cape Town and giving birth there. Years later Georgiana unburdened her still palpable grief to Helen Story. The trigger to do so was the receipt of a letter from Helen informing her that she and her husband, Robert, had also lost a much-wanted baby. Helen's letter seemed to have acted as a catharsis: all Georgiana's pent-up sorrow broke down. Doubtless she shed a few tears as she replied to her dear 'Nellie':

> I was indeed grieved my dear Nellie, to hear of the poor
> infant's demise for your sakes . . . I could truly sympathize
> with you, for language refuses to utter what I experienced
> when mine died in my arms in this dreary land with no
> one but Molloy near me . . . I know I have not made use of
> those afflictions God designed . . . I thought I might have
> had one little bright object left to solace all the hardships
> and privations I endured and have still to go through. [8]

As newly created resident magistrate, Jack Molloy had been empowered by Lieutenant Governor Stirling to provide certain services to the Swan River colony. His area of jurisdiction was Augusta, and later the Vasse and Leschenault, and his official duties included exercising a general superintendence over all the district, acting as justice of the peace when required, inspecting roads, buildings and other works, and receiving and forwarding all requests for land grants. He was to keep salary and cash accounts on the usual forms, transmit them every month, keep an account of all persons residing in his district and render an accurate report on them at the close of each year. [9]

This meant a great deal of paperwork for which Molloy needed Georgiana's help. However grim the conditions, the Molloys could not give up. Having burned his boats and left the army, Captain Molloy still clung grimly to his hopes of a good future if they worked hard enough. A man used to duty and command, he was proud to have been appointed representative of the young Queen Victoria.

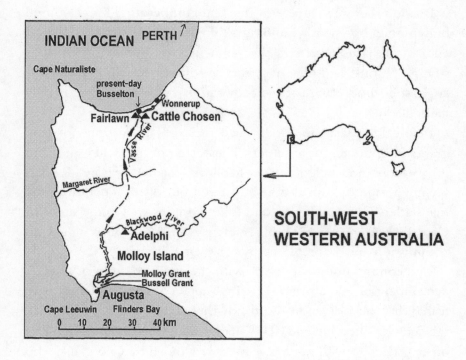

Even though her husband had not yet selected his land, Georgiana set about establishing a garden at Augusta. Near her tent, she sowed the mignonette and other seeds she had brought with her from England, the yucca lily bulbs her mother had given her, and peach stones and grape pips she had brought from Cape Town.

The felled trunks of the jarrah were turned into boards and slowly the Molloys' small timber house took shape. It had a veranda, a separate kitchen and scullery to reduce fire risk, a thatched roof and an outside bathroom with a bucket shower. There were separate living quarters for Elijah and Ann Dawson, the only servants to live with the Molloys. By the end of August 1830, the Molloys were able to camp in the shell of their future home.

The Molloys found fish were plentiful and easy to catch; ducks, herons and swans provided meat. Swan, cockatoo and parrot pies became delicacies, as did kangaroo tail soup. None of the settlers along the Blackwood River went hungry to begin with, but they begrudged the time spent hunting and fishing when there was so much land clearing and building to be done.

It soon became apparent that the pioneering life favoured brawn and those with building skills over those with a classical education. James Turner, the semi-literate builder with four strapping sons, had the necessary resources to build himself a large, solid house with stone foundations, which he patriotically named Albion.

Before long Captain Molloy had received applications for land grants from fifteen more settlers. They came from a wide spectrum of society and included the Molloys' former servant Robert Heppingstone (who had bought himself out of his indenture), and free settlers George Layman and John Cook, as well as the surveyor Captain Kellam and his brother Henry. Kellam soon resigned his commission and was replaced by surveyor Edwards.

The community slowly grew with the arrival by ship of another detachment of soldiers sent there by Captain Stirling, who may have feared that the indigenous Wardandi-Bibbulmun might try to attack the settlers. They included Dr Charles Simmons, a young medical officer, whose arrival must have been welcomed by Georgiana, who was soon pregnant again. But more disappointment was in store, and Georgiana miscarried early in the pregnancy. In a sign of how things would be for her at Augusta, she went into labour alone and unattended, with her husband and Dr Simmons away.

By now the busy Bussell boys had built themselves a small wooden house they named Datchet, after a hamlet in southern England. Around the house they planted beds of potatoes which, to their dismay, would not grow and remained as small as marbles. Only after a disastrous farming season did it become apparent that the soil of Augusta was unsuited to agriculture. Jarrah trees were the only thing that grew well.

On the north of the settlement of Augusta, along the line of what was officially known as Osnaburgh Street, now stood the houses of James Turner, the Bussells and the Molloys, all facing out over Seine Bay, with Flinders Bay and the landing place to their left.

As the Augusta settlement developed, Sunday services were held on the Molloys' veranda. But Georgiana was very lonely, missing her adopted sisters Maggie and Mary Dunlop and Helen Story. She had now lost two babies, and pined for someone at Augusta with whom she could replicate the close female friendships she had enjoyed in Scotland. She wrote to Helen telling her how homesick and isolated she was, and added that the soldiers and their wives were a rowdy, drunken crowd. Their drunkenness was made worse by the fact the men were issued with a daily allowance of rum, supplied by the army quartermaster on the orders of the British Government. Rather than joining in with the drinking parties, both the Molloys and the Bussells spent their evenings separately, reading by candlelight.

Georgiana comforted herself with the thought that the Bussell sisters, when they finally arrived, might bring her the company she craved, and by daydreaming about beautiful gardens, including those of Rosneath Manse and the Dunlops' garden at Keppoch House.

ಳೆ ಳೆ ಳೆ

The Bussell boys had their own problems: they were running short of money. They had been awaiting a transfer from their mother in England, which should have reached them in the final months of 1830. But the Bussells seemed to be dogged by bad luck, and the transfer went astray, leaving the boys practically penniless. Exacerbating their situation, because the crops had delivered a poor yield, food had to be ordered in quantity and sent down from Perth by cutter.

With their money running low and anxious about their future, John Bussell set about making exploratory trips along the Blackwood River. He reached the conclusion that they would do better further up the Blackwood on a promontory he named the Adelphi, which was surrounded on three sides by water rendering it safer from attack by the Wardandi–Bibbulmun. The Bussells applied for and received an additional land grant there.

Eventually the transfer of money did arrive but it was an anxious time for the Bussells, during which Jack Molloy was both kind and generous to them. As he had been the one to persuade John Bussell to emigrate, possibly the captain felt some responsibility for them. He lent them seed corn to plant and agreed to temporarily employ their manservant Pearce, which would mean one less mouth for the Bussells to feed.

He also tried to find Charles a government job, so they would at least have one salary coming in, and persuaded Lieutenant Governor Stirling to let Charles Bussell act as government storekeeper at Augusta. By September 1831 Charles was earning a salary and the Bussells could afford to take Pearce back so he could help them finish the two small houses they were building for their mother and sisters, to be ready when they arrived.

Possibly anxiety over money may have caused differences of opinion between the Molloys and the Bussells, but relations between the two families began to deteriorate from about this time. The Bussell boys and Georgiana differed sharply in their approach to the Wardandi, a clan of the large Bibbulmun-speaking group whose territory stretched south from Perth down as far as Flinders and Geographe Bay.

When the British newcomers had first waded ashore and pitched their tents at Augusta, it was the beginning of the wet season and the Wardandi had moved inland to avoid the rain. When they returned in the drier months and found strangers on their land, the Wardandi interpreted the white-skinned men and women as ghosts of their long-dead ancestors whom they referred to as *djanga*. The trusting Wardandi hospitably showed the new arrivals springs of fresh water. They also indicated that there were grassy plains further north on the Vasse River which flowed into another bay (Geographe Bay), larger than the one at Augusta. The Wardandi's tribal lands, made rich in supplies of food through their fire-stick farming methods, seemed abundant and they had no qualms about sharing their game and fish.

For their part, with very different ideas about property and ownership, most of the settlers saw the Aboriginal people as a threat to their wealth creation and certainly not with rights of their own. The hardworking Bussell boys were dismissive of the Wardandi because to their eyes they did not farm or improve the land.

In contrast, Georgiana, who was principally concerned with laying out and planting the garden around her house, came to admire the Wardandi for their knowledge about the native plants she was just beginning to appreciate, and she attempted to learn a few words of their language so she could converse with them.

In early 1831, Georgiana discovered she was pregnant for the third time. She decided to rest as much as possible this time, determined not to lose this baby. With the Heppingstones, the best of the servants whom the Molloys had brought out with them, gone to take up their own land, Jack Molloy was left with only Staples the gardener and Elijah Dawson to perform the farm work. Georgiana had the increasingly unwilling Ann Dawson, who was also pregnant, to help her with their primitive arrangements for washing, cooking and carting water from the nearby Blackwood River. House cleaning seemed endless and the floors were often coated with fine sand as they were so near the beach.

Jack Molloy was busy morning, noon and night, either supervising the increasingly wider area he was responsible for or visiting the administration in Perth to meet some official request or other. Georgiana had to double as housewife and resident magistrate's wife, and in his absence to attend some of his duties. Her husband's returns home were occasions for great rejoicing.

On 2 November 1831, Governor and Mrs Stirling arrived for an overnight stay at Augusta. Despite the fact that Georgiana was only a week away from giving birth, it seemed she managed to prepare an excellent dinner for the Stirlings and provided a host of delicacies, duck and a variety of fish. The Stirlings greatly admired the large garden Georgiana had designed and planted.

For Georgiana the educated conversation of Ellen Stirling must have been a pleasure. It is likely that the festive meal took place by candlelight rather than in the gloom of the evil-smelling slush lamps they normally used. Conversation around the dinner table presumably ranged over subjects such as whether Perth would go ahead as the capital of the new colony, the planned balls and other entertainments of the settlers, and the exciting overall prospects for the new settlers. At some stage in the visit Georgiana must have mentioned to Ellen Stirling that she was collecting seeds from native plants, writing down details of their habitat, flowering season and the names by which the Wardandi-Bibbulmun called them.

Possibly at this juncture, Ellen Stirling may have mentioned her bachelor cousin, Captain James Mangles, a retired naval officer and a fellow of the prestigious Royal Geographical and Royal Societies. Mangles was passionately keen in cataloguing rare plants and collecting their seeds. He had made a trip out to Western Australia earlier that year and taken home with him the seeds of some native plants. Possibly Ellen Stirling said nothing to Georgiana but thought to herself that she would write and tell her cousin he had at Augusta a fellow enthusiast for his 'botanising' studies. In any case, it would be a letter from Ellen Stirling's cousin, Captain Mangles, which would alter Georgiana's life considerably.

The Stirlings stayed overnight in a vacant house and then with their entourage boarded their ship and headed north to Perth. Five days after the Stirlings departed, on 7 November 1831, Georgiana gave birth to a strong, healthy girl. They named her Sabina Dunlop Molloy, after Georgiana's best friends, the Dunlops of Keppoch House.

In view of the lack of medical help at Augusta, it was fortunate that Sabina turned out to be a healthy and contented baby. Georgiana found she greatly enjoyed the business of mothering, but with a baby to breastfeed and care for and none of the labour-saving devices we take for granted today, housework and mothering were time-consuming and tiring.

There was mending, sewing, carting water, boiling it up, washing, cleaning, cooking and salting down of meat, as well as hours of food preparation, with no frozen or tinned foods to rely on. It was the task of every housewife to make slush lamps or candles to light the house. Georgiana also had to run the dairy and look after their farm whenever her husband was away. All this work she had never imagined herself doing with a child to raise, let alone under such primitive conditions. By now Ann Dawson had turned sulky, did as little work as possible and dreamed only of the day when she and her husband, Elijah, would be free of their indentures and could work their own land.

In November 1831, John Bussell accompanied surveyor Edwards on an overland expedition northwards to Geographe Bay. There they found the 'fine grassy plains' the Wardandi had indicated, and local people who kindly showed them good waterholes. The Vasse River area seemed far better suited to agriculture than the heavily timbered country around Augusta and the Blackwood River.

John Bussell wrote a long report on their expedition. He handed it to Captain Molloy, who invited John to the house to discuss making an application to exchange part of their extensive land grants at Augusta for better grazing land at the Vasse. It was remarkable that these two men were considering moving their operations after expending such huge efforts to settle at Augusta. Government Resident Magistrate Molloy had just named the streets of Augusta,[10] and taken out a further land grant on a site he called Molloy Island in the Blackwood River.

But the Augusta settlement was far from flourishing. By February 1832, supplies of flour in the government store were running short and the price of flour had soared in Perth as well. The settlers were eating wild spinach, parrot pie and pigweed stew, and shooting kangaroos to survive. Finally, at the end of May, a transport ship called the *Sulphur* arrived, bringing the hungry settlers fresh supplies at reasonable prices.

With Jack Molloy's eyes also now resting firmly on the Vasse, the following November he sailed for Perth to apply for over 12,000 acres of land there for himself, leaving Georgiana and Sabina to fend for themselves yet again. Feeling depressed, lonely and overworked so near Christmas, Georgiana wrote a long and revealing letter to Maggie Dunlop. She told of her delight in little Sabina but indicated strained relations with their neighbours over a wandering cow that the Bussells had shot:

> This life is too much both for dear Molloy and myself . . .
> I have all the clothes to put away from the wash; a baby
> to put to bed; make tea and drink it without milk as they
> shot our cow for trespass; read prayers and go to bed
> besides sending off this tableful of letters.

She discussed their prospects, but obviously found it hard to see beyond the workload she was burdened with. She also confided in Maggie about things which she could not tell anyone else at Augusta where she had to keep up appearances as resident magistrate's wife, representative of the Queen and Governor in the area.

She told Maggie how:

> Molloy again went last Monday to view his large grant of land at the Vasse — a most pleasing country and answering with truth to the description given of its park-like appearance, with long waving grass, and abounding also in kangaroos.
>
> In the interim a vessel has been in, which has given me not only my own, but Jack's letters to write — which I am unable to do — as at the beginning of the week I was confined to my bed from over-exertion . . . I must unbosom myself to you, my dear girl . . . I am, of necessity, my own nursery-maid . . . I told you how it would be: I should have to take in washing and Jack carry home the clean clothes in a swill [a tub to hold pig-food]. The last of this has not yet happened, but between ourselves, dear Maggie, the first is no uncommon occurrence . . .
>
> I wish I had you here to help me. What golden dreams we used to have about your coming to stay with me! How would you like to be three years in a place without a female of your own rank to speak to or be with you whatever happened?

At one point in her letter Georgiana, once acknowledged as the prettiest girl in Cumberland, jokingly refers to herself as 'poor worn-out Mrs Molloy'. Missing Maggie, Mary and Helen very much, she signed the letter to Maggie 'With unabated affection from your sincerely attached sister'.[11]

***

The settlers hoped that in 1833 life would be easier. The Bussell boys looked forward to the arrival of two of their sisters early in the year.

They were a close-knit family and perhaps they also expected that the women would make their domestic situation less messy and chaotic.

On 26 January 1833, 26-year-old Frances ('Fanny'), only one year younger than Georgiana, and high-spirited 20-year-old Elizabeth ('Bessie') Bussell arrived in Perth, with their youngest brother, Lenox, their former nurse, Phoebe Bower, and another servant, Emma Mould. The girls spent six happy weeks in Perth being entertained left, right and centre.

Like their brothers, the Bussell girls had boundless stores of energy. There were at that time few attractive single women in Perth, so the girls were deluged with invitations, including several to functions at Government House. Had the sisters stayed in Perth they would doubtless have received proposals of marriage. But the Bussell girls had a strong sense of family and were determined to sail south to Augusta and keep house for their bachelor brothers.

Directly he heard his sisters had arrived, John boarded the colonial schooner *Ellen* in Flinders Bay and sailed north to Perth, to escort his sisters down the coast.

Georgiana was excited at the thought of some female company at last. She had insisted that the girls should not begin life at Augusta in the rough bachelor quarters of their brothers and went to great pains to prepare for them the empty house of Lieutenant Dawson, which was often used as a guest house.

Fanny, a great chatterbox, and the spirited, vivacious Bessie were surprised by John's bushwhacker appearance when he arrived in Perth wearing 'canvas trousers made by his own hands . . . hair and beard both long . . . and moustaches enough to give a bandit look'.[12]

John and his sisters left Perth aboard the *Cygnet* in mid-April, arriving at Augusta on 20 April 1833. The following day Fanny wrote to her mother and told her that Captain Rolleston, the *Cygnet*'s captain, had been very attentive and they had dined with him frequently. Their trunks had arrived in good order, and both she and Bessie were well and thrilled to see their brothers, 'our own darlings', after such a long and anxious separation.

Their ship had landed them at sunset about a kilometre away from the three most important houses in Augusta — those of the

Molloys, the Bussells and the Turners — and Fanny described how they had followed a winding footpath lined by peppermint trees and with the unfamiliar scent of wild rosemary and pelargoniums. The path was bordered by low sandhills which muffled the sound of the waves, and the sky slowly faded from red to pink and pale lemon. They passed the farm labourers' allotments, with their little wooden cottages, until they reached the Blackwood River.

John and Alfred Bussell carried the luggage and Fanny was escorted by the current surgeon, Mr Green, although she had been warned by John that Mr Green was still yearning unrequitedly after Ann Turner, the daughter of James Turner, who had married the previous year. It was almost dark by now but Fanny saw that 'the river was broad and beautiful and the country more richly wooded than the English imagination can conceive'. She continued:

> Mrs Molloy came out to receive us with her little Sabina
> in her arms, looking so youthful and interesting. Her
> home is very comfortable and she is so active. We
> are to stay here for a few days, but as she has not
> accommodation for us she has fitted up one of Mr
> Dawson's houses so nicely, a French bed and all sorts of
> land comforts. A vase of sweet mignonette upon the table
> . . . and a large wood fire blazing on the hearth cast a
> cheerful light around. We spent a very pleasant evening,
> dear Charley [brother Charles] and Mr Green being of
> the party, though I must say that all [word indecipherable]
> with respect to him are futile, so let there be no
> speculations.[13]

(Clearly Mrs Bussell was as keen as Georgiana's mother had been to marry off her daughters.)

Georgiana did not describe the Bussell sisters in her letters but we know from a watercolour made of the Bussell family before they left for Australia that the girls were slim and attractive with dark curly hair and dark eyes.

Fanny and Bessie were too excited to sleep and walked over to see the boys' house. They were shocked to see how thin their brothers had become through working hard to establish themselves on the land and living off the very simple things they could cook for themselves. They found their brothers had only had very rudimentary help from Pearce. Their little wooden house was filthy and 'resembled a bandits' cave' with hammocks suspended from the ceiling. Casks and barrels of all description lay around. They found young Alfred and Vernon eating rashers of salt pork and pancakes without the help of knives, plates or forks. Dirty clothes and dishes were piled everywhere.

The brothers and sisters embraced, laughed and talked, fired off questions and hardly listened to the answers. By now the moon was rising, far larger than in the northern hemisphere, so they all went for a walk on the beach. Fanny wrote to her mother that she was thrilled 'by the wildness and grandeur' of their new surroundings.

The following day the Bussell sisters set to with a will to clean up the mess. It was even worse than the girls had thought. Fleas and bugs infested the boys' bedding. Washing dirty clothes was a difficult job without running water, and they had to cart buckets of water to the kitchen and heat it on the wood-fired stove. Fanny and Bessie could manage cleaning very well but had to learn from Phoebe Bower, who was too old to do heavy work, exactly how to bake bread and starch and iron clothes.

They cleaned up the mess the boys were living in but the sheer amount of housework would eventually get Fanny down. After a few weeks she burst into tears thinking that without any running water washday would last from 'Monday till Saturday'.

The Bussell girls, daughters from a vicarage, now had to learn a complete new range of skills — how to ride horses, groom them and harness them to the plough and how to row the boat which their brothers had constructed to cross the river. But the girls were young, strong and healthy and found they loved outdoor life. They were proud of the way they tackled the vegetable garden and planted neat rows of potatoes and other vegetables, and looked forward to harvesting them.

Though she found them pleasant enough, Georgiana did not forge the close friendships she hoped she would with the Bussell sisters. Besides the fact that they were busy attending to their brothers and the farm, it appears Georgiana had little in common with them.

Georgiana enjoyed playing and listening to classical music on the piano. Fanny also played the piano but preferred popular songs, while Bessie loved books but had little ear for music. Georgiana enjoyed cultivating flowers and reading poetry and religious tracts. The Bussell girls were far less intellectual. They enjoyed books but had very different tastes in literature from Georgiana.

Fanny and Bessie were to prove better suited to outback life than Georgiana. By now Pearce had served his indenture and had had enough of pioneering and running short of rations. When another whaling ship came into Flinders Bay he sought employment as a deckhand and departed on it. The girls pitched in to do farm chores as well as housework, and even helped their brothers build post and rail fences. Their good health and high spirits meant they could work all day from dawn to dusk, sharing the housekeeping, the butter and cheese-making, feeding the turkeys, ducks and hens, and working in the large vegetable garden. Their many cheerful hands making light work must have made the loneliness Georgiana and little Sabina suffered even more difficult to bear.

In May, however, the household split up. Bessie went upriver with Emma Mould and many of the household goods to live at the little wooden cottage the boys had built at the Adelphi. John, Vernon, Alfred and Lenox were often at the Vasse. Chatterbox Fanny stayed behind to look after Charles at Augusta.

⁂ ⁂ ⁂

For all her hardship and loneliness, Georgiana was beginning to appreciate her new surroundings. A few months before her bitter letter to Maggie Dunlop, she had written to her sister Elizabeth not only of the 'heavenly clime' she was now living in, but in some detail about the brightly coloured birds that surrounded her and the flowers and leaves of the native plants she had observed. Georgiana loved the warmth and the sunlight and described in a letter to Helen Story how she would sit on her veranda surrounded by the sweet scents of her flowers and shrubs.

While she was most interested in her flowers, Georgiana also turned her expertise to the Molloys' crops. Their first wheat crop at

Georgiana Molloy and the Bussell women would have used irons like these. Those on the top row were heated on the stove. Those on the lower shelf were filled with hot coals. None had any temperature control.

Augusta had been ruined by the fungal disease known as rust. To avoid this happening again, before their second crop was sown in 1833, Georgiana organised for the gardener, Staples, to soak all their seed corn in salt water then dry it off. The result in June was the best harvest at Augusta.

That year, due to a fire at Kitty Ludlow's home, Georgiana was able to obtain the resident services of crippled Kitty Ludlow who also suffered from epilepsy. Kitty was the wife of a labourer who had an alcohol problem. Although her help was limited, Kitty was able to provide baby-sitting assistance and do dressmaking for Georgiana. She was also company for Georgiana when Jack Molloy was away.

Each afternoon Georgiana left Sabina in Kitty Ludlow's charge and the little girl would sit on Kitty's lap by the fireplace. One day, a mud-brick wall beside the fireplace collapsed following a prolonged rainstorm. Fortunately Sabina, who was about to run to the fireplace where Kitty was sitting, had instead stayed with her mother. Upset but relieved, Georgiana suffered the realisation that she could have lost another beloved child if the wall had fallen on Sabina.

Georgiana was now pregnant for the fourth time and grateful for the help Kitty could provide, but it was not to last. Kitty became increasingly subject to epileptic fits. She foamed at the mouth, rolled on the floor and her weakening condition alarmed and distressed Georgiana. Each fit left her worse than before. Kitty's mental processes gradually clouded and her physical condition weakened until she was condemned to Molloy Island where she died early in 1834, raving and insane.

As was so often the case, Captain Molloy was away and it fell to Georgiana to organise the burial of Kitty's decomposing body one night with a couple of farm labourers present. Burning torches on sticks illuminated the pathetic scene. Georgiana read the burial service aloud in a clear steady voice. The torchlight in the darkness of the surrounding bush accentuated the remoteness of their tiny outback settlement and the deep silence that surrounded them.

❧ ❧ ❧

The story of the first European settlers at Augusta and the Vasse is one of determination, resourcefulness and resilience to the blows of fate. Unfortunately for the Bussells, who continued to be dogged by bad luck, on 5 November 1833 their thatched cottage at the Adelphi caught fire. 'The kitchen chimney was blazing fiercely and the ridge-post on fire. It was no use to try water,' wrote Bessie later that night to Fanny, explaining what had happened.

Risking her own life, Bessie had remained inside the blazing building and threw everything she could lay hands on out of the windows before fire destroyed it. She wrote to reassure Fanny that she had managed to save her precious books, diaries and clothes, but her underclothes and corsets (which 'nice' girls of the period wore even in the heat) and her boots, all irreplaceable in the outback, had been lost.

> Ally [Alfred] and Len [Lenox] pulled out the piano, tables and chairs. I ran to look after my crockery . . . I was endowed with unnatural strength, took your [Fanny's] mattress, my own and your bedding and rushed out of the room . . . Ally got into the loft through the ceiling and . . . threw down the boxes helter skelter. All [the] needles, tapes, bonnets, ribbons, pins are lost. All your shoes are safe. I have not a pair left, nor a bonnet . . . Len saved the medicine chest . . . All the Bibles and the Byron are safe . . . The piano got very hot after it was out. The music [is] safe, desks and workbox . . . The looking glasses are safe. I wish it was daylight. It is the longest night I ever knew.[14]

After the fire destroyed their thatched cottage, the Bussells left the charred ruins and removed most of their remaining possessions by boat. They rowed back to join Fanny and Charles at Datchet, still expecting their mother and sister Mary to join them from England later that year. Their misfortune provided one pleasure for Georgiana — they lent her their piano, one of the few generous acts Georgiana ever received from the Bussells.

⚘ ⚘ ⚘

The local Wardandi women admired Sabina's blonde hair and chubby features and Georgiana sometimes let Sabina play with their children. However, Georgiana still faced the occasional problem with the Wardandi. As the settlers continued to shoot the wallabies and kangaroos the Wardandi relied on for food, tensions rose about supplies. Early in February 1834, in Captain Molloy's absence twenty Bibbulmun-speaking people from further south arrived at the Molloys' home. The men were naked, except for cloaks of kangaroo skin, and armed with spears and waddies, and they aggressively demanded potatoes from Georgiana's garden.

Georgiana described in a letter to Helen Story how she had been too afraid to show her fear. Masking it well, she smiled brightly at them as though she did not have a care in the world:

> The tall man, perceiving that I was not intimidated, cut
> the air close to my head with his wallabee stick. I stood it
> all, taking it as play but I heard the whizzing stick and
> expected Dawson, the child or I should be struck. He then
> . . . drew a piece of broken glass bottle close to my cheek.
> I smiled and trembled, and said 'Dirilia' or glass, meaning
> that I knew they used it for sharpening their spears.[15] He
> rubbed his fore-finger in his hair until it was covered with
> the fat and red earth with which they rub themselves and
> poked it right into my face. Yarner, a great thief, pointed to
> the potatoes and wanted Dawson to give him some.[16]

Elijah Dawson refused to give away their precious supply of potatoes. The Aborigines were clearly annoyed they had not been given any and refused to leave. The same man who had threatened Georgiana took hold of little Sabina by the leg and seemed about to drag her away with them. Georgiana was terrified for her daughter but realised it was safer if she continued to hide her fear. She had learned a little of the Bibbulmun language and said very firmly, '*Ben-o-wai*' (Be gone).

Georgiana then tried to retreat, but the tall man turned and followed her. She knew that by now the Bibbulmun were afraid of firearms, and while Elijah Dawson drew some water for them, Georgiana managed to locate her husband's pistol. Without saying a word she laid it on a table 'where they could see it'. This had the desired effect of making the men leave.

They moved to the next house to try to intimidate the Bussell sisters into giving them potatoes, since they knew the Bussell boys were away at the Vasse River.

Fanny and Bessie had planted their precious potatoes with their own hands and refused to give any away. Georgiana had meanwhile sent Elijah Dawson over to Datchet. When they saw him, the Bibbulmun took a few salt cellars (so they could use the glass to tip their spears) and departed. Fanny and Bessie quickly reported the theft to Georgiana, who sent soldiers after them. The salt cellars were retrieved under threat of bayonet and returned to the Bussells.

Two days later the same Wardandi–Bibbulmun returned with smiles and a freshly killed wallaby which they gave to Georgiana and the Bussell sisters as a peace offering.

✎ ✎ ✎

On 13 April 1834, John Bussell and his younger brothers loaded everything they could in the way of farm equipment aboard the schooner *Ellen* at Flinders Bay, which was to sail them round to Geographe Bay and a new life at the Vasse. The boys left Fanny and Bessie at Augusta, and took Phoebe Bower with them to do the housekeeping and, by agreement with Captain Molloy, Elijah Dawson accompanied them to help with ploughing.

John had planned things so a second shipment of valuable household and farm goods from Perth would arrive at Geographe

Bay while they were there. Many of these were irreplaceable in Western Australia. They included goods Mrs Bussell had sent out from England to Perth as she packed up their belongings in preparation for her own long trip out. She had then organised for the cargo, once it arrived at Fremantle, to be loaded onto the *Cumberland*, a coastal trader ship bound for Augusta. The leaky old vessel sank off the West Australian coast without trace in a storm, drowning several crew members. Under this further blow the family now had to start pioneering at the Vasse, living in the same minimal way they had done at Augusta.

Georgiana gladly gave the Bussells certain items to compensate for the loss of their household goods aboard the *Cumberland*. However, she was disappointed that the Bussells seemed unwilling to give anything in return for all the help she and her husband had provided. She commented that she found the Bussells 'close-fisted' and mean. Perhaps the damage had been done when they had first met and the Molloys had travelled in first class and the Bussell boys in steerage class — creating the impression that the Molloys were wealthy and could afford to be generous, and that the Bussells had no need to give anything in return. (Ironically enough, because the pioneering life was easier with a large and healthy family, and a sound sense for grasping opportunity, and because Captain Molloy expended much of his time and energy on government business in return for a minute salary, the Bussells would eventually become far wealthier than the Molloys.)

Georgiana puzzled over the Bussells' meanness. Like them she had once been affluent but had lost money and status after her father died. But she had a warm and generous nature and would not allow genteel poverty to make her any less generous to those in need.

ﬖ ﬖ ﬖ

From the first moment in 1834 when young Mary Bussell arrived with her mother in Perth she disliked colonial life. Mary had been fretting over a failed love affair in England and was also resentful that Patrick Taylor, a tall, dour Scot she had met on board the *James*

Pattison on the voyage to Perth, was not regarded as 'eligible' by her mother, who did her best to discourage their shipboard romance.

Mary Bussell and her mother finally arrived at Augusta aboard the *Ellen*. Mary, annoyed at having been made to leave Perth, found that she hated the isolation of Augusta, and the constant round of hard physical work, and complained incessantly to anyone who would listen.

Georgiana was unimpressed by the Bussell family matriarch, thinking Mrs Bussell foolish to have consigned the family's goods to such an ancient and unseaworthy vessel as the *Cumberland*. No wonder it had sunk on the way to Augusta. She was also upset that her generous loans of replacement items and her offers of friendship had met with so little response from the Bussells. She described in a letter to her mother how the Bussells accepted everything she gave or loaned them and added 'you will hardly believe they have made no return; nor have Molloy or myself ever broken their bread'. Disillusioned by her neighbours' apparent parsimony and lack of gratitude, Georgiana described the Bussells 'as perfectly selfish and inconsiderate as any people I ever knew', a judgment which seems to have been borne out by subsequent events.[17]

While his brothers toiled at the Vasse, Charles Bussell, still earning good money as storekeeper, remained in Augusta with Bessie, Fanny, his mother and Mary, along with the servant Emma Mould. In spite of his pronounced stammer Charles managed to seduce Emma, and after discovering she was pregnant Emma begged him to marry her. But Charles Bussell saw himself as a gentleman and never had any intention of marrying a servant. He denied he was the father. Emma had previously announced she was pregnant to another settler which turned out to be false. This time it was true. The Bussell family was extremely unsympathetic and blamed Emma for her plight. Since there were no welfare payments for single mothers, Emma's position was bleak.

Mrs Bussell, the clergyman's widow, showing a distinct lack of Christian charity, called Emma 'a most abandoned creature' who 'had violated every commandment'. The bossy matriarch turned penniless Emma out of the house when she was eight months pregnant and had nowhere else to go.

In the end it was Georgiana who showed true Christian charity by taking in the pregnant Emma Mould and helping her give birth to a baby whom Emma named Henry John. Although Charles Bussell continued to deny paternity, oddly enough the family demanded to keep Emma's baby. As soon as she recovered from the birth, however, Emma moved away to Perth where she got a job in a private house, eventually marrying a settler named Thomas Sweetman.

⪼ ⪼ ⪼

The arrival of Mary Bussell and her dragon of a mother in Augusta in October 1834 came only four months after Georgiana herself gave birth to another daughter, whom she named Mary Dorothea. Like her sister Sabina, Mary was a healthy, robust baby, and thrived in her mother's care.

Georgiana delighted in her new child, but she was soon tragically reminded of her isolation and distance from her family in England. In September she received a letter with the tragic news that her sister Elizabeth Besley had died.

News of her sister's premature death shocked evangelical Georgiana deeply, and her religious nature worried that Elizabeth, although married to an Anglican curate, had not been sufficiently pious. She wrote to Helen Story grieving for Elizabeth and the state of her soul, and hoping her unmarried sister Mary and her mother would change their ways before her mother died as well.

With two children to care for, Georgiana was also finding that she was no longer as strong as she had been. Carrying a heavy baby around made her lower back ache and she had sleepless nights when Mary Dorothea suffered teething problems. However, she managed to retain some sense of humour and wrote of her rapid weight loss that 'I have every day expected to see some bone poking through my epidermis'.[18]

While Georgiana tended to her growing family, the Bussells began the exodus from Augusta to the Vasse. In September 1835, the adventurous Bessie Bussell set out on horseback with John, Alfred, Vernon and Lenox, to take up residence at the Vasse in the rudimentary shelters they had so far constructed. The brothers had made frequent return visits to Augusta from the Vasse River and must have fired Bessie's enthusiasm for hard pioneering.

But even someone of Bessie's spirit and determination might have quailed a little as she set off on the 100-kilometre journey on horseback into the unknown.

The young men and Bessie camped out in mosquito-infested country. Bessie dealt with hordes of flies that swarmed over her eyes and lips by wearing a veil over her sunhat. They rode with 'the dogs frolicking around their horses' feet', dined under the stars and slept rough for the night.[19]

Crossing deep creeks in long skirts presented a problem but Bessie took it all in her stride. She wrote how 'I was sent into the bush while [the boys] changed their trousers'. In those days 'nice' girls could not wear trousers, for fear of being thought immoral, so Bessie had to ride side-saddle and wade across the creek in her long skirt which sopped up water like a sponge. She had to traverse swamps where the horses were in danger of being 'completely sucked into the mud'.

When Bessie's horse stumbled and nearly threw her, her brothers had to come to her rescue. Worse was the fact that her pale skin became badly sunburnt, despite her hat and veil. She described her face as 'burned to the red of a Virginia creeper in August'. But her brothers were proud of Bessie's courage and determination, and of the fact that their sister, who had never had anything to do with horses in England, had taught herself to ride so well in such a short time.

The Bussells kept themselves cheerful by singing, laughing and telling stories. They slept under the stars, cooked a breakfast of freshly caught fish and pancakes, which Bessie ate with her fingers from a saucepan lid instead of a plate.

Later, when writing about her big adventure to her wealthy cousin Capel Carter in England, Bessie seemed to take a delight in telling Capel how she was living the sort of life that would have been impossible for a girl of her class and background in England, milking their cow, churning butter and caring for farm animals.[20]

On the second and last night of their overland trek, Bessie was forced to sleep with her back propped against a tree, as by now she was so stiff, saddle-sore and sunburnt that the pain prevented her lying flat.

Eventually the group arrived at the place the Wardandi-Bibbulmun called Windelup (place of the digging sticks — implements carried by the women), where they would finally settle. The Bussells' land had been named Cattle Chosen by John Bussell, because Yulika, one of their best milking cows, having been lost for almost a year, was found there in 1834 accompanied by a valuable calf. Yulika was grazing contentedly in a pretty spot near a bend in the river.

The brothers had been working Cattle Chosen for more than a year now. John had decided they should build a main house for the family, with a smaller house for himself and Sophie Hayward, the girl he hoped to marry in England.

In January 1836, the houses were ready for the remainder of the family to move into from Augusta. The wattle-and-daub walls were fully plastered (Alfred by now having become proficient at plastering) and the furniture was installed. Books stood on shelves down the length of the room and the precious piano, retrieved from Georgiana Molloy, stood under the window. One long window overlooked the river; from the other they could watch their 'beautiful sleek cattle, horses and goats'. Mrs Bussell had her own room while the sisters shared a dormitory, as did some of the boys in this experiment in communal living. In her journal, written as a family history, Bessie described how:

> The great bell erected just before our windows awakens us
> from our slumbers just before daylight. Breakfast is
> prepared. After breakfast the boys separate to different
> duties; John and Len to carpentry and building, Vernon to
> the garden, Alfred to the cows. Bessie prepares vegetables
> for dinner. Mary clears away the breakfast and arranges the
> sitting room and Fanny goes to the boys' rooms to make
> their beds and look after the fleas, which we are gradually
> exterminating. Our duties are divided into three

departments, cook, housemaid and chambermaid; offices
we change monthly. Bessie's bell summons us from our
work and the dinner-hour is a welcome break. Then comes
feeding the turkeys and the ducks and hens. Plates and
dishes are washed and put away and then there is a little
rest with a book, which often falls from a tired hand.[21]

The girls' afternoons were spent helping Phoebe to wash and fold
the clothes and churn the butter made from their cows' milk:

We work until the setting sun calls in our animals to be
fed and settled for the night. The boys come in and soon
our last meal is in progress. The cows are all milked, the
horses praised and petted and then we sit down to our
bread and milk supper.[22]

By the end of their first year at Cattle Chosen, the Bussells owned
thirteen cows, eight goats, and four horses as well as numerous hens,
ducks and pigs. Surplus butter, potatoes and cheese was sent by boat
to the Swan River settlement, where it brought good prices in the
market. The Bussells also traded their produce with American
whalers who put into Geographe Bay in search of fresh water.

The Bussells could reflect with satisfaction on their fortune now,
but they identified one major obstacle to their advancement: the
Wardandi-Bibbulmun whose land they were exploiting. For an
initial period at Augusta the Bussells had enjoyed reasonably
harmonious relationships with the Wardandi. They made them
presents of flour and potatoes and showed them how to make
damper and bake the potatoes in the ashes of a camp fire. But once
the Wardandi found game in the area less plentiful, they turned to
other food sources — the settlers' cattle and crops. The response of
the Bussells was to shoot at the 'heathen natives'.

Although they were happy to use the local knowledge of the
Wardandi people and take over grassland that had been produced
by their burning off, the Bussells made no effort at all to
understand Aboriginal customs, folklore or beliefs. They were
offended by the Wardandi's nakedness and by their odour — the

Wardandi rarely washed, and greased their bodies with animal fat to keep warm and daubed their matted hair with red ochre. The Bussells mistrusted 'the natives', and, with labour in such short supply, were put out that the Wardandi refused to work in return for food. Along with many newcomers, the Bussells regarded the indigenous people as little better than animals.

The Bussells' limited tolerance for the Wardandi was also tested by the fact that the grassy Vasse (Windelup) area where they had established Cattle Chosen attracted large numbers of Bibbulmun-speaking people from near and far, who would make camp and hold noisy corroborees close to the Bussells' house. All night long the family could be kept awake by the noise of the clapsticks, the drone of the didgeridoo and the thumping of bare feet accompanied by wails and cries. It made the Bussell women very nervous indeed.

One night, when most of the family was away, Bessie noted in her diary, 'The natives nearly drive me out of my mind . . . The noise they make puts conversation out of the question . . . [the word 'native'] is fraught with fatigue, fear and anxiety.'[23]

In December 1836, the schooner *Champion* arrived at the Vasse with Lieutenant Henry Bunbury on board in charge of a group of soldiers. Bunbury, who had shot and killed Aboriginal men in the Avon district east of Perth, supported the Bussells in their increasingly violent stance against the Wardandi. For their part, the Wardandi-Bibbulmun could not understand the concept of owning land and regarded food sources as communal. Clashes were inevitable and would end in the demise of all clans of the Bibbulmun.

Enmity between the locals and the settlers escalated into open conflict when Leonard Chapman, another Vasse settler, found one of his calves missing. Chapman and the soldiers shot and killed nine Wardandi men and wounded two more without having any evidence that the Wardandi men were guilty.

Having employed Phoebe Bower and Emma Mould, the Bussells did not need to employ Aboriginal house girls. Had they done so, and got to know them as individuals, they might have developed a much warmer relationship with and appreciation of

Aboriginal people, as was the case with Emma Withnell, Jeannie Gunn, Evelyn Maunsell and Atlanta Bradshaw. But instead conflict escalated: soon the Bussell boys and Bessie came to see themselves as waging a war on the Wardandi. The brothers were convinced that killing some of them would teach the rest a lesson. And the aim of war is death to the enemy.

On 2 July 1837 Bessie remarked in her journal, 'The natives announced that a hostile tribe [probably another group of Bibbulmun] is making a descent on us. How will all these wars and rumours end?' Faced with the danger of an attack, those young hot heads, Charles, Alfred and Lenox, assembled a range of guns and ammunition and Lenox even attempted to build a cannon using ball cartridges. However, the cannon exploded into pieces when Lenox tried it out for the first time.

On 30 July the Bussell boys took the 'war' one step further. They and other settlers went out on a punitive raid and shot dead five Bibbulmun men and women whom they feared were about to attack them. They also left many more Aborigines badly injured.

⁓ ⁓ ⁓

Back at Augusta Georgiana's life continued in her ceaseless round of cooking, cleaning, washing and ironing, feeding hens and what she described as 'the odious drudgery of cheese and butter making'. Georgiana was worked off her feet from dawn to dusk without domestic help. In addition to household and farm chores, without the services of a governess she had to find the time to give young Sabina, now a very active little girl, reading and writing lessons. If Georgiana took time off to write to Helen Story or Maggie Dunlop or to her own family, the sewing and mending piled up beside her work basket. She told Helen:

> I must either leave writing alone or some needlework
> undone . . . I never open a book and if I read a chapter
> on Sunday, it is quite a treat to have so much leisure . . . I
> have not a cap to put on my child's head.[24]

Now thirty years of age, pregnant again and working harder than she had worked in her life, Georgiana complained that she had no time to make baby clothes. Each new pregnancy sapped her strength and brought her more work. And always with her was the anxiety of something happening to her children.

To Georgiana's horror, in November 1835, two months before the Bussells left for Cattle Chosen, Sabina had developed convulsions and fever. Georgiana nursed her little daughter devotedly day and night until she recovered. But she lost faith in Mr Green, the inept surgeon who diagnosed that Sabina was suffering from sunstroke. Georgiana must have wished desperately there was a competent medical practitioner within reach.

Captain Molloy's frequent absences on resident magistrate's business coupled with Georgiana's pregnancies meant the Molloys were much slower to set up a new farm at the Vasse than the Bussells and other settlers. Whenever he could, Captain Molloy would travel to the Vasse property where he was building a homestead for the family, some five kilometres away from the sea, overlooking the Vasse River.

As more Augusta residents left for the Vasse, Georgiana's isolation and loneliness increased. The few visitors who arrived by ship were generally poorly educated and talked about nothing more stimulating than 'grubbing out stumps, whaling and harpooning'.

Her main comfort, besides her children, was still her flower garden. The seeds and the yucca lilies Georgiana had brought with her flowered abundantly, giving the effect of an English cottage garden. Flowering creepers climbed in profusion over walls and verandas, as did vines grown from the seeds she had brought from Cape Town, and the peach trees which she had grown from stones she had brought with her flourished. She sent new seeds home to her mother to show her what had become of those wedding presents of seeds and bulbs, and described her West Australian garden with pride.

Sometimes in the evening Georgiana took her children to the beach. While they played, she sat and daydreamed about happy days at Helen Story's stone manse at Rosneath, and listened to the sound of the waves of the great Southern Ocean pounding over the sandbar.

In April 1836 a much-wanted boy — heir to the Molloys' hard-won acres of land — was born. The Molloys were thrilled and named him John after his father. Little John grew into a handsome, fair-haired toddler — their pride and joy. They talked about how he would eventually inherit the land they were wearing themselves out clearing and cultivating.

Georgiana's life was also about to gain another new absorbing interest. One day in November 1836 she received a letter, with a box of English seeds, sent by Captain James Mangles, the cousin of Mrs Stirling. Ellen Stirling had forwarded the captain's letter in which he asked if she would be kind enough to collect and send to him in England some seeds from native plants for his plant collection, together with her notes on them, and he would pass some on to other leading collectors.

Captain Mangles had inherited a vast annual income from his father, who, like Ellen Stirling's father, was also a director of the prosperous East India Company. Mangles no longer needed to work and could afford to spend his time writing books on plants from exotic locations and importing specimens. He also owned a large and beautiful garden near London and corresponded regularly with other garden owners and horticulturalists. His hobby had put Captain Mangles in touch with the curators of major botanical gardens around Britain.

Before making his trip to Australia in 1831, Captain Mangles had offered to obtain new and exotic specimens for the collections of the Royal Horticultural Society, for various English botanical gardens and for the home of the Duke of Devonshire, Chatsworth in Derby, the gardens of which were run by the noted horticulturalist and garden designer Joseph Paxton. Mangles had been fascinated by Western Australia's profusion of wild flowers but had not had time to travel further south to collect additional specimens.

Now Captain Mangles had sent out by ship a box, a *hortus siccus* album and the letter in which he very politely asked Mrs Molloy to fill the box with the seeds and pressed flowers of her local plants and write notes on them. He would pay the cost of shipping them to England.

Georgiana took Captain Mangles' request very seriously indeed. For the next six years she would follow his instructions and, in doing so, gradually develop an encyclopaedic knowledge of the flowers and plants of the south-west of Western Australia. She was happy to think she was contributing in some small way to the process of scientific exchange.

Although her free time was limited with three children to care for and teach, and her household and farm duties to attend to, she took the job on with enthusiasm. She packaged and labelled seeds in small muslin bags and, whenever possible, added pressed leaves and flowers of each specimen with her notes on the plant and its medicinal properties, if known. She would also add the native name, which members of the Wardandi, who were always very helpful, would tell her.

Georgiana had found an outlet for her enthusiasm for Australian native plants. She had made no real friends at Augusta and found no one who shared her religious preoccupations. Now at last she had someone as fascinated as herself to communicate with about native plants of the area — an expert with access to a vast library of horticultural reference books. Captain Mangles, a man of roughly the same age as her husband, in touch with Britain's major botanical gardens and horticulturalists, could supply her with additional horticultural knowledge.

By March 1837 she had collected enough specimens to fill a small box. She sent them off to Mangles with a letter full of thanks for the seeds he had sent out, and humility in accepting the job he proposed. Georgiana was not to know that this first shipment would go astray and never reached Mangles.

In the months following Captain Mangles' letter requesting her help, Georgiana became absorbed in her new interest. She sewed more little muslin bags for next year's seeds, and found and tagged the plants whose seeds she and her children would collect once they had ripened. Georgiana's children helped her on her rounds of inspection, because, as she later wrote to Captain Mangles, their eyes were so much closer to the ground they often found samples she had missed.

By this time Georgiana was employing young Charlotte Heppingstone, which gave her more time to get out and 'botanise' than during the whole of the previous six years. Georgiana was aware of the need to pack seeds carefully to survive the long sea journey and still be useful for propagation. It was this careful preparation and handling that would impress Captain Mangles when he received her first shipment. He had already received packages and boxes from other collectors at the Swan River in very poor condition but would be delighted with those sent by Mrs Molloy and the quality of the information that she provided when he eventually received some.

Captain Mangles and his vast store of botanical knowledge became Georgiana's connection to the outside world: they offered her the chance of a new and more fulfilling life.

The Molloys' move to the Vasse was scheduled for 1838 and Georgiana was determined to send Captain Mangles as many seeds and research notes from Augusta as possible before starting to collect and annotate the plants of the Vasse region. She had been told by several of the settlers that the vegetation and the climate were very different at the Vasse. She was looking forward to a new challenge but had grown to love the mild climate and the beauty of Augusta and was sorry to be leaving them.

And then, in November 1837, without warning, when beloved little John was nineteen months old, came the tragedy of Georgiana's life.

One morning after breakfast, the family and Charlotte had dispersed to their various household duties. Georgiana went to the outside kitchen to bake and to churn the butter. Suddenly she noticed that little John was nowhere to be seen. Worried that he might wander into the bush and get lost she had fastened a little bell to his belt but she could not hear its ringing.

Desperate with fear, Georgiana checked to see if John was with Charlotte or with her husband. They told her they had not seen him since breakfast. Georgiana's mind turned to the well, a stone's throw from the house. 'Do not frighten yourself, he never goes there!' her husband tried to reassure her. But John *had* gone there and fallen down, and all their attempts to revive their little boy were in vain.

The shock of John's death brought on a deep depression in Georgiana, who by now was pregnant once more. She was unable to eat or sleep, endlessly reproaching herself for her only son's fate. She stayed inside the house and brooded on her baby's death. Everywhere she went in the house she saw her lovely little boy. There was no clergyman to absolve her from the terrible pain she took upon herself; her suffering was so profound she could not even write about it to her family.

The herbariums and the big collecting boxes stood empty for weeks. Slowly Georgiana regained some vigour and resumed her family duties, but little John's death was never far from her mind. It was a couple of months before she began a letter to Captain Mangles apologising for lack of communication. In the course of the preceding twelve months, Georgiana had composed one letter to Mangles, accepting his request. Now, in the aftermath of the tragedy, she was able to describe the painful details of little John's death to him, a stranger, more easily than she could to her sister or to Helen Story:

> We have recently been overwhelmed with the most bitter
> loss of our darling infant and only son of 19 months by
> the aggravated death of drowning. Painful as it is to record
> — distance of time and space compels me . . . Charlotte
> going to the well . . . pulled out that darling precious
> child, lifeless, his flaxen curls all dripping, his little
> countenance so placid, he looked fast asleep but not dead;
> and we do not believe he really was so until some
> minutes after . . . We tried every means of restoration, but
> to no effect. And that lovely, healthy child, who had never
> known pain or sickness and who had been all mirth and
> joyousness the last time we beheld him together, was now
> a stiff corpse, but beautiful and lovely even in death.[25]

Possibly writing about her dead child acted as a catharsis for Georgiana and unburdening herself to Captain Mangles allowed her to begin 'botanising' again. It was as though subconsciously she turned away from death in favour of life, represented by the flowers and seeds she was once more passionately collecting and documenting.

From now onwards her letters contained no more pious statements on spiritual questions and instead she concentrated on 'botanising'. She visited her chosen collecting grounds with her daughters up to several times in a single week, waiting for the ripening seed pods to burst, so that she could harvest the seeds at their peak. Mindful of how many children had been lost in the bush and starved to death, Georgiana never let her beloved little girls go seed collecting without her.

Georgiana asked her husband to bring new plant specimens back when overseeing the clearing of their land at the Vasse and the building of their new house. She also persuaded soldiers from the garrison to collect seeds for her, and tackled her collecting with precision, dedication and professionalism. She documented various medicinal plants, along with the uses to which the Wardandi put them. Several types of berries and roots were used to cure sore eyes, others healed skin rashes and fevers.

With Georgiana's pregnancy advancing, the Molloys' plans to move to the Vasse had to be delayed again. The family's continuing stay in Augusta near the graves of her dead children was some compensation for Georgiana, who was still losing her neighbours. The garden she had planted so carefully with her English seeds and her yucca lilies was by now at its best.

To provide much-needed entertainment in the outback for her husband and children on summer evenings they would move the little piano-organ she had brought with her out onto the grass. There she would play classical or religious music to her family in the moonlight with the broad sweep of the Blackwood River, fringed by the cream-coloured trunks of peppermint trees, gliding past in front of her. Her music was occasionally punctuated by the harsh call of black swans overhead, while the night air was heavy with the scent of her English garden flowers.

In June 1838 Georgiana gave birth to another daughter, her fourth baby to survive. The labour was a difficult one and did not produce the son she had hoped for, but a beautiful and healthy little girl, whom they named Amelia.

Georgiana was delighted that Sabina could now read and keep herself amused. By the end of winter she had also managed to teach four-year-old Mary Dorothea to read. But she worried that no ships were coming into Flinders Bay to collect the annotated specimens she had packed with such care for Captain Mangles in England. She was eager to hear his opinion of her collecting work and her research notes and to know to which botanical gardens he had sent the seeds.

As spring advanced Georgiana's health improved. She could not resist taking the children seed and flower collecting once more in the bush where, she told Captain Mangles, they 'ran like butterflies from flower to flower'.

It was months since Georgiana had begun her long letter to Captain Mangles following John's death, and packed her boxes and *hortus sicci*, and still no ship had called to pick them up. Finally, in November 1838, Georgiana consigned Captain Mangles' two precious collecting boxes to Ellen Stirling for onward shipment to her cousin in England. They would not reach him until early 1839. He was delighted by their carefully packed contents of seeds, pressed flowers and leaves and by Georgiana's annotations.

❧ ❧ ❧

In May 1839 the Molloys finally made the move from Augusta to the Vasse. A few days before the family's departure (some five years after the Bussells had gone there in April 1834), Georgiana planted a red rose on her beloved son's grave. She uprooted her favourite plants and put them in a saddle bag so she could take them with her by row boat and then on horseback. She was sad to leave the magnificent Blackwood River with its pelicans and the tall peppermints overhanging the dark water which mirrored their reflections. She was also reluctant to leave her first matrimonial home, her beautiful garden and the graves of her dead children.

It took a day for the crew of a visiting whaler to row them some fifty kilometres up the Blackwood River. They camped overnight and cooked a meal over a camp fire. The girls found it very amusing, although Georgiana had a heavy heart as she nursed her baby.

Captain Molloy had arranged for them to be met by horses and soldiers stationed at the Vasse who would escort them the 100 kilometres to their new home. With two young children and a baby, their progress was slow. Georgiana carried little Amelia in a wicker pannier attached to one side of the saddle, with her precious plants in a pannier on the opposite side. Sabina and Mary Dorothea rode donkeys. They spent two more nights camping in the bush and Georgiana and the children were totally exhausted by the time they reached the Vasse River on 10 May.

The new house which Georgiana named Fairlawn proved a big disappointment. Captain Molloy, it seemed, was a better soldier and magistrate than an architect. Although Georgiana's family was now much larger than when they had built the first house at Augusta, their new home was roughly the same size as the old one and had fewer windows. None of the small windows were fitted with glass, as Molloy had been unable to obtain any, so insects swarmed in.

The temperatures were much hotter during the day and colder at night than at Augusta and she missed the sea views. Georgiana found the surrounding countryside of the Vasse, with its flat grassy plains, uninteresting. While the Bussell boys had seen acres of rolling pastures, which would bring them wealth by fattening cattle, to Georgiana's eyes the semi-stagnant Vasse River was a poor substitute for the broad, sweeping expanse of the Blackwood and those magnificent stands of jarrah at Hardy's Inlet.

Her first thought on arrival was to find moist soil where she could bed the plants taken from her beloved garden at Augusta. Slowly she grew used to living in the colder climate of the Vasse. In spring she was thrilled by the profusion of wild flowers, which she thought even lovelier than those at Augusta. And in time she made friends with a Wardandi man named Calgood and gave him food in return for his help in collecting Vasse plants and seeds for her.

By now the Bussells were doing very well at the Vasse. As the district grew, so their income increased and they were able to employ labourers. They started thinking of more ways to make money from their land, and eventually came up with the idea of breeding and shipping horses to India for the British Army, a venture which would prove highly profitable.

But white settlement and land clearing meant diminishing food supplies for the Wardandi. As Europeans shot and killed the kangaroos and wallabies they relied on, so they continued to raid the settlers' stores in search of flour, tea and sugar, which provided them with an easy source of nourishment.

In February 1842, members of the Wardandi-Bibbulmun stole flour from the Bussells' flour mill, along with several goats. A warrant was issued by John Bussell for the arrest of the suspects. They were taken prisoner but escaped, with the Bussell brothers in pursuit. Charles shot and killed a Wardandi man named Erigedung but was acquitted of any wrong doing at a magisterial inquiry.

A month later, on 10 March, while investigating the theft of six kilograms of Bussell flour, Charles stated how, in order to frighten a seven-year-old girl called Cummangoot, who had been turned in by another tribesman, into confessing the crime, he had pointed a gun at her. The gun discharged and Charles shot her in the stomach. The unfortunate little girl died the following day. Charles was indicted and tried for manslaughter in Perth but was let off with a fine of only one shilling. He expressed no remorse for his actions.[26]

The callousness of the Bussells towards the Wardandi-Bibbulmun distressed Georgiana. She was one of the few pioneers of the Vasse who tried to understand Aboriginal culture with its richness of legends and ceremonies and their use of native plants for medicinal purposes.

_ℓℓ_ _ℓℓ_ _ℓℓ_

Strangely enough, in view of the fact that Georgiana and John Bussell were opposed in many of their views, Georgiana gained a good friend in John's wife, Charlotte Cookworthy Bussell. In 1837 John had returned to England intending to marry Sophie Hayward, the young heiress with whom he had had an understanding since childhood and with whom he had kept up a correspondence. But unknown to him, Sophie was having second thoughts about migrating to Western Australia to live under the same roof as bossy

Mrs Bussell. In his letters John had insisted that, even when they married, his mother would be in charge of their communal living arrangements, and that Sophie must consult Mrs Bussell on every aspect of their domestic life. John's attitude says a great deal about Mrs Bussell's firm hold over her sons.

John had been distressed to arrive in England and learn that mutual friends accused him in front of Sophie of being a fortune-hunter. He broke off the engagement, desperately hurt by such accusations. Miserable and depressed, he also feared that, with the shortage of suitable single girls in Western Australia, his chances of finding a wife who would undertake the hardships of pioneering the outback were limited.

While recovering from his broken engagement in England, John met an attractive, intelligent and practical young widow, Charlotte Cookworthy, who had recently suffered a great deal herself. Charlotte proved a sympathetic confidante. Perhaps because she had been married before, Charlotte considered the prospect of a demanding matriarch at Cattle Chosen less intimidating than young Sophie Hayward had, or perhaps she was prepared to take more risks to improve her circumstances.

Within three weeks of their first meeting in August 1838 Charlotte and John had married — but not without difficulty and drama. After the death of her first husband, Charlotte had become a member of the Plymouth Brethren, who then ex-communicated her for marrying John, an outsider to the sect. Complications ensued when the Plymouth Brethren refused to release Charlotte's three children, intending to raise them themselves. John and Charlotte were forced to kidnap her children from the sect before they took a ship for Western Australia.

Charlotte's arrival at Cattle Chosen brought an end to Georgiana's terrible loneliness and led to something of a rapprochement between the Molloys and the Bussells. As there was as yet no bridge across the Vasse River, Charlotte, who lived on the opposite side to the Molloys' house, rowed across the narrow river to pay Georgiana a visit. The two women, one fair and one dark, embraced each other and began a friendship which was to enrich both their lives.

Charlotte commented in her diary on Georgiana's delicate complexion and the fact that on the table Georgiana had placed a beautiful bunch of wild flowers. When Charlotte complimented her on the beauty of the floral arrangements, Georgiana said that she could not 'bear to be without flowers in the room'.

⅋ ⅋ ⅋

The year before the Molloys moved to the Vasse, Bessie Bussell had married, but remained living at Cattle Chosen. Her husband was a young surveyor named Henry Ommanney, nephew of Rear-Admiral Sir John Ommanney on his father's side, while Captain

Lithographed drawing of Cattle Chosen at the Vasse River showing the Bussells' vegetable garden and home.

James Mangles was his maternal uncle. Henry was there to survey the districts of Leschenault and the Vasse River. In a case of instant attraction, Henry married vivacious, capable Bessie only a few months after their first meeting.

Georgiana must have been told of the match by her husband when he went on one of his trips to the Vasse and she conveyed the news to Captain Mangles.

In December 1839, Georgiana received Captain Mangles' first reply, congratulating her on the excellence of her collecting and assembling of the specimens. He told her how pleased curators at the Royal Botanical Gardens at Kew and Chelsea had been with the seeds she had packed so carefully, and mentioned that he had sent some seeds to Joseph Paxton, as well as other major British horticulturalists, who had been delighted with them.

In appreciation, Captain Mangles sent toys for the girls, books, some scented soap and other valued gifts the isolated settlers in their far-flung colony could never have bought. Georgiana did not want financial reward and did not expect academic credit for her research. She was happy that at last she had a friend and collaborator who shared her interests. She wrote humbly, thanking Captain Mangles for his 'disinterested liberality and kindness to those you have never seen, and who are not able to make you any return'.[27] Like most women of her era, Georgiana still failed to realise her own worth and worried whether she was able to do a capable enough job of documenting all the new species to satisfy Captain Mangles.

Georgiana was now impatient to start sending more Vasse dried flowers and seeds to Captain Mangles. She had an enormous box made up measuring one metre long by sixteen centimetres deep to export her specimens.

But an interruption to her collecting routine and to the creation of a handsome new garden at Fairlawn came in March 1840, when Georgiana's sister Mary Kennedy arrived. Georgiana had not seen her sister for ten years. As a visit to the family in England was out of the question, she had been imploring Mary to make the long trip out to the Vasse to stay with her. Now at last Mary had done so.

New arrivals were always fascinating in such a restricted society and Mary was invited to visit the Bussells, where Fanny and Mrs Bussell found Georgiana's mercenary sister 'far more congenial than Mrs Molloy'. But Mary remained unimpressed by the Bussells and their way of life. She ignored the remarkable beauty and tranquillity of the Vasse and its rich flora and fauna.

Mary told her older sister she was foolish to work like a slave for her husband and live in the wilds without entertainment or amenities, especially as she was now pregnant again. Even so, Miss

Kennedy searched in vain for a wealthy husband, possibly hoping she might find one at the Vasse — despite its primitive way of life and her claim that colonial life was boring and aged women prematurely.

In May 1840, the cook Georgiana had secured to provide meals for the farm labourers and the family, left, lured away to work for the Bussells. Captain Molloy was, as usual, away on government business when Georgiana went into labour. Doubtless not wanting to involve the alcoholic army surgeon Mr Green, Georgiana was assisted by her unmarried sister, who knew practically nothing about childbirth, and Ann McDermott (nee Turner), who had also recently arrived at the Vasse. Neither of them appreciated that a germ-free delivery was vital, something not understood generally before the work of Dr Ignaz Semmelweiss and Joseph Lister into asepsis.[28] With their help Georgiana gave birth to her sixth child, a healthy baby girl whom she named Flora, the Latin for flower.

The birth, once again without benefit of antiseptic conditions, good antenatal and post-partum care, left Georgiana with a debilitating uterine infection known as puerperal (childbed) fever. For a month she lay sick and exhausted, attended by Mary. As Georgiana's temperature soared, Fanny Bussell left her own work at Cattle Chosen and her sister Bessie, now Mrs Ommanney, who was also on the point of giving birth, to provide some nursing assistance to Mary Kennedy. Georgiana began haemorrhaging. With no medical help, and amateur nursing, Georgiana's recovery was very slow.

Even in her delirium, Georgiana had worried about her collecting, especially the seeds of the *Nuytsia floribunda*, or Christmas tree, which were just ripening. As the pods burst and scattered the seeds very quickly, they had to be collected at the right moment: Georgiana had been hoping to send specimens to Captain Mangles and had placed muslin bags around the pods to catch them. She now hoped the friendly Wardandi would harvest them for her.

In June 1840, while she was still recovering, Georgiana heard from Captain Mangles again. Impressed by the seeds and detailed research notes Georgiana had already sent him, he had forwarded out by sea a magnificent gift of two microscopes and a telescope. She was delighted that Captain Mangles was also commissioning from her an article about the flora of Western Australia for *The Floral Calendar*, a British horticultural magazine he edited. Georgiana felt honoured by his request, especially since at that time women were rarely invited to contribute to academic journals and were banned from joining most learned societies.

Modest as ever, she replied to Captain Mangles, telling him:

> I shall with unfeigned pleasure attempt to gratify you in writing in the 'Floral Calendar', but really feel you have over-rated my poor exertions . . . But I will glean all I can, and pray my health may permit of my making those much enjoyed floral excursions.[29]

With no wealthy husband in sight, Mary Kennedy had had quite enough of nursing, child care and deprivation in the outback. As soon as Georgiana showed signs of improvement, she packed her trunk and sailed back to England.

Race relations in the Vasse area continued to decline. The hot-headed and impulsive Vasse settler George Layman became involved in a dispute over stolen damper with Gaywal, an Aboriginal elder whose daughter had been raped by a settler. Gaywal was seen as a trouble maker and had already been accused by the Bussell brothers of spearing their cattle. The argument between Layman and Gaywal turned into a fight in which Layman was speared and died of his wounds.

The causes of the argument, of course, lay far deeper than the mere theft of some damper. No doubt Gaywal was a trouble maker but he was also seething with anger over the rape of his daughter by one of the settlers and the fact that his son-in-law was in gaol awaiting a charge of killing another settler for the rape of another Aboriginal woman.

The response of the settlers was brutal. Led by Captain Molloy and the Bussells, a search party located an Aboriginal camp where they shot dead seven of the Wardandi. Gaywal escaped but was later hunted down and also shot dead.

Captain Molloy was made guardian of the four Layman children, which meant even more work for the harassed Georgiana. She consoled Layman's widow and her children, and once more showed her generosity by inviting them to stay as her guests at Fairlawn for several months. Mrs Layman and her children were far too scared of Wardandi vengeance to stay in their own house.

Women were still greatly outnumbered by men at the Vasse, as they were at other West Australian settlements. Widowed Mary Layman was courted by young Robert Heppingstone, son of the former servant of the Molloys. Eight years younger than Mary and from a very different background, he nevertheless married Mary and she left Georgiana's home and moved into her own house with her new husband.

~ ~ ~

Governor James Stirling had left Western Australia in mid-1839 with his wife. His replacement was Governor John Hutt, who had previously served with the East India Company. In November 1839 Governor Hutt had made his first official visit to the Vasse River, staying with the Government Resident Molloy and his wife.

As hostess at dinner Georgiana had had time to talk to Governor Hutt and discovered that he was also interested in the wild flowers of the district. Before long, Georgiana had received an introduction from Governor Hutt to a Mr Ludwig Preiss, a visiting German botanist. She hoped to learn a great deal from him and so she invited Preiss to stay. Unfortunately he turned out to be pompous and self-important, unlike Georgiana who underestimated the value of her own contributions to horticulture. In the event, Preiss learned a great deal more from Georgiana than she did from him. He failed to keep his promise to send her specimens of seeds and plants, but he took eagerly all those she offered him.

In December 1841 Governor Hutt, his valet and three accompanying soldiers revisited the Molloys in their somewhat primitive accommodation at the same time as the Reverend John Wollaston was staying with them.

The Reverend Wollaston, clergyman to another struggling settlement of south-west Western Australia called Australind, was also a keen amateur botanist. In the course of his three days with the Molloys, Wollaston noted in his journal that he would have liked to have them as neighbours — he wrote that they were 'uncommonly generous and motivated by less self-interest than anyone else in the colony'.[30]

Wollaston and his son John were also drawn to Georgiana by their common passion for botany. They admired her greatly for her botanical knowledge and dedication to collecting and studying plants.

Wollaston felt sorry for Georgiana who, since Charlotte had left to get married, was working harder than a maid servant. As Georgiana had no domestic help she had to cook a dinner suitable for a governor on a wood stove helped by her nine-year-old daughter. She also had to play the role of elegant hostess at table and keep the conversation flowing. Then later that night she had to heat the water and help the governor's valet wash and dry the dishes and greasy pans. Wollaston noted in his journal how:

> I could not help remarking to the Governor one morning, as Mrs Molloy passed in our view from the house to the kitchen, with the dinner dishes in one hand and her youngest daughter without shoes or stockings, in the other, how distressing and laborious must be the female emigrant's lot, who has in her native country been used to the common comforts and plain cleanliness of genteel life . . .
>
> . . . The Molloys are at present without servant of any kind, and if it had not been for the loan of the steward of one of the ships in the bay and the Governor's servant, they must have done everything for us themselves. As it was, Mrs Molloy, assisted by her little girl, only nine years old, had to attend to everything in the cooking way. Although the dining room has a clay floor and opens into the dairy, the thatch appears overhead and there is not a

single pane of glass on the premises . . . yet our
entertainment, the style and manners of our host and
hostess, their dress and conversation, all conspired to show
that genuine good breeding and gentlemanly deportment
are not always lost sight of among English emigrants.[31]

As there was still no church at the Vasse, the Reverend Wollaston held a service at the Bussells' home, Cattle Chosen, where he baptised the Molloys' youngest daughter. In his journal he remarked that 'Mrs Molloy was a perfect botanical dictionary'. Indeed, by that time Georgiana knew a large amount about the wild flowers of the region. Yet she was still eager to learn more whenever she could tear herself away from her exhausting and unending round of household chores.

Georgiana soon made contact with the captain of a British whaling ship at Geographe Bay, which was heading to England. The captain agreed to transport the precious collecting boxes containing seeds and notes addressed to Captain Mangles, who would pay the freight when they reached England.

By now, however, Georgiana's husband was becoming less supportive of her hobby. He suggested gently she should spend more time on domestic affairs and less time collecting flowers and seeds for Captain Mangles.

Despite her husband's lack of enthusiasm, Georgiana persisted. She kept watch on the precious seeds of the beautiful golden-orange flowers of the *Nuytsia floribunda* and began daily collecting trips in order to be there when the seeds ripened in April or May. Some she saved for Captain Mangles and with pride planted a few in her own garden at the Vasse, which was developing nicely.

In March 1842 Georgiana discovered that she was pregnant again. It seems clear that no doctor had warned Jack Molloy of the danger to his wife of bearing a seventh baby. She was dismayed but hoped that this time she would have a male child. She became tired and listless, and suffered severe bouts of morning sickness, but she continued to collect seeds for Captain Mangles.

'I should like nothing better than to kindle a fire and stay out all night . . . as I should be ready for my work early in the morning . . . but the natives are much greater than white people in flower seed hunting,' she wrote to Captain Mangles early that winter.[32]

It was mid-winter before Georgiana managed to pack and send her final shipment of seeds and pressed flowers, along with her notes on them. This shipment contained over 100 different specimens of seed, all neatly sorted, labelled and tied with pink tape around tiny brown muslin bags, together with notes describing them and their habitat, in the hope they would be officially classified.

It seemed that Captain Mangles had mentioned Georgiana's name to some English botanists and moves were already afoot to name a flower species after Mrs Georgiana Molloy, the woman who had done so much to enrich the botanical gardens of Europe and who had not received due credit for her work. It was proposed by the West Australian botanist James Drummond to name a species of grevillea *Grevillea molloyae* to honour her research and collecting work but this never eventuated. However, the naming of the tall, fragrant *Boronia molloyae* secured Georgiana a measure of botanical immortality.

By November 1842 Fairlawn deserved its name. Following Georgiana's design, a grassy lawn reached down to the river's edge, and vines and fig trees had been planted. In her final letter to Captain Mangles she wrote proudly, 'I believe I have sent you everything worth sending.'

Three weeks before Christmas, Georgiana's seventh child, another girl named Georgiana, was born.

Captain Molloy was by now desperately worried about his wife. Mr Green, the local medic, was sent for but arrived dead drunk. As was the custom at this period, he probably made a vaginal examination without first washing his hands with antiseptic. Once again the birth was difficult and the prolonged labour exhausting for the mother. Once again Mr Green proved so incapable that Captain Molloy begged Alfred Bussell to fetch another doctor. Alfred galloped on horseback to Leschenault but both the doctors there had too many urgent cases to be able to leave them.

Not until the following day did Alfred return with a third doctor, Dr Henry Allen, who dismissed the alcoholic and incompetent surgeon Green and treated Georgiana himself. However, by now it was too late. Georgiana was skeletally thin and her condition improved only marginally while her childbed fever continued throughout the month of January 1843. Before the discovery of antibiotics there was no sure way to heal childbed fever which grew steadily worse.

When the Reverend Wollaston visited the Vasse in January, he was alarmed by Mrs Molloy's condition. As the days grew hotter Georgiana suffered even more. Her temperature soared. From then on, Georgiana, weak and exhausted, realised she was dying. She worried as to who would rear her young daughters. She begged her husband to see that Mary Layman, now Mrs Heppingstone, her nearest neighbour, would care for the baby once Georgiana was dead.

Georgiana hung on in this condition for weeks. The Reverend Wollaston visited Fairlawn again on 27 March 1843 and noted in his journal that 'Mrs Molloy will lose her life for want of nursing', although the real damage had been inflicted by the doctor who delivered her baby, but Wollaston did not realise this. His own mood was bleak. Wollaston's wife was also 'weak and worn', and she and his two daughters were starting to suffer from the effects of ophthalmia from too much sunlight on their eyes. He added a warning note that around the Vasse region and further afield many of the Bibbulmun were dying from imported diseases, in particular from influenza.

John Ferguson, a West Australian settler and a former surgeon and carpenter, was sent for and arrived at the Vasse only to find poor Mrs Molloy's back covered in ulcerated bedsores and one of her legs paralysed from a blood clot. He and Jack Molloy attempted to make her a water bed out of a water trough covered with an old mackintosh coat to ease the pressure, and for a short time Georgiana had some relief.

Skilled medical care could have saved Georgiana. But there was none. She never blamed her husband for the fact that her final pregnancy was responsible for her childbed fever at a time when about sixteen per cent of all mothers died in childbirth. Even in her last days she loved him deeply and no doubt believed that her short life had been lived to the full through her family and her botanical work.

By now Wollaston was so alarmed by her condition, he reminded the dying Georgiana that she should 'set her house in order', by which he meant she should confess her sins and be administered the Last Sacrament. After doing this Wollaston returned to his home at Picton where his own wife was sickly, saddened by the fact he would never see Mrs Molloy again and worried about the fate of her daughters.

As Georgiana's fever increased, she slipped into unconsciousness and died on 8 April 1843. She was only thirty-seven. She was buried in a paddock close to her beloved garden at Fairlawn, her grave surrounded by the tall, white yucca lilies she had loved.

Gentle, scholarly Georgiana Molloy was a martyr to medical mismanagement in the pioneering era. She could have had a splendid future as a botanist of international repute had women been more respected as scientific researchers — and had Captain Mangles given her credit for her research and collecting skills. Had Georgiana survived the birth of her last child, she would have learned that the seeds and information she had sent in her detailed letters and notes to Captain Mangles were greatly valued in plant nurseries and botanical gardens at Kew, Chelsea, Edinburgh and Dublin, as well as in other major botanical gardens in Europe and North America. Unfortunately only a few curators were told that these seeds had been collected by a woman botanist — most believed mistakenly that Captain Mangles himself had collected and annotated them.

Neither Captain Mangles nor Professor John Lindley, Professor of Botany at London University and Secretary of the Royal Horticultural Society, bothered to acknowledge her name in their publications.

Based on Georgiana's work from her first shipment of seeds and plants but still omitting any mention of her name, Professor Lindley wrote 'Sketch of the Vegetation of the Swan River Colony', which was published in London to great interest as an Appendix to Edward's *Botanical Register* in 1839. Lindley knew of Georgiana's existence and in a letter to Captain Mangles described how 'Your friend Mrs Molloy is really the most charming person . . . and you the most fortunate man to have such a correspondent. That many of the plants are beautiful you can see for yourself.'[33]

Because she was female, Lindley never mentioned her name once in his book, yet he published her work. The great Joseph Paxton at Chatsworth was sent Mrs Molloy's seeds but probably never knew her name.[34]

⊱⊰⊱⊰⊱⊰

After Georgiana's death, the pioneer women of the Vasse cared for her children. Mary Heppingstone, widow of George Layman, was extremely supportive, and she and her husband, young Robert Heppingstone, virtually adopted little Georgiana during the early years of her life.

Once she was old enough, Georgiana's daughter and namesake went back to live at Fairlawn and acted as housekeeper to her widowed father. She became engaged but her fiance, J.K. Panter, nephew of a governor of Western Australia, was killed by Aborigines while exploring the Roebuck Bay area. Georgiana's last child never married and remained at Fairlawn looking after her father. She died in 1874.

Georgiana's closest friend, Charlotte Bussell, looked after the elder girls and did her best to be a surrogate mother to them. All her daughters had Georgiana's peaches-and-cream complexion and her blue-grey eyes, and were described as 'five daughters who . . . possess a grace and dignity and ease of manner which would do honour to the most refined society', by Archdeacon Matthew Hale. She would have been proud of all of them.

The Archdeacon visited the Vasse River in November 1848 and fell in love with Sabina Molloy. A strikingly handsome man, he proposed to young Sabina and she accepted him. They were married from the home of Charlotte Bussell and moved to Perth, where Hale eventually became Bishop of Perth.

Mary Dorothea Molloy married an aristocratic Englishman named Edmund DuCane and accompanied him to England, becoming Lady Mary Dorothea DuCane after her husband was knighted.

Amelia Molloy married William Bunbury, son of Lady Richardson Bunbury, and lived at Beechlands, about five kilometres from Busselton. Their descendants remained at the Vasse on a property named Marybrook on land that was once part of Captain Molloy's grant. Flora Molloy married William Brockman, a member of one of Western Australia's leading pioneer families.

The Bussell boys eventually achieved their aims and became financially secure, and by 1914, the start of the Great War, the Wardandi–Bibbulmun were seen no more. The neighbouring town of Busselton is named after the busy Bussells.

Fanny Bussell refused a proposal of marriage in Perth and returned to help her brothers at Cattle Chosen, where she managed the dairy on a profit-sharing basis. She married, relatively late in life, settler Henry Charles Sutherland and went to live at Crawley, now the site of the University of Western Australia. Her husband died four years later and she returned to end her days at Cattle Chosen. Bessie Ommanney remained at Cattle Chosen, had five children and a long and happy life.

The erratic Lenox Bussell who had built the cannon to kill the Wardandi became an alcoholic and died the same year as his mother, in 1845. Lenox's alcoholism may have explained his unstable behaviour and his violent treatment of the local Wardandi, two of whom he killed merely for stealing flour. Charles Bussell worked in Perth as a storekeeper and died in 1856.

John and Charlotte Bussell spent long and happy lives at Cattle Chosen. John died at the age of seventy-two. His grieving widow, Charlotte, could not bear to remain at the Vasse without him, so left widowed Mary Bussell in charge and sailed back to Europe. She spent her final years in Paris. Today descendents of Charlotte and John Bussell occupy Cattle Chosen, a historic property.

Jack Molloy never remarried. He extended Fairlawn and built a cottage in the grounds so his children and grandchildren could visit. In 1850 he made the long sea voyage back to London, where he was received cordially by the Duke of Wellington at Apsley House on Hyde Park Corner (known as No. l, Piccadilly), which a grateful British nation had given the Iron Duke. The Duke presented Captain Jack Molloy with a Peninsula Medal in addition to his Waterloo Medal and asked him if farming in Western Australia had made him rich. Captain Molloy replied that unfortunately it had not. The captain also called on Sir James Stirling, the man mainly responsible for the Swan River disaster, but there is no record of their conversation.

When Captain Molloy returned to the Vasse, he found Western Australia experiencing a recession and a run on the banks. Due to repeated requests for help from the colonists who complained of the shortage of labour, in 1856 the British Government sent out shipments of convicts to be used on road works and public buildings, but with the promise that equal numbers of free settlers would also be sent out to the struggling colony.

Aged eighty-seven, Captain Molloy died the year after the first shipment of convicts and free settlers arrived in Western Australia. Jack Molloy had the sadness of seeing his wife and two of his children die before him but at least had the satisfaction of seeing the colony, which he and Georgiana had struggled so hard to pioneer, starting to prosper.

Out of all of these diverse characters and their achievements, it is Georgiana Molloy who arouses the most interest. Her fame has increased in recent years as more attention is paid to women's achievements in science. Georgiana's most striking epitaph as a botanist came from the noted British horticulturalist George Hailes, who had grown magnificent show specimens of West Australian flowers and native trees from the seeds Georgiana had collected and annotated in her years of botanising. In a letter of condolence to Captain Molloy, Hailes wrote with admiration:

> Not one in ten thousand who go out into distant lands
> has done what she did for the Gardens in her Native
> Country.

CHAPTER 2

COURTESY NATIONAL LIBRARY OF AUSTRALIA.

Emma Mary Withnell

1842 – 1928

THE SPINIFEX PIONEER WHO BECAME THE 'MOTHER OF THE NORTH-WEST'

On 24 March 1864 the sailing ship *Sea Ripple* took Emma and John Withnell and their two children on a dangerous journey from Fremantle to the north-west of Western Australia to take up a land grant of 100,000 acres (40,500 hectares). With them were Emma's elder brother John Hancock, her sixteen-year-old sister Fanny, John's younger brother Robert Withnell and three farm labourers. They had packed on board a large quantity of farm equipment, household items, enough tea and sugar to last for six months and Emma's precious medicine chest, which would prove invaluable. Also on board were 650 sheep, and cows, poultry, sheep dogs and horses, including John Withnell's pride and joy — his Clydesdale stallion, which had cost him £300 (about the equivalent of the price of a luxury car today).[1]

Twenty-one-year-old Emma was pregnant with her third child but was delighted they were finally on their way to the De Grey River plains which her cousin, the famous explorer Francis Gregory, had promoted as 'fertile land suitable for pioneering'. A steady breeze filled the sails and the *Sea Ripple* made a speed of over six knots. The captain of this three-masted barque the Withnells had chartered for their family and their livestock reckoned they would reach their destination in a fortnight. Little did he — or the Withnells — realise that disaster was about to strike. They would never reach the De Grey plains or the river of the same name (today the area around thriving Port Hedland).

≈ ≈ ≈

George Hancock and Sophia Gregory, Emma Withnell's parents, had been among the diverse group of free settlers who emigrated to the Swan River in the early 1830s aboard the British sailing ship *Warrior*, one of many specially chartered vessels to bring 2290 free settlers to Western Australia from different parts of the British Isles. George and Sophia met for the first time on board ship. George was eighteen years old while Sophia was only seven. Like the Molloys who were also aboard (see chapter one), the Gregorys had paid good money for stock in return for grants of land along the Swan River.

Some of the more prosperous Swan River migrants, like the Gregorys, had brought with them luxury items such as pianos, oil paintings, porcelain dinner services and silver cutlery — unaware that what they needed most as pioneer farmers were ploughs, harrows, spades, seeds and livestock.

Arriving at Fremantle the unfortunate migrants had been forced to camp on the beach, as there was no accommodation. In a desperate search for fertile land, many, like the Molloys, took up grants in other parts of Western Australia. The Gregory family, however, stayed around the Swan River, eventually receiving a grant in the Avon Valley.

The Hancocks were not so illustrious. George's father, John, came out on the *Warrior* as an indentured carpenter to retired soldier Captain Francis Byrne.[2] Like the Gregorys, Captain Byrne also obtained land in the Swan River district and the Avon Valley.

After working out his indenture John Hancock became licensee of the Mermaid Hotel and also worked with his sons in his own sawmill. He too was eventually granted land, some of which he also took up in the Avon Valley.

John Withnell's father, William, was a stonemason by trade. His wife, Martha, earned a little extra money by weaving. The Withnells came from a social strata much lower than that of the Gregorys. They had run a few cows on their land in Lancashire — their ancestors had been yeoman farmers for centuries — but the Industrial Revolution had adversely affected their modest way of life. The Napoleonic Wars had brought inflation and unemployment in their wake and the future seemed depressing to this hardworking couple who were ambitious but lacked capital. Emigrating to Western Australia must have seemed a solution to their problems.

In the autumn of 1829 William and Martha Withnell boarded the emigrant ship *Nancy* with their two children, six-year-old John and five-year-old Mary Ann. Martha was expecting another child when the Withnells sailed from Plymouth. On 9 January 1830 their ship dropped anchor in Cockburn Sound, Western Australia. They were rowed ashore and took shelter in a cave where Martha gave birth to another son, whom they named Robert.

After a great deal of hardship the Withnells took up land in the York area. Due to their limited finances, their eldest son, John, did not attend school but worked for his father, helping him establish their farm. When John was only sixteen his father died, and he had to support his widowed mother and run the farm as best he could. He gained practical experience in farming but as he could not read or write, his expectations were modest. Certainly he moved in very different spheres from the parents of the girl with whom he would fall in love.

⚜ ⚜ ⚜

George Hancock and Sophia Gregory had married in 1839, nine years after they'd first met on board the *Warrior*. Sixteen months later, their son John Frederick Hancock was born. On 19 December 1842 their first daughter was born and named Emma Mary. The family grew until eventually George and Sophia had five sons and six daughters and a prosperous farm near Beverley.

Emma developed into a tall, long-legged teenager with pleasant rather than beautiful features. She wore her long blonde hair pinned in a knot on top of her head. Highly intelligent, hardworking, resourceful and responsible, she had been taught history, geography and science by her educated mother and had inherited her love of books and reading. She enjoyed caring for others and whenever her younger siblings fell sick, she helped nurse them through childhood ailments, such as whooping cough, mumps and measles.

By the time Emma was sixteen, the Hancocks were running Boyadine, a large farm near the West Australian settlement of York. Burly John Withnell owned a much smaller adjacent farm called Hillside. He enjoyed visiting Boyadine and became good friends with Emma's older brother John. On his visits to Boyadine, John was introduced to Emma, whom he thought very attractive. He knew her parents might not approve but, fascinated by this delightful, lively girl, was unable to keep away.

If George Hancock noticed that John Withnell seemed to spend a great deal of time talking to his eldest daughter, the fact that she had mentioned she thought John attractive would have worried him even more. George did not enjoy the thought of his clever young daughter marrying an illiterate man almost twice her age. George had worked hard to make something of himself and was now a considerable landowner. He hoped that Emma would marry well, as he himself had done. Although George had no objection to John as a friend for his son, he could not see him as a worthy son-in-law.

Emma was aware that her parents looked down on the Withnells, but that did not stop her from being attracted to John. She recognised him as hardworking and highly intelligent. When John eventually found the courage to ask her for her hand she accepted him, announcing to her father, 'When you have seven daughters and they are all as plain as me, you should be grateful for an honest man, even if he *is* poor, to take one of them off your hands,'[3] — rather cleverly playing on the fact that daughters cost money.

Emma was by no means plain but neither was she a raving beauty. Perhaps her father tried to talk Emma out of what he believed was potentially a disastrous marriage to a man unworthy of her. Doubtless he told her she was not nearly as plain as she made out and could do far better for herself. Maybe tempers flared and harsh words were exchanged. But Emma's mind was made up. She wanted John Withnell for a husband and nothing would change that.

Emma and John were married on 10 May 1859, when Emma was only seventeen. The newlyweds moved to Hillside into a single-storey stone and mud-brick cottage with a thatched roof, which John had built himself. They worked hard to develop their land and make their new home attractive. But Emma was frequently left alone, with John having taken up more land to clear and cultivate some distance away from Hillside. They were ambitious and were prepared to work extremely hard to achieve their goals.

ℓ ℓ ℓ

By the early 1860s, large pastoral leases for riverside land in the area that came to be known as the Pilbara, about 1200 kilometres (as the crow flies) north of Perth, were available to applicants who could stock the land with sufficient cattle and sheep. To induce them to move to virgin territory, settlers were offered their first year free of rent. Settlement had begun after the publication of a very favourable report on these areas by the Royal Geographical Society of London. This initial report, which included a detailed map of the area, was made by Emma Withnell's cousin, the distinguished explorer Francis Gregory (later knighted for his work). In his report, Gregory stated that the area had good water and fertile soil and was highly suitable for grazing sheep. There were also possibilities for a pearl-diving industry on the coast.

The north-west region of Western Australia that was opened up for settlement encompassed more than 400,000 square kilometres[4] and eight-year grazing leases for vast acreages were offered on easy terms — *provided* intending settlers were prepared to stock their land and build a house on it immediately.

Emma, whose parents had been sent a copy of Gregory's report, read from cover to cover her cousin's account of the area. Her interest aroused, she made enquiries and learned about the favourable terms the West Australian Government was offering.

As the water supply at Hillside was poor and the Withnells were struggling to make John's farm pay, Emma thought it would be an excellent idea to sell Hillside, invest the money in livestock and sail north to set up a new farm there. Acreage in the north-west was to be granted proportionately to the amount of stock the settler possessed, so the fact that the Withnells owned a quantity of livestock would give them the right to take up a large tract of fertile, well-watered land on the De Grey River plains, an area specially praised in the Gregory report.

John Withnell may not have been able to read but he had a good grasp of finance and quickly saw the merits of his wife's idea to improve their lot without the outlay of large sums of capital. He started to make plans. They, with their two children and a large quantity of sheep and farming equipment, would charter a ship and sail north to virgin territory and establish a large farm there.

After four difficult years of hard work trying to make Hillside pay, with Emma's enthusiastic support John sold the farm. The Withnells invested practically all their capital in cattle, sheep and horses for their new farming venture. Emma was only twenty-one, full of energy and ideas and prepared to brave the unknown, even though she realised she might be the only European woman in a large area with no doctor near at hand. But she was convinced she could cope, and excited by the prospect of a new and more productive life with the man she loved.

John had earned enough to pay £650 (a great deal of money at that time) to charter the 187-ton *Sea Ripple* for the perilous voyage north and invest the remaining profits from the sale of Hillside in their pioneering venture.

Stocking up for the long sea voyage to Port Walcott took some time. By the time the *Sea Ripple* was ready to sail, Emma was six months pregnant. Her worried parents begged her to wait until after the baby was born and join John later, once he had established a home. Emma refused to listen to their fears, convinced that 'the Good Lord would look after her'.

The chartered vessel had restricted space and with so many farm animals in the hold, the atmosphere soon became foetid and smelly.

Engraving of the Sea Ripple, *the ship on which the Withnells sailed to Nickol Bay.*

But the ship made good headway in the steady breeze and at first everything went well. However, ten days after its departure from Fremantle the *Sea Ripple* was becalmed near the port of Cossack (then known as Tien Tsin, after a Chinese ship that had been wrecked there). For days they floated over calm water without making any progress. The stench of the animals in the hold increased and the burning hot sun made life on board uncomfortable.

At last dark clouds appeared on the horizon. Minutes later a gust of wind rippled the surface of the sea, the sails bulged again and the ship started to move. But the wind rapidly became a gale. Soon the sea became a boiling cauldron, tossing the *Sea Ripple* around like a walnut shell.

In panic the crew reefed in the sails, battened down the hatches and ordered passengers to remain in their cabins. While the wind howled around the rigging, the helmsman struggled to hold the ship steady. There was chaos on deck and much of the Withnells' precious cargo was swept overboard. For hours the gale whipped the waves into giant peaks and troughs, terrifying the children.

Finally, the helmsman lost control of the rudder. The *Sea Ripple* was blown in a north-easterly direction towards the shore, about 140 kilometres beyond Cossack on Nickol Bay. John and Emma watched in horror as the ship drifted towards a reef which suddenly emerged in front of the bow. Then, with a crushing sound and a violent shudder, the ship struck the reef. Water flooded into the hold through a gaping hole in the hull. The animals panicked and some were trampled to death.

The gale abated as quickly as it had blown up. While the crew tried to establish order on deck, the tide went out and the ship became lodged on the reef and would not budge. As the sea level dropped, so the ship gradually started to lean to one side. Eventually, the deck was sloping at such a steep angle that it was impossible to walk on it. The petrified sheep in the hold slid into a heap on the lower side, and many suffocated under the weight of those that lay on top. Others broke down the hatches and managed to escape, some plunged headlong overboard and drowned or became engulfed in the slimy mud and suffocated.

In haste, the crew lowered one of the tenders and seven months pregnant Emma, Fanny and the children were rowed to the nearby

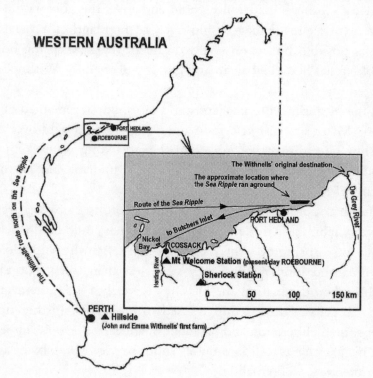

WESTERN AUSTRALIA

shore. Treacherous mud flats, extending for hundreds of metres from the shore, had to be crossed on foot to reach higher ground. Black sticky mud oozed through the women's shoes as they carried the children to a small island surrounded by mangroves and still more mud — but to their dismay it was impossible to reach the mainland from that point.

They sheltered from the fierce heat under a canopy they rigged from a tarpaulin supported by driftwood. Before long they were bitten by hundreds of tiny sandflies.

The surviving stock was taken from the ship to the edge of the mud flats, but more sheep stuck fast in the black sticky morass and perished. Many of those that managed to make it to the island wandered off again and drowned in the incoming tide. It was agonising for John and Emma to watch the animals they had worked so hard to raise perish before their eyes.

The men helped to fix the hole in the ship's hull but the work could only be done at low tide. As a temporary measure the captain decided to fother a spare sail with tar and cover the hole with it. He wanted to get his damaged ship back to Fremantle for repairs as soon as possible, but was forced to wait for the next spring tide to be able to get her afloat again and unfairly blamed the Withnells for his predicament.

In the meantime, Emma, Fanny and the children remained on the island.[5] Mattresses, blankets, food and water were brought over from the ship. The sun was so fierce that their drinking water, kept in a wooden keg, became so hot it was almost undrinkable. At night, swarms of mosquitoes descended upon them.

After a couple of days, the stench from rotting carcasses became so overwhelming that the women and children could hardly bear it. Finally, on a spring tide, the men managed to get the ship afloat.

Emma and John realised they were less than thirty kilometres south of their destination, the De Grey River, but the captain, angry over the damage to his ship, refused to take them further north. After some deliberation and payment of another £100 he agreed to take his passengers 140 kilometres south to Cossack, which lay on his route back to Fremantle.

After three days of sailing into the wind, the *Sea Ripple* finally arrived at Nickol Bay — then known as Butchers Inlet. Late in the afternoon of 14 April they anchored in deep water a few kilometres offshore.

The following day John Withnell and the other men went ashore in one of the ship's tenders to inspect the area. The remaining stock, including John's precious stallion, were loaded into the second tender and taken ashore as well. Emma, Fanny and the children remained on board and waited for John's return.

While the others looked after the greatly depleted flock of sheep, John walked on ahead to assess the possibility of settling in that area, which seemed to grow nothing but spinifex. Towards the end of the day he arrived at a nearby sheep station, managed by William Shakespeare Hall, known locally as Shaky. Shaky was an eccentric but kind-hearted man with a bushy black beard. He knew the region well, having been a member of Francis Gregory's exploring party in 1861. Shaky kept a journal in order to keep his employer, the wealthy landowner John Wellard, informed about the events on his station. His diary entry for 15 April 1864 reads:

> Withnell arrived at Station about 7 p.m. Heard one gun
> from *Sea Ripple* at 8 p.m. previous night and would have
> gone down had there been a second.[6]

The following morning Withnell and Shaky went down to the shore. Shaky instructed two of his men to follow them in a bullock dray containing a dinghy and an eight-gallon (thirty-six litre) barrel full of drinking water. John and Shaky returned to the *Sea Ripple* in the dinghy while the other men remained to look after the Withnells' horses, bullocks and other livestock.

The next day all the passengers and what was left of their goods were taken ashore. They disembarked on a strip of beach, called Upper Landing, which was separated from *terra firma* by a large swamp. This time the women were saved from having to wade through murky water and mud because Shaky had arranged for two horses to be waiting for them on the beach.

On 17 April Shaky recorded in his diary:

> Two boats came on there [the beach called Upper
> Landing], one with Mrs. Withnell and children, without
> breakfast or a drop of water and in the blazing hot sun,
> and the poor little children crying for some [water].
>
> I told Mrs Withnell the bullock dray was at the head of
> the marsh with 8 gallons of water waiting for her . . . I
> put Mrs Withnell's sister on one horse, with one child,
> carried the other and gave Mrs Withnell my horse
> [loaded] with bundles on to lead, so off we went with
> men following with such little things as they could carry.

Most of their goods were left on the beach inside a timber and canvas enclosure the men had built, believing it was above the high-tide level. Fortunately the most important items like tents, bedding and food were carried across the swamp by the horses and men.

After crossing the swamp they quenched their thirst and placed their luggage on top of the waiting dray. Shaky then led the party to Dig Down, an isolated spot about ten kilometres from their landing place, near the mouth of the Harding River. There they found shade trees and a waterhole containing drinking water. Tents were pitched which would be their living quarters for the next five weeks.

A few days later, John Withnell, John Hancock and one of Shaky's labourers rode back to near where they had been shipwrecked, in the hope of finding some of the missing sheep and horses. Frequently they needed to consult their copy of the map drawn by Francis Gregory. In the meantime Emma, Fanny and the Withnell children stayed at their camping spot. Shaky kept an eye on them and, on one occasion, led the whole family to his house to shelter them from a deluge of rain.

Three weeks later John Withnell and his companions returned with the sad news that they had been unable to find any trace of their lost stock. But John also had good news. They had found an excellent spot for permanent settlement about sixteen kilometres further along the Harding River beside a deep natural pool in the river.

When they did a final head count of the remaining stock, John found to his dismay that only eighty-four ewes, two rams, one horse and one cow had survived, plus a few chickens and ducks. Luckily, their sheep dogs were still alive and Emma's medicine chest was intact.

؎؎؎

With the help of Shaky, who by now had become a good friend, the Withnells and Hancocks moved camp upstream from Dig Down to a place called Yeeramukadoo pool (place of the wild fig) by the Ngarluma Aborigines whose hunting grounds it was.

On arrival Emma saw a green hill on the skyline and named it Mount Welcome, claiming, 'it gave us shelter, peace and rest at last'. She made them all kneel and thank God for saving them from the shipwreck. So Yeeramukadoo became the site of the Withnells' first home, which they named Mount Welcome Station.

They had to camp for many more weeks until John could build them a house on their site. Emma was now too near to giving birth to be able to assist. They had very little furniture left, so John fashioned a strong chair out of whale jawbones, which he had found on the shore.[7] Their shoes wore out and could not be replaced so Emma's resourceful husband made a variety of clogs using straps of sheepskin nailed to the upper side of wooden soles. He also made a baby's cradle out of half a water barrel.

On 1 June 1864, only a week after their arrival at the Harding River, Emma and John's third son was born, the first European child to be born in the north-west of Australia. Unfortunately for Emma, John was not a great help — all he knew about birth was pulling calves out of cows with a

COURTESY ROEBOURNE MUSEUM. PHOTO TISH LEES.

Emma Withnell's whalebone chair made by her husband, John.

rope. Accordingly, Emma's younger sister, Fanny, who was only sixteen, helped deliver the baby by following Emma's instructions. Although the little boy was born under primitive conditions, the remarkable and stoic Emma remained calm and brave throughout and their child, whom they named Robert Harding DeWitt Withnell, arrived safely.

In mid-June the men returned to the landing spot on the beach to retrieve the rest of the goods. They found another gale had blown up since they left and had swamped the enclosure. The heavier items — crates with farm equipment, tools and some of their household goods — still remained on the beach, but they were horrified to find that the remaining possessions, including the children's clothes and all those for the new baby, had been washed away by an exceptionally high tide. Most of the stores Emma had chosen so carefully had also disappeared into the sea. They managed only to salvage some of the flour and sugar. 'We kept the sugar for the children and fortunately the cow had calved so at least we had fresh milk,' wrote Emma.[8] Unfortunately the flour turned out to be full of weevils.

John, aware that he had lost most of their money in the shipwreck, now worried that no matter how hard they worked they would *never* recover their capital. He became depressed, saw himself as a failure and even thought of giving up and going back to Perth. Emma restored her husband's self-confidence by insisting she trusted him completely and saying she knew they would do well. The resilient Emma insisted they must continue with their original plan of setting up a farm with their eighty-four remaining sheep. She was determined they would not return home to her parents as failures.[9]

With Emma's encouragement, John continued building their new house. It was a very basic structure, made from locally available materials — walls of stone, held together with river clay. Cajuput trees, which grew along the river, were used to make posts and roof-framing. The roof was thatched with the ubiquitous spinifex. Later, once the roof started to leak, wooden shingles were installed instead of the spinifex.

In September 1864, they sheared their sheep amid great rejoicing. The following month their precious hand-washed wool was sent to

Perth aboard a vessel called the *Stag*. Emma's sister Fanny, her brother John Hancock, and Robert Withnell returned home aboard the same ship. Two of their farm hands, having complained that Mount Welcome was too isolated, also returned to Fremantle.

The Withnells and their one remaining labourer were now alone in the vast undeveloped region. Emma felt desperately lonely — and found it was hard work running the farm and caring for three young children without the help of her younger sister. She described how in the outback, 'There is always the awful loneliness. It must be hard for newcomers for the work is hard and the lonesomeness at times terrible.'[10]

From the start Emma was determined to maintain friendly relationships with the local indigenous people known as the Ngarluma. Two of the women, Nungerdie and Thoodoo, became her devoted helpers in the house and came to love the children.

For her part Emma respected the Ngarluma women when she saw how many miles they had to walk to find edible roots, tubers, berries and seeds to pound into a paste. They turned the paste into a kind of flour and made small cakes or patties from it, which they roasted on the fire to supplement the game the men had caught. When she had been at Mount Welcome for some time, Emma could see why the Ngarluma women appreciated the occasional gift of flour from her as it saved them many hours of hard work. And she understood why they were sometimes tempted to take food or bulbs from her garden which they regarded as a communal resource.

Whenever Ngarluma women came to visit Emma and her new baby she gave them presents of tea and sugar. They were happy to help care for her children in return. Often the Ngarluma women would ask Emma to take out the pins and let her hair down and they would touch it, admiring its softness and pale golden colour.

The Ngarluma women took Emma to swim in the river. They also invited her to attend food-increase ceremonies or women's corroborees. In return, Emma frequently treated their sores with ointments from her medicine chest and bathed sore eyes with borax, earning the reputation of 'Medicine Woman' in the process.

Emma and her husband were also known as 'Boorong' and 'Banaker' which, in the Ngarluma language, were terms of great respect.

Although Emma loved her husband dearly, cherished her children and had great respect for the Ngarluma women, she longed for another European woman to talk to. Since that was impossible, she coped with loneliness and isolation by working extremely hard. She rose early each day to avoid the worst of the heat. There were all the farm duties to attend to as well as the usual household chores. With no shops handy or workers available, clothes, household items, farm equipment, fences, and so on had to be made by hand.

Mutton was their staple diet, and fruit and vegetables were scarce or non-existent. Ships bringing them fresh supplies and seeds for a vegetable garden took a long time to make their way up the coast. On one occasion, the supplies of dried goods, tea and sugar Emma had ordered from Perth were lost.

In the long evenings by candlelight, Emma taught her husband how to read and write. At first John found it difficult but persevered and eventually was able to write his own business letters.

There were, however, consolations for living in one of the most isolated regions of Australia. The wild flowers were beautiful, the soil around their house was fertile and Emma cultivated a fine ornamental garden. But she had less success with her vegetable garden; as soon as she planted seeds or bulbs the Ngarluma dug them up and ate them.

❧ ❧ ❧

The Withnells had been 'squatting' (occupying without government permission) on the land along the Harding River for nearly six months when John became anxious to have the lease of his selection formalised. With Emma's help he submitted an application for lease of 10,000 acres (4000 hectares) and applied for the lease of 100,000 additional acres (40,500 hectares) on the Sherlock River. Emma's brother John had promised to take the necessary action to expedite the lease on behalf of his brother-in-law, as soon as he arrived back in Perth. On 20 July 1865, a lease in the name of John and Emma Withnell for 10,000 acres of land fronting the Harding River was approved.

Emma was confident they would obtain a lease on the land on the Sherlock River as well and was impatient to look at the area. She and John loaded their children and camping gear onto a dray and travelled the fifty kilometres to view their prospective property. Emma was delighted to see that it was both beautiful and fertile, with the Sherlock River running through the centre. Hoping that one day they would go and live there, she selected the spot where she wanted a homestead to be built.

A few months later their second lease was granted and John put a large flock of wethers (castrated rams) on the vast property, sunk a well and made plans to build a dwelling there as soon as they had enough capital to do so.

Hard as Emma and John worked, it became apparent that building up their farm could take years. So John decided to diversify his interests.

Collecting valuable pearl shells from the beaches and the seabed of Nickol Bay appealed to him. Although he hated being separated from his family, John now spent a lot of time at Nickol Bay where he started his own pearling operation, leaving Emma to manage the station.

Employing the Ngarluma as divers, he collected pearl shells and when there were enough shipped them to Fremantle. Occasionally John found a precious pearl in one of the shells which provided him with extra income. On his visits home to Mount Welcome, John brought some of the most beautiful shells with him and gave them to Emma. Gradually her collection grew and eventually she became an expert on pearls and pearl shells.

John, being a farmer at heart, longed to work his land rather than collect pearl shells. Leaving one of his labourers in charge of the pearling operation, he returned to Mount Welcome. He found that under Emma's capable management the farm had done well. Their flock was gradually increasing due to successful breeding and through Emma buying additional stock when she had the money to do so.

≝ ≝ ≝

During the 1860s more settlers came to the area. Several development schemes were started but most of them foundered, with the new colonists taking the first ship south to Fremantle or returning to England, saying the land was impossibly harsh.

The Denison Plains Association was one such scheme, which had been formed by Melbourne investors in order to take up huge tracts of virgin land at the head of the Victoria River (East Kimberley) and further north at Roebuck Bay (the future site of Broome). Under its resettlement plan, in May 1865 a party of British settlers arrived in Fremantle by the sailing ship *Warrior*. They were told the grim news of failures of other pioneering ventures at Roebuck Bay, but were determined to sail northwards all the same.

This group included a surveyor by the name of Wedge, his wife and five children, and it may well have been their salvation that their ship was blown into Nickol Bay. Short of drinking water, the passengers decided to land and settle there instead of proceeding to Roebuck Bay.

The arrival of a ship was related to Emma by the Ngarluma women. She had now been in the isolated north-west for thirteen months and when she heard that women and children were camping on the shore she insisted that they all be brought to Mount Welcome to rest and recover. It had been so long since Emma had seen a European woman, she was thrown into confusion and worried that she had no suitable clothes in which to receive her guests. Normally she wore old working clothes, pulled her hair back and plaited it into a pigtail. Now she realised she could not greet total strangers like this; they would think her eccentric. She must play the role of gracious hostess as her mother would have done.

Emma pulled her shipping trunk out from under the bed, rummaged in it and brought out her best outfit, which had survived the shipwreck. She held up a faded silk dress with a lace collar that had been fashionable when she left Perth, all those years ago. She found the hooped crinoline which went under it, and some frilled petticoats, put them on and slipped the silk dress over her head. She pinned on a brooch which her mother had given her; it had belonged to her English grandmother and she comforted herself with the thought that if the new arrivals were 'gentlefolk' they would recognise that she too came from a similar milieu.

Emma untied her long hair, brushed it out and did her best to put it up in an elegant chignon. She longed for a woman friend and knew that this first meeting with the strangers could be important in making friends. And so, dressed in a gown that had been the height of fashion over a decade earlier, Emma laid the table with her few remaining pieces of good china and awaited her visitors.

When she heard Shaky's bullock team pull up in the yard, she watched eagerly as a pleasant-looking woman with five children and a young governess descended from the dray. Emma was so excited that she burst into tears of joy. Rather than playing the grand lady and waiting to be introduced, impulsively she ran out of the house and hugged Mrs Wedge and her children. She was overjoyed when they returned her embraces and seemed equally pleased to see her.

She ushered them all inside, sat them down and poured out cups of tea all round. She discovered that, like her, Mrs Wedge had endured a terrifying sea voyage and been through a severe storm. The two small Wedge boys played with the Withnell children. When the Ngarluma children approached giggling nervously, they were invited by the boys to join in their games.

Emma was delighted when the Wedges settled at Roebourne and the two families became good friends.

❧ ❧ ❧

In 1864, a year before the Wedges arrived, a party of eighty-four people had drifted into Camden Harbour north of Roebuck Bay. They were quickly followed by a resident magistrate named Robert J. Sholl who was accompanied by a staff of surveyors and police. Like many others in the north-west, this settlement also failed for lack of water and harsh conditions and was abandoned in 1865. Sholl was ordered south to Nickol Bay.

Sholl and his family arrived from Camden Harbour at Nickol Bay that same year. The Sholls had to take an exhausting fifteen-kilometre walk along the hot and dusty road to the new settlement at Roebourne where they decided to visit the Withnells before pitching their tents.

Sholl wrote to the Colonial Secretary in Perth, reporting his arrival and giving his impressions of Mrs Withnell as a kind and efficient woman:

> I landed at once with some of the passengers and set forth on foot in the direction of Mr. Withnell's station on the Harding, about 10 miles from the beach. We were kindly received by Mrs Withnell, her husband being absent from home at the time.
>
> I landed horses and stores at Butcher's Inlet beach [Nickol Bay]. As we were frightened of the tide, Mr. Gall carted our stores to high ground. The natives are a fine lot of men, their conduct is good and from the first settlement until now, have been able to help the settlers.[11]

An official residence was built for the Sholls, only a few hundred metres away from the Withnells' house.

The Withnells were a constant source of help and companionship to Magistrate Sholl and were frequently mentioned in his journal:

> December 5 1865: Withnell with two drays came bringing wool and water.

> December 15: Withnell cleansed and deepened the well. There is sufficient for shepherding the flock and water at a hole two miles away. This morning he started off with his bullock dray. Withnell is a most indefatigable man and took the bullock and horse teams to the landing for goods.

> December 28: Spoke to Withnell [to ascertain] if he would oblige us with meat from his station.

> April 2 1866: Kind Mrs Withnell sent cooked fish, the natives had caught a large one.

It is significant that in Sholl's records the ladylike Emma is referred to as 'Mrs Withnell' while John is not dignified by the title 'Mr' but is simply 'Withnell'.

With the influx of settlers to the Nickol Bay area, the town of Roebourne was formally established in 1866, and the district of Nickol Bay gazetted in 1871.

Mount Welcome Station presented a problem for those, including Robert Sholl, who were required to draw up the town allotments. The part of the property where John Withnell had built both his homestead and other outbuildings was right in the middle of the proposed new town. The solution found was to grant the Withnells six acres (three hectares) on which their buildings sat as a town allotment and compensate them for the loss to their run by granting them another lease on land adjoining Sherlock Station. The Withnells were now owners of a suburban lot.

With the approach from sea to the new town of Roebourne so difficult, John Withnell saw a new opportunity for business. On arrival ships had to put up with the inconvenience for passengers of having to anchor in deep water several kilometres offshore. Passengers and their luggage had to be rowed in a dinghy to the beach. Then they had to cross marshes before making the long walk to the settlement. Entrepreneurial John Withnell saw the possibilities for earning income by building a flat-bottomed lighter. For a fee, he would convey new arrivals and their luggage directly from the ship along the Harding River to the fledgling town of Roebourne.

While the lighter brought in some income, it was not enough and John saw other opportunities in the developing town. With Emma's approval and assistance, he opened a butcher's shop-cum-general store which could supply not only the new settlers to the area, but the increasing number of pearlers and other itinerant workers.

The influx of people to the Roebourne area, including Malays who participated in the fledgling pearling industry, also brought disease, and tragically for the Ngarluma, smallpox. In 1866 a smallpox epidemic broke out amongst the Ngarluma. Emma did whatever she could to reduce their suffering, including vaccinating many against the disease.[12] Nevertheless hundreds of workers and tribespeople died. Their rotting corpses were found on beaches and among the mangroves and Emma feared cholera or typhoid would result. She managed to persuade the Ngarluma *not* to follow their normal practice of mummifying corpses by exposing them to sunlight, but to bury them immediately, in order to reduce the possibility of more disease.

✧ ✧ ✧

A welcome event for Emma the following year, 1867, was the return of her sister Fanny and her brother John Hancock. Fanny, now Mrs George Fisher, already had one child and came north to join her husband, owner of Mount Fisher Station. Because there was as yet no home for them on Mount Fisher, Fanny and her husband lived in a cottage at Roebourne. It pleased Emma very much to have their company. Emma's brother John by now also had a wife and two daughters. He had come north to manage a property which he called Woodbrook.

On 10 February 1867, Emma's first daughter was born, a most welcome addition to a family with three sons. They called their beautiful baby Emily Ellen. Emma felt weak and ill after the birth and it took a long time for her to recover, partly because of a shortage of fresh vegetables leading to vitamin deficiency. The Withnells had had little success with their vegetable garden and orchard, and the settlement was still dependent for many supplies on trading vessels arriving from Fremantle.

The year 1867, however, was a disastrous one for coastal shipping. Seven ships were lost in the treacherous and uncharted waters along the coast of Western Australia. The most tragic loss for the Withnells was that of the 117-ton *Emma* (named after Emma Withnell by its owner Walter Padbury). Forty-two people perished aboard, many of them from Roebourne including young Treverton Sholl, much-loved son of Magistrate Robert Sholl.

As well as losing several close friends in the wreck of the *Emma*, the Withnells also suffered considerable financial loss. Golden sovereigns to the value of £148 (all the earnings from the Withnells' sales of meat Magistrate Sholl had bought for government staff and increasing numbers of prisoners in the local gaol) and their entire wool clip for that year sank to the bottom of the sea. Several bags of valuable pearl shells also went down with the ship.[13]

With the loss of such an amount of money as well as potential sales, the Withnells were forced to sell their store. They grieved with the Sholls and the other Roebourne families for their lost relatives but the continual round of farm and home duties kept them occupied.

On top of this, from 1868 to 1872 severe droughts devastated the Roebourne district and water reserves dried up. The Harding River virtually stopped running, and only a few muddy waterholes remained. Many sheep and cattle died of thirst or for lack of food, while the condition of the remaining livestock became pitiable. The Ngarluma also suffered from the shortage of drinking water and from assorted ailments which Emma nursed as best she could.

By the end of 1868 Emma was pregnant again and pleased that her sister Sophia had arrived in Roebourne and would be there to help with the birth. Sophia was also a great comfort to the Sholls, becoming firm friends with Robert Sholl's daughter Penelope. The two took many rides together and visited each other often.

On 25 August 1869 Emma gave birth to another boy. If the start of a new life gave her hope that their fortunes might turn, she was mistaken. With another mouth to feed and a larger family to care for there were more demands than ever on her time. Then the forces of nature hit with a vengeance.

In 1869 the area suffered from a cyclone, bringing much needed rain, but also causing havoc. Warned by the friendly Ngarluma, who instinctively knew that a 'willy-willy' was on its way, the settlers battened down. They put heavy chains across their roofs and attached these to boulders, a precaution that saved many structures and lives.

The cyclonic rain brought only a short reprieve from the drought. In the cycle of life and death, death seemed to be pre-eminent. In February 1871, Emma's younger sister Sophia fell ill from hepatitis and died on 10 April. She was only twenty-one. Not until 1875 would a doctor come to work in the area. Sophia's death was followed by another shock for Emma — the death of her father down south.

Then on 20 March 1872 the most devastating cyclone ever to strike Roebourne and the surrounding areas occurred. Again the pioneer settlers took all possible precautions, but this time they were to no avail. The whole town was virtually flattened and left a ruin.

Outside the Withnells' house the wind roared, uprooting trees and tossing them around like matchsticks. Emma, who was in the last months of another pregnancy, told her children to lie under the beds and the dining table. They were to wait for the cyclone to pass. It was a long time doing so. There was a brief silence as the eye of the cyclone passed overhead. Emma urged little Emily Ellen and the boys to escape to the only outbuilding that was still standing. In despair and mounting terror she discovered that her baby son was missing.

After the lull the wind began to howl again, this time even stronger than before. Fortunately the wooden outbuilding withstood the onslaught.

After a few hours the cyclone passed. Panic-stricken Emma and John went to look for the missing toddler. Finally they found their baby boy wedged tight between two rocks, where the gale-force wind had blown him. Miraculously, neither the baby nor any of the other children was seriously hurt, but Emma had received a deep gash on her wrist from a flying piece of wood.

Emma's sister, Fanny Fisher, who had three children by now, was not so lucky. After the cyclone destroyed the Fishers' cottage and the roof had collapsed, Fanny was found lying unconscious, her baby dead in her arms. In fact, poor Fanny suffered another terrible blow when, a few months later, she lost her other two children through a water-borne disease which may have been typhoid or blackwater fever. The final blow came seven years later when Fanny's husband, George, sailing home from Perth was shipwrecked and lost his life.

After the storm, Magistrate Sholl, still grieving for his dead son, found his recently completed house also in ruins. Like other Roebourne people, he had to resort to living in a tent until his house was rebuilt.

The Harding River, normally a sluggish stream, had changed into a torrent of murky brown water and was overflowing into the adjoining pastures. When John and Emma went to inspect the damage to their property they discovered many of their precious sheep that had managed to survive the drought had been drowned. In addition, some 600 valuable wethers had been lost from Sherlock Station. Once again Emma and John showed courage and resilience in overcoming their setbacks. With dogged determination they started to rebuild everything that had been ruined by the cyclone, replenished their stock and continued farming. Emma's medicine chest remained safe and she was able to go on treating her own children and those of other settlers.

Four months after the cyclone Emma gave birth to twin boys, Horace and Ernest. Their house was still not completed and it is almost beyond belief that 29-year-old Emma was able to look after and feed two babies and five other children without a proper roof over her head.

But despite the hardships and the setbacks Emma managed to maintain her faith in the future and her keen sense of humour. She was always able to laugh at her own mistakes. Once, when John was away on a pearling expedition, she saw lurking in the twilight what appeared to be the menacing figure of a man. She picked up her rifle and called out, 'Who's there?'

Receiving no reply, Emma took aim and fired — and hit one of her own long-skirted dresses which was swinging in the breeze on the clothesline.

≈ ≈ ≈

With the continuing arrival of settlers at Roebourne, John Withnell recognised the dangers European men posed to Aboriginal women. John placed the Ngarluma camp at Mount Welcome out of bounds to Europeans at night and insisted that anyone who raided the camp for girls or tried to barter them for alcohol would be punished according to Ngarluma custom.[14]

The Ngarluma women came to respect the Withnells for doing their best to protect them but some of the new settlers experienced deteriorating relations with the local Aborigines. The newcomers complained that the Ngarluma were pilfering from them and sought retribution from the magistrate. On one occasion Sholl's men went to investigate but found that the settlers' complaints were unfounded. Like elsewhere in Australia, the Aborigines felt that as the settlers were shooting their kangaroos and other game, they had a right to take food in return. Nevertheless, the Withnells found themselves caught in the middle when one Aboriginal man was charged and locked up in John's wool press in the period before the prison was built in 1866.

Emma was deeply concerned about the condition of the Ngarluma, especially the Aboriginal pearl divers. Extremely good underwater swimmers, they were being exploited and forced to stay too long below the surface, placing their lives at risk to bring more profit to the owners of the pearling luggers. Emma suggested to Sholl that legislation should be brought in to limit this. Sholl agreed. Acting on information supplied by the Withnells, the now retired magistrate drafted a proposal that led to the passing of the 1873 Pearl Shell Fishery Regulation Act to protect Aboriginal and Malay divers.

❧ ❧ ❧

Two more sons were born to the Withnells during their busy years at Mount Welcome Station and to the chores of cooking, sewing, mending and midwifery with which she was helped by her faithful house girls Nungerdie and Thoodoo, Emma now added the duties of teaching, using old newspapers instead of textbooks to instruct the children to read. She described in a letter to her parents how 'I brought my children up in Christian faith and without most of the refinements of civilised life'.

By 1879 Emma had been the matriarch of Mount Welcome Station for fifteen years, bearing nine children and running their farm with her usual efficiency and good humour. She had endured cyclone, drought, epidemics and, in 1878, a fire which destroyed many wooden structures on the Withnells' property and once again necessitated an extensive rebuilding program. Now their homestead was surrounded by dozens of houses — in effect, their six acres were now in Roebourne itself and they felt hemmed in. Roebourne had become a sprawling, noisy town — no longer was Mount Welcome Station the quiet and peaceful spot where the family had settled fifteen years ago. During the day, bullock drays rattled over rugged stony roads; at night brawling and loud laughter at Roebourne's public houses kept Emma and the children awake.

Emma and John decided it was time to move away from the area. They sold their now flourishing property on the Harding River to their friend Robert Sholl and moved to the much larger Sherlock Station. In anticipation of the move, a large homestead had been completed on the spot Emma had selected years earlier.

By this time Emma and John's land holdings had dramatically increased from the original lease of 100,000 acres to 307,000 acres (124,000 hectares), which would provide sufficient land for their sons to farm as well. At Sherlock Station, named for the river which watered the property,[15] Emma developed beautiful gardens. Both she and John were happy to be away from the hustle and bustle of the town of Roebourne, now known as the 'capital of the north'.

In time Emma bore two more children. Of her eleven children only the first two had been born with the help of a doctor. Her others were delivered by Emma herself directing Fanny or Sophia, or more often her husband who was assisted by her devoted Ngarluma house girls, Nungerdie and Thoodoo.

Emma and John remained at Sherlock Station for nine years, by which time their eldest sons were well capable of running the farm under their father's supervision.

Despite many setbacks from the harsh climate and the occasional cyclone, they enjoyed pioneering the vast north-west area which they and Walter Padbury who started a sheep station in 1863, and John Wellard, had been the first to settle and develop. They had set off for the north with 650 healthy sheep but due to the shipwreck had been left with only eighty-four ewes, two rams, a horse and a cow. But they had never lost hope in the future — and now thanks to a great deal of hard work, courage and determination they possessed 20,000 sheep, 130 horses and 150 head of cattle and were regarded as very successful pioneers.[16]

The Withnells had seen many changes to the area and by 1885 isolation from civilisation was no longer such a problem. The Overland Telegraph Line now linked Roebourne, Geraldton and Perth, and many more people would arrive once gold was discovered in the Pilbarra in 1888.

By that year, however, John's health had started to fail. He was now sixty-five and suffering from asthma. His right leg had been badly damaged in a fall and he had been advised he needed to live close to a hospital. He was now happy to hand over the running of the property to several of his sons and his capable son-in-law, John Meares.

At forty-five Emma was still healthy. However, she was concerned about her husband's health and was also anxious to have good schools for her younger children and opportunities for them to take up careers other than farming.

In September 1888, John and Emma finally left their beautiful Sherlock Station homestead. They said goodbye to the local Aborigines who gathered around the homestead, keening and mourning for the departure of the children they had come to love. Emma embraced her two faithful helpers, Thoodoo and Nungerdie, who gave her a beautifully woven dilly bag as a present. When they passed through Yeeramukadoo — the place of the wild fig — now Roebourne, they also said goodbye to their Ngarluma friends, who wailed a mournful farewell to the much-loved Boorong and Banaker.

As their ship drew away, the wharf at Nickol Bay was crowded with settlers who had come to wave goodbye to Emma Withnell, 'the mother of the north-west', her husband and the younger children, Herbert, William, Lilla and Grace.

❧ ❧ ❧

Emma and John settled in the Perth suburb of Guildford. Through hard work they had made enough money to retire in comfort, although Emma would continue to assist those in need and help deliver babies free of charge whenever she was asked to do so.

Most of their elder children remained in the north, eventually marrying and providing the couple with grandchildren.

Karratha Station near Port Hedland, formerly owned by the Withnells.

Their eldest son George, who had come north with them on that fateful boat trip in 1864, remained single. At thirty-four he married a Guildford girl named Ellen Amelia Worth, of whom Emma had become very fond. To celebrate the marriage of their first born, Emma and John gave a splendid ball at Guildford Town Hall.

John Withnell died in May 1898 in his seventy-fifth year. The following year Emma, always a shrewd investor, bought a half share in Karratha Station on the Maitland River (near today's Port Hedland), together with three of her sons. The property had been originally selected for their eldest daughter, Emily Ellen, who in 1886 had married pastoralist John Meares and given Emma and John their first grandchild. Eventually the widowed Emma rented out her Guildford residence and built herself a delightful new and smaller house, called Esselmont, at Northam.

For the next thirty years Emma divided her time between staying with her sons and daughters in the north-west, in her own house at Northam or with relatives in Perth. She joined the Karakatta Club and became an excellent public speaker. She was interviewed by journalists and historians who wanted to know what outback life had been like in the early days of the Pilbara.

Emma was one of the first women to be appointed a justice of the peace in Western Australia and was praised by the Premier, Sir James Mitchell, for her role in pioneering the region.[17] The Withnell family developed a total of eleven pastoral properties and Emma's descendants still run some of these stations.

In spite of their initial difficulties, Emma and John Withnell founded a dynasty which spread out across the rapidly developing state of Western Australia. Sons, daughters, grandsons and granddaughters all inherited the determination, enterprise and energy of Emma and her husband. Emma was proud of her eleven children and considered their successes in life ample repayment for her care and affection.

❧ ❧ ❧

In May 1928 Emma died of cholecystitis at the Mount Lawley home of her eldest son. She was buried in the Anglican cemetery at Guildford beside her husband. Nine of her children attended her funeral. Premier Sir James Mitchell gave the eulogy and said: 'Emma Withnell has been placed amongst the state makers of Western Australia in appreciation of the work she has done for her homeland.'

All her life Emma had been an imaginative yet supremely practical woman. She helped her husband in their many enterprises with determination and foresight. She was a woman in advance of her time — in an era when relations between Europeans and Aborigines were often hostile, she believed in establishing friendship with the local indigenous people and saved the lives of many Ngarluma during an epidemic of smallpox.

All those who have profited from the pearling industry around Broome and the vast mining wealth of the Pilbara area (which now exports one-eighth of the world's iron ore) owe Emma Withnell a debt of gratitude. Indeed, it was one of Emma's sons, James Withnell, who, in 1888, discovered the gold-bearing lode which started the Pilbara gold rush and eventually led to other mineral discoveries in the area. Another son ran an iron foundry as a sideline.

The name Withnell appears on street names and in small parks in many parts of the north-west of Western Australia — at Withnell

Emma Withnell's granddaughter Judith Stove standing beside the memorial to Emma near Roebourne.

Hill, Withnell Bay, and at Karratha and the more modern mining towns of Dampier and Port Hedland. It also appears on a plaque set amid a cairn of stones near Roebourne that acts as a memorial to Emma. The cairn was erected by the Country Women's Association, an organisation which has been of immense benefit to women in remote areas, and with which Emma Withnell was associated in her later years.

Due to the 'tyranny of distance', very few people in the eastern seaboard of Australia know the name Emma Withnell, although she was one of our greatest female pioneers, an entrepreneurial, enterprising and determined woman, as well as a dedicated humanitarian and a generous human being.

The plaque in Roebourne commemorates 'the mother of the north-west' who dared to take on the challenge of developing that formerly wild and remote region which has brought economic success and prosperity to the thriving state of Western Australia.

CHAPTER 3

Atlanta 'Attie'
Hope Bradshaw
1866 – 1929

MOTHERING 'SEVEN LITTLE AUSTRALIANS' AT ALICE SPRINGS

In 1899 33-year-old Atlanta Bradshaw and her children undertook a hazardous journey from Adelaide across the red desert at the heart of Australia to take up residence at Alice Springs Telegraph Station.[1] Atlanta's husband, Thomas Bradshaw, had been appointed superintendent of the telegraph line as well as its postmaster. He was replacing Irish-born Francis Gillen who had been at the telegraph station for seven years and left to work on a book about Aboriginal desert peoples.

The Overland Telegraph Line was considered a technological marvel for its time. Alice Springs Telegraph Station played a vital role in transmitting the latest news from London, via undersea cable, to Australia. From Darwin (then known as Port Darwin), messages were passed through stations at Pine Creek, Katherine, Daly Waters, Powell Creek, Tennant Creek, Barrow Creek, Alice Springs, Charlotte Waters, Oodnadatta and several more stations to the head office at Adelaide, where Thomas Bradshaw had been employed as night superintendent.

As a boy Thomas Bradshaw had migrated to Australia with his family from southern England to the Portland area in Victoria,

CENTRAL AUSTRALIA

where he grew up and joined the telegraph office.[2] He later moved to Adelaide and worked as a telegraphist at the General Post Office rising to the position of night supervisor.

In 1887, aged twenty-eight, Thomas married tall, raven-haired Atlanta Allchurch, a capable, resilient and hard-working 21-year-old, with a mind of her own. Atlanta enjoyed cooking and loved children. Soon she had four of her own, becoming a loving and devoted mother.

Perhaps in wanting a large family Atlanta was compensating for her lonely childhood. Her sea captain father was often away from home for long periods. In fact, Atlanta had been born at sea off the Cape of Good Hope. Her mother had been accompanying her husband, captain of the SS *Atlanta,* on its way to South Australia, and Atlanta was named after the ship.

Atlanta and Thomas eventually set up home in Halifax Street in Adelaide; however, late in 1898, feeling the toll of working at nights, Thomas decided on a career change. To Atlanta's dismay, he signed a contract to run the Alice Springs Overland Telegraph Station.

Once appointed Thomas had to set out almost immediately. In March 1899 he left by train for Terowie, farewelled by his wife and children — clever dark-haired Winifred Doris (Doris); plump little Katherine Constance ('Consie'); lively Edmund Mortimer ('Mort'), and cuddly Jack (christened Eric Ivan), the baby of the family.

At Terowie, Thomas had to change trains and go on to Oodnadatta. As there was no road across the desert beyond Oodnadatta he was to go by horse and buggy through rough country to Alice Springs. This leg of the journey would take Thomas five or six weeks, camping out every night. Once he arrived he had to prepare suitable accommodation for his family who were to make the same journey at a later date.

The idea of camping for weeks in the desert with a baby, a toddler and two lively elder children did not exactly enchant Atlanta. But she loved Thomas and lived in an era when the duty of a good wife was to follow her husband wherever he went, so she was determined to make the best of their situation at the telegraph station. She may also have remembered the times when her father was away for long periods at sea, and determined *her* children would not have an absentee father.

Atlanta's neighbours in Adelaide were horrified to learn she was off to the outback. Her parents were also extremely concerned. At that time 'ladies' did not go to the outback. But Atlanta shrugged off their fears. Perhaps she thought that if Francis Gillen's wife Amelia ('Minnie') had been able to stick it out, then so could she.

But the more she heard about the dangers and hardships of the outback, the more worried Attie Bradshaw must have felt. Wives of Thomas's former colleagues whispered about poisonous snakes and polluted water and told her the story of Carl Kraegen, the first superintendent at the telegraph station who had died of thirst on the journey out to Alice Springs to start operations. They also told her about poor Superintendent Flint, who died of rheumatic fever.[3] Nor could she have helped worrying that there would be no doctor or midwife for hundreds of miles.

Thomas had sought to calm his wife's fears by telling her they would have the very latest medical textbooks and that a doctor could be consulted over the line if the children fell sick. He would transmit messages to the doctor in Morse code and wait for his reply, or he could contact the nurses at the new hospital at Port Darwin.

Atlanta had reminded Thomas there was schooling for their children to consider. In those days no one ever dreamed of a School of the Air. Women in the outback had to educate their own children or, if they could afford it, employ a governess. To pacify Atlanta, Thomas had promised they too would employ a governess. Although they could not afford to pay her very much, Atlanta succeeded in engaging Bertha Easom, an enthusiastic and attractive young woman in her early twenties who wanted a change from working in an office.

Thomas was also aware that Atlanta had a soft spot for her younger brother Ernest, who had had trouble settling down to a steady job. So he promised he would find the young man a job with the telegraph station and he too could live with them. That thought cheered Atlanta up. She loved Ernest, her boisterous handsome young brother, and hoped he would soon settle down to a regular career and get married.

Eventually the sad day came when Atlanta had to leave her parents and her dear sister Emily. Bertha joined them on the station platform. With four children under the age of eight, Atlanta must have been relieved to have some help on the long and harrowing journey ahead of her.

The first leg of their journey from Adelaide took them to hot, dusty Terowie. Here they boarded the narrow-gauge train called the Ghan, named for the Afghan camel drivers who had opened up the outback and continued to deliver goods there by camel train. The Ghan was pulled by a steam engine that belched out smoke and soot. Cups of tea were made en route from the boiling water of the engine and passed down the train.[4] Legend had it that if ever the engine packed up and food ran out, passengers lived off whatever game the engine driver was able to shoot.

Along their way, the train stopped overnight at Quorn and at Hergott Springs, where thankfully they all piled off into hotels for the night. (Hergott Springs, named after a German settler, would in World War I be renamed Marree.)

Finally, after four days' travel, they reached the terminus at Oodnadatta. Oodnadatta was a bleak, dusty place, consisting of a combined telegraph station and post office, a campsite of Afghans, Hindus and smelly camels, a bush pub and a tented mosque.[5] The sandhill countryside around the town was monotonous and arid, consisting of spinifex grass, saltbush and small rocks called gibbers.

Atlanta was delighted to see the tall figure of her husband waiting for them at Oodnadatta railway station. He was accompanied by Bob Crann and George Hablett, two telegraph station employees, as well as two vehicles: a buggy drawn by five horses and a buckboard drawn by four. There was also a team of spare horses to pull the vehicles in shifts as the going was so rough it exhausted the animals.

George Hablett's eyes opened wide at the sight of pretty young Bertha. He searched around to see if she had any girlfriends, demanding plaintively, 'What's the use of only bringing one? You should've brought a cartload and let 'em loose up here.'[6]

They managed to purchase some freshly baked bread and stowed it away in the tucker box, a contraption of which Thomas was very proud. He had had it fitted out specially with separate compartments for salt beef, butter and other supplies for the journey. The buckboard was a flimsy open cart with a hard wooden seat across the front and a full-width shelf underneath it designed to take the heavier luggage, the tents they would pitch each night, their valises, Atlanta's steamer trunk, the tucker box, their cooking utensils and the blanket rolls on which they would sleep. The buggy was more substantial. It had springless horsehair seats and took several passengers. Objects such as canvas water bags and gridirons for grilling food over the camp fire were strung underneath.

It was some 500 kilometres of desert to Alice Springs. Atlanta sat in the buggy beside the driver, Bob Crann, with baby Jack on her knee. Mort, Consie, Doris and Bertha squashed together in the back. There was no canopy to protect them from the burning sun so Atlanta and the children wore hats which they had to hold fast to their heads when the wind blew. Thomas rode on the buckboard beside George Hablett and an Aboriginal groom, with the line of packhorses and spare horses following behind.

The eighteen-day journey, rattling and bouncing over uneven and stony ground in a buggy with steel-framed wheels and bad springs, was extremely tiring for all of them. Space in the overcrowded vehicle was at a premium. There were no shops to buy food so they had to make do with their meagre supplies, and nor could they carry fodder for the horses. Finding fodder and water for the horses was the priority for every camp, and each evening it would take a long time to feed, water and hobble them, and then erect the tents and start the cooking. The process had to be reversed each morning.

Each day they drove until dusk by which time the horses were exhausted. Their first camp was at a place called the Swallow. Alas, their dinner was vile — salt beef and bread — and would only get worse as the butter melted and turned rancid and the bread bought in Oodnadatta turned stale and rock hard, like the seats of the buggy. Atlanta spent an uncomfortable night on the blanket roll, the ground hard and unresisting as she lay worrying about the baby beside her. To cap it all she lost a brooch which friends had given her as a farewell present. She could have wept with vexation but bit

A buckboard or produce wagon, designed to be pulled by two horses. It had an unsprung seat and was a most uncomfortable vehicle.

back her tears and continued with unloading and loading the luggage, feeding the baby with condensed milk and checking the children.

In spite of Atlanta's efforts, as the journey continued the meals grew almost inedible. The children, bored and weary, grizzled that the food was horrible, with Doris refusing to eat a thing.

At first the ground was the colour of ochre and very monotonous. The closer they came to the original Alice Spring discovered by John Ross in the dry river bed of the Todd, the more varied the landscape became. Soon there were no more gibber rocks. Spinifex, grey-green mulga and eucalypts dominated the rich deep red of the earth, sometimes enlivened by the dark green feathery foliage of the desert oak. Bob Crann explained that this strange tree, unlike anything Atlanta had seen in Adelaide, had only one long single taproot which served to make the tree drought-proof. Aboriginal women would dig around it for ants after rain when the insects became engorged with a honey-like fluid. The women killed the ants by snapping off the heads then drank the sweet fluid in the bodies.

On the morning of 23 May, Atlanta felt anxious when she realised she had forgotten to send a card from Oodnadatta for her sister Emily's birthday. It was too late now to rectify the oversight. 'I wish I could send her a telegram,' she said ruefully.

'Go on,' Thomas said. 'You want to send a telegram — all right, I'll send it for you.'[7]

Atlanta thought her husband must be suffering from delusions brought on by sunstroke. But she decided to humour him and wrote out a loving message. Thomas took the piece of paper, went to one of the saddles on the packhorses and returned with linesmen's clamps — two curved pieces of metal which he fixed around his boots. Putting Atlanta's message in his pocket he straddled the nearest telegraph pole and proceeded to climb it like a monkey, much to the amazement of his children.

Reaching the top of the pole, Thomas took some tools from his pocket and, hanging on for grim death, did what he had seen other linesmen do — tap into the wire. Clinging on by his foot clamps he managed to send the telegram to Emily, care of the Adelaide Telegraph Office. Atlanta was astounded and said so once Thomas had descended from the telegraph pole looking pleased with himself.

As the journey continued they traversed ninety kilometres of dangerous sandhills, furrowed by the wind into regular patterns. In this country summer temperatures could reach as high as 50 degrees Celsius in the shade and many men had died of thirst. The horses plodded on with an occasional drink from the canvas water bags, but supplies were dwindling fast. Bob Crann warned them that there was a danger the water at isolated Alice Well and Deep Well might be polluted by dead animals, and this could lead to typhoid and dysentery.

As the water supplies decreased, Atlanta had to ration them. She did her best with the spoiled food from the tucker box but there was no denying the meals were unpalatable. The only thing she and the children enjoyed eating were the crisply baked hot Johnny cakes (small round dampers) that George Hablett made out of flour, water and salt, and cooked in the ashes of the fire rather than in the awkward camp oven. As the outer layer of the Johnny cakes tended to be crusted with charcoal, George filed the burned bits off with a rasp he kept for the horses' hoofs. Atlanta was delighted to see the children eating something with pleasure rather than with groans and grimaces.

Eventually they came through the sandhills and to deep-red rocks which marked the entrance to canyons and ravines. At the family-owned Alice Well Cattle Station they stopped to rest the horses. Here they were given a meal of salt beef and freshly baked bread by the pioneer graziers William Hayes and his wife. Atlanta was amazed by the primitive living conditions of the Hayes family. She had assumed they must be wealthy as they owned large mobs of cattle, but she was surprised to see dirt floors and their dining-room walls papered with yellowed, fading old newspapers. So this was life in the Never-Never.

After a short break, it was back on the road again. The children were delighted by the mobs of red and grey kangaroos, which bounded away from them in a series of leaps. Their little convoy passed through Heavitree Gap where two white policemen and six Aboriginal constables were stationed, near the camps of the gold and ruby miners who were starting to flood into the area. It would not be long before the miners realised that the 'rubies' they found were only garnets, worth very little. In spite of this, the rumour persisted that where there were garnets there *must* be gold. Some desperate types were wheeling their digging equipment on barrows or handcarts and Thomas feared they might have guns in their swags.[8]

Along the skyline they saw range upon range of purple-tinged granite mountains, with deep shadows on their flanks — the incredibly beautiful MacDonnell Ranges. As they clip-clopped through the red heart of Australia, the horses followed a line of wooden poles embedded four feet deep in the earth. Thomas told the children these poles had been dug in by hand by European linesmen who had lived in camps out here for months at a time.

At last the cavalcade reached the tiny hamlet of Stuart, which would eventually be renamed Alice Springs, after the telegraph station closed its operations beside the original Alice Spring and moved to Stuart where most of the population were living.

In 1899 when the Bradshaws arrived, Stuart consisted of one hotel — the Stuart Arms — two general stores, a saddlery and three houses. One lone European woman, Mrs Charles Meyer, wife of the owner of the saddlery and harness shop, lived there. Atlanta had been looking forward to meeting her; however, they were told that Mrs Meyer's second child was expected at any time and in the absence of a midwife, desperate Mrs Meyer had made a full day's buggy drive out to Hermannsburg Mission,[9] more than 100 kilometres away on the Finke River. There she would be cared for by the missionary women, including Mrs Frieda Strehlow, rather than impose on Mrs Charles Brookes, the police constable's wife, who lived with her husband and four children in the camp at nearby Heavitree Gap.

Hermannsburg Mission had been set up by missionaries from Wurttemberg, Germany, in the 1870s. Like Thomas Bradshaw and

Ernest Gillen, missionary Carl Strehlow was a man of wide interests who learned to speak Arrernte. Strehlow was compiling an Arrernte–English dictionary, putting the Arrernte language into written form and translating the Bible into Arrernte. He was trying to turn Hermannsburg Mission into a self-supporting community with a date-palm plantation that would bring in money.

Mrs Meyer, Mrs Brookes and Frieda Strehlow at Hermannsburg were the only educated white women to live in the red centre area when Atlanta arrived.

Over the last three kilometres to the telegraph station, Atlanta gave thanks they had come through safely. None of the children had fallen from the buckboard, been bitten by a snake as they slept on the ground, or been poisoned by the decaying food. Relieved that their long arduous journey was nearly over, she could now admire the beauty of the ranges and marvel at the purity of the air — so clear it made rocks half a kilometre away look as though you could reach out and touch them from the buggy.

At the edge of the Todd River they saw a small camp of Arrernte. Naked dark-haired women and children with tousled blonde hair and dark eyes came out to look at the party and point at them with excitement. The Bradshaw children waved back as the buggy carried them on to where they caught the first glimpse of their new home — a cluster of nine stone buildings with thick walls and tiny windows that housed the staff and telegraph machinery. Some buildings still had their original palm thatch while others had roofs of corrugated iron.

Lined up beside the station office were the male telegraph operators: Mr Field, Mr Squire, Mr Middleton and Mr Jago, all wearing their best suits and waiting to greet Atlanta. As the telegraph station had to be manned all the time, these telegraph operators worked in shifts around the clock so the messages could get through. The men smiled and doffed their hats rather than shaking hands with her. Two shy Arrernte women dressed in their Sunday-best white blouses and skirts, and a traditional white *chillara* headband, which kept their hair out of their eyes, were introduced to Atlanta. Tryphena (Tryff) and Dolly had previously

PHOTO © JAKE DE VRIES, PIRGOS PRESS.

Hermannsburg Mission where Frieda Strehlow acted as midwife to Atlanta Bradshaw's friend Annie Meyers.

worked for the Gillens. The women smiled and spoke in pidgin English, calling Atlanta 'Quei' — 'senior woman' in the Arrernte language.

Thomas led his family to the station master's house with its wide verandas and showed them the blacksmith's workshop and stores, the separate post and telegraph office, the stables and the buggy shed. The station master's house was now almost thirty years old, had ant-bed floors, and badly needed renovating, Atlanta thought. Doors needed to be fitted to many of the rooms, she decided.

In order to both minimise fire risk and reduce heat in the main house in summer, the station master's kitchen was a separate building. It was joined to a dining room which had a large dining table covered with a green baize cloth. The room was fitted with a fireplace because in winter the nights could become very cold indeed.

Since the station master's house lacked running water, whatever was needed for drinking and washing had to be hauled up by hand in buckets from the Alice Spring waterhole along the Todd riverbed. Atlanta did not find it reassuring that the designers of the house had fitted the exterior walls with holes at eye-level so bullets could be fired at marauding Aborigines. But she was reassured by her husband that the Gillens had enjoyed excellent relations with the Arrernte people so shots had never been fired through these slits.

≈≈≈

The former superintendent, Francis Gillen, was one of a handful of people who had treated the Arrernte as rational human beings. He was disgusted by the cruelty some of the white and native police showed to the Arrernte.

The Aborigines regarded the Gillens as friends and genuine protectors. They had initially been suspicious, after their bitter experience of being hunted and killed by so many European men. However, after Gillen brought a private prosecution against a police constable for cruelty to Aborigines, he won their trust. Unfortunately, the case became a *cause célèbre* when the police paid a leading barrister to act for them and Constable Willshire got off. Nevertheless, it established Gillen as a champion of Aboriginal people.[10]

As an active Protector of Aborigines, Gillen had become very close to the Arrernte, and had been invited to secret ceremonies and

COURTESY BERNARD SPILSBURY.

Alice Springs Telegraph Station.

initiated into their ways. His 'skin name' among them was 'Oknirrabatta' or 'Great Teacher'.

Like Thomas Bradshaw, Gillen had had a passion for photography. In his eight years at the telegraph station he studied and photographed the Arrernte, who were possibly the friendliest and most artistic of all the Aboriginal peoples of the red centre.

A turning point in Gillen's life came when he met the Oxford-trained Walter Baldwin Spencer, who was a professor at Melbourne University. Professor Spencer was the official zoologist and photographer on the 1894 Horn expedition to central Australia financed by a wealthy mining magnate and investor in the fabled Broken Hill silver mines, William Horn. Horn was a keen amateur anthropologist, who also wished to investigate the land between Oodnadatta and the MacDonnell Ranges for possible mineral wealth.

Spencer realised that Gillen could supply him with invaluable information for his projected book on the Aboriginal people of central Australia. On the return journey, Spencer stayed behind at the telegraph station after the rest of the Horn expedition had departed. At nights the two men smoked their pipes and talked a great deal. Before Spencer left for Melbourne he invited Gillen to become joint author with him on a book about the Arrernte, the Papunya and Loritja of central Australia. Gillen agreed.

Spencer returned to the telegraph station the following year when Gillen 'arranged' for a corroboree to take place in his honour. The ceremony would feature in Spencer and Gillen's book *The Native Tribes of Central Australia*, a work which would make the pair of them famous. Eventually Gillen left Alice Springs in order to work on his contributions to *The Native Tribes of Central Australia*. He wrote with empathy about the Arrernte's legends and their ancestral Dreamtime, which bound them so firmly to the land.[11]

Gillen had worked hard to improve conditions for the Arrernte at a time when 'dispersing Aborigines' was a convenient euphemism among Europeans for murdering them. The Bradshaws would continue this tradition of helping the Arrernte, especially in times of drought when their game and supplies of plants and seeds ran low. Clustered around the Alice Spring waterhole, they would be fed from huge pans of boiled rice by Atlanta.

Thomas Bradshaw did not continue Gillen's anthropological research but using his glass-plate camera became a brilliant photographer of the red centre of Australia. Gillen had also taken photographs but they were not of the same quality as the glass plates of Thomas Bradshaw, whose strength lay in the composition of his subjects, the high quality of his photographs and their recording of pioneer days around Alice Springs.

Thomas also took photographs showing the family enjoying picnics at local waterholes, with magnificent reflections apparent in the water from the red rocks of local beauty spots, including Standley Chasm and Emily Gap. The unique landscape of the area inspired him and he became one of the period's great photographers.[12]

❦ ❦ ❦

Due to its vast distance from markets the telegraph station had to be as self-supporting as possible: it had to grow its own vegetables, raise its own beef and mutton, and keep goats for milk. There were no grocery stores to go to in time of need. Dry goods like tea, sugar and rice, and all tools and fabrics came from Adelaide by camel train but only *once a year*. Atlanta had the responsibility of keeping an inventory of stores to feed and clothe the family, staff and station Aborigines, as well as supplying outback travellers who called in for purchases, and of making up the huge annual order which was telegraphed to Adelaide.

In addition to the four telegraph operators, regular station staff included blacksmith George Hablett and stockmen Bob Crann and Harry Kunoth. These men could also turn their hands to telegraph line work. Additionally there were four linesmen who went outback to keep the lines repaired, and a station cook, 'Cookie' Lloyd. An elderly man named Billy Crick acted as station gardener. Billy had planted sweet potatoes very successfully, and could grow carrots and cabbages in winter, but in the fierce summer heat had had no success with green vegetables, which withered and died, putting the Bradshaws and staff at the station at risk of scurvy — the dread of pioneer wives and mothers.

Atlanta found the summer heat overwhelming. In midsummer the temperature could reach up to 50 degrees Celsius and the only fans available had to be operated by pulling on a rope. She never came to terms with living in an unscreened house plagued in summer by flies and mosquitoes. It was impossible to escape from these insects or from the ants which infested the kitchen and pantry. Flies swarmed inside the house, settling on lips, eyes and every scrap of food they could find. After dark the flies quietened and then came the second shift, the mosquitoes, attracted by the light from candles and oil lamps.

While the telegraph office would not pay for insect screens it did pay wages for two or sometimes three local Arrernte house girls to help Atlanta clean, cook and run the house for her large family, and for the staff of boys, shepherds and water carriers — all of whom needed supervising. The house girls were liable to disappear without warning to go walkabout or take a long period of leave for 'sorry business' if a family member died. As frustrating as this was, Atlanta had to accept it. Going walkabout was like going on a pilgrimage, an essential part of Arrernte cultural life. Besides, how could girls who had lived a nomadic life be expected to know how to lay tables or do the ironing and avoid scorching delicate clothes with an iron that had to be heated over hot coals? Few of them had ever been inside four walls before, or seen a knife and fork; most did not know what cupboards or toilets were for and thought the spring water too precious to be employed for washing their bodies.

On the other hand, the Arrernte women could do many things European women could not do — like tracking people through the desert or carrying loaded pitchers of water without spilling a drop, balancing them on their heads with the aid of a *manguri,* a circle or coil of woven hair and emu feathers. Their skills had been honed over centuries to ensure survival in a harsh land where Europeans died because they could not find bush tucker for themselves, as the Arrernte could.

Atlanta found two of the women, Rungee and Amelia, much more dependable than the others and they became indispensable to her as her family increased in number. Amelia was the illegitimate daughter of an Arrernte woman and English-born Jack Pavey, who had worked for the telegraph line but did not wish to know about his daughter. The telegraph station had accepted responsibility for this delightful little girl who had become so fond of Atlanta's predecessor, Amelia Gillen, that she had renounced her tribal name and wanted to be known as Amelia.[13]

The Gillens had raised Amelia, and taught her to read and write. They had considered taking her with them when they left Alice Springs, but in the expectation of Francis Gillen being off work for a year while he finished his share of *The Native Tribes of Central Australia,* the Gillens feared it would be too much to take on additional financial responsibility for young Amelia. So Amelia remained at the telegraph station, where she became the charge of the Bradshaws.

Amelia would live happily with the Bradshaws for the nine years they spent at the telegraph station and blossom from an attractive lively child into a confident and beautiful young woman. Atlanta, who became very fond of Amelia, would form a lifelong bond with her, having come to rely on her and the much older Rungee through three difficult pregnancies and the children's illnesses.

Perhaps the Bradshaws felt that in an almost exclusively male society they had a duty to protect a young Aboriginal girl until she was old enough to decide who she wanted to marry. Much later, after the Bradshaws left, she would accept the marriage proposal of Harry Kunoth. A devout, mission-educated Lutheran, Harry never said a word about his feelings for Amelia until he considered her old enough for marriage.

Another of Atlanta's charges was another part-Aboriginal child who had been entrusted to the care of the telegraph station management during the Gillens' time there. Mumpaguila had been found abandoned as a baby, her nose and mouth stuffed with sand, making it

PHOTOGRAPHED BY JAKE DE VRIES FROM A DISPLAY AT THE OLD TELEGRAPH STATION MUSEUM.

Amelia with Edna Bradshaw.

difficult for her to breathe. One of the staff had cleaned her up and brought her to the telegraph station, where she had been fed, clothed and given a bed in the corner of the kitchen by Cookie Lloyd.

Thomas Bradshaw was not very happy about this arrangement. He wanted the youngster returned to the Aboriginal camp to be cared for by her own people. But, Doris recounted, as 'none of [the Arrernte women] were prepared to look after her my father always relented and allowed her to stay with Cookie', who fed her in his kitchen.[14]

Left to her own devices, when not in the kitchen with Cookie, wild little Mumpaguila roamed around by herself, often getting up to some mischief or other. At one time the station goats were apparently failing to give milk. Atlanta's sons Jack and Mort found that Mumpaguila had been drinking it, after catching her with a jam tin full. She flung the milk in their faces and ran away to the hills for several days before returning to the telegraph station rather than to the Arrernte camp.

Fifty years later, Doris and Consie Bradshaw visited Mumpaguila in an Adelaide hospital. By that time she was 'a very dignified, patient woman', although dying of cancer of the throat. Doris learned that Mumpaguila had been flown to Adelaide in three hours, 'over country through which we toiled for nearly three weeks'. In the intervening years Mumpaguila had settled down, married and raised a family, grateful for her life having been saved.

In learning to deal with her Aboriginal staff, Atlanta had to exercise patience. One of their most perplexing customs related to kinship rules, and Atlanta's experience of this was remarkably similar to that of Jeannie Gunn (see chapter four). Out on the veranda were wash tubs where the family washing was done with water carried from the spring by Mick the Aboriginal water boy. Since Aboriginal men were forbidden to look at or talk to particular women who were closely related to them, some of the house girls would scatter when Mick arrived. While these complex kinship rules were initially difficult for the Bradshaws to understand, they always led to lots of games and laughter among the Arrernte women, as they fled Mick and the washing suds.

It was not only the Aboriginal staff who gave Atlanta headaches. If her daughter Doris's descriptions of his meals are to be believed, Cookie Lloyd, whom Atlanta inherited from the Gillens, must have been one of the outback's worst chefs. He looked the part, at least, in his tall white cap and coat, and he could turn out tolerable bread and yeast buns in the men's kitchen. Apart from that his menus were monotonous and his cooking lacked flavour; everything the men were given was overcooked. As he was known to have a vile temper they kept quiet. Cookie's favoured dessert was a stodgy sago pudding, which he served five or six times a week, although the men hated it and sometimes threw it out of the window when Cookie was not looking.

After eating Cookie Lloyd's first meal, Atlanta decided she would do all the cooking for her family herself. She also found it hard to make the Arrernte wash their hands, another reason why she insisted on preparing and cooking the food. Many white children died in the outback from stomach infections and dysentery, so it was likely Atlanta worried about her own children.

Atlanta did her best in the hot kitchen on a temperamental stove which lacked any form of temperature control. As was so often the case in the outback, beef and mutton from the station herds were plentiful, and there was always a good supply of chops, steak and roasts. Sometimes, for a change, Atlanta would make the children an outback delicacy known as Burdekin Duck. This consisted of thick slices of cold roast or corned beef dipped in a milky batter to which finely chopped onion was added and then deep-fried in fat to produce delicious fritters. But fresh fruit was scarce or non-existent. As a special treat the family ate tinned fruit such as plums until the rations gave out.

Tea was the standard drink in those days and most pioneers automatically boiled all their drinking water fearing it might be polluted and thus cause dysentery or blackwater fever. But the water from Alice Spring was clear, unpolluted and rich in calcium, and in times of drought attracted Aboriginal groups from a wide area to camp around it.

❦ ❦ ❦

Another task Atlanta assigned herself was to set to on her hand-operated sewing machine to make clothes for the Arrernte women so they would not go about stark naked. She made five dozen skirts out of blue serge she found in the store. She could not give individual fittings but made them to a one-size-fits-all pattern with a drawstring waist.

The women liked clothes that kept them warm in winter but tended to discard them in summer and preferred brighter colours, like red and emerald green. One woman shrewdly complained that the dark blue skirts made the women look 'Allasame longa crows'.[15] Eventually many of the skirts ended up as headbands for the women's husbands. The headbands were thought to prevent headaches and were regarded as essential by the Arrernte.

The house girls wore white blouses, skirts and headbands. Atlanta insisted that the girls leave their uniforms behind before going back to their camp, a practice Amelia Gillen had initiated, knowing from bitter experience that the uniforms would be given or gambled away. During the heat of day the girls had a siesta and often slept in the red dirt surrounded by their beloved dogs, another reason for leaving their white uniforms at the station.

≈ ≈ ≈

Between her household duties and looking after both her family and the telegraph station's Aborigines and staff, Atlanta was kept busy. In her memoir of their time there, Doris Bradshaw paints a picture of her mother as dutifully tending not only her own family, but to many of the station Aborigines with food, medicine and, if that failed, attention.

The government had supplied the Bradshaws with a large medicine chest in which were old fashioned remedies like glycerine (used with honey as cough medicine), Condy's crystals (an antiseptic), castor oil (for constipation), olive oil (to soothe sores), laudanum, carbolic acid, iodine, pulverised charcoal (for bad breath), quinine (for malaria), bismuth, essence of ginger (for stomach disorders), digitalis (for heart attacks and, oddly enough, recommended for the treatment of piles) and borax (for bathing sore eyes). Doris recorded how a constant stream of people would present to Atlanta with real or imagined illnesses and all would be helped. Atlanta tended various ailments including many cases of sore eyes from sunlight suffered by the Arrernte, who arrived at the front door of the house. There were also sad cases of children who had fallen into the camp fire and had been badly burned.

As well as doctoring the Arrernte, Atlanta had to nurse her own family when they became sick. Atlanta's worst fears were realised when her son Mortimer developed a high fever and coughing fits, less than a year after they arrived at the telegraph station. His symptoms were telegraphed to Adelaide. A reply from doctors there suggested Mort had whooping cough. Over the line in Morse code the doctor prescribed doses of castor oil and belladonna, chlorate of potash, and hot fomentations to be applied to the little boy's chest.

Atlanta carried out the doctor's instructions but still Mort's condition did not improve and his temperature stayed high. Soon the poor boy had an ulcerated mouth, blurred vision, swollen glands and great difficulty in swallowing. Atlanta was beside herself with worry. Her son was far too ill to be moved. Messages sped back and forth along the wire to doctors in Adelaide and Port Darwin and soon Mort was diagnosed with diphtheria. Her son became so ill that Atlanta was in despair. She stayed in his room at night and wore herself out nursing him and worrying whether the prescriptions of doctors in distant cities, who had never examined the patient, could be effective. Mort was desperately ill with diphtheretic paralysis for three months, during which time Atlanta massaged his limbs daily while suffering all the anguish of a mother lacking medical help.

Not long afterwards Doris developed rheumatic fever with terrifying bouts of fever known as 'night sweats'. With her condition deteriorating and the doctor on the telegraph line vague on treatment, the Bradshaws sought help by getting in contact with a former hospital matron, wife of a station owner in Katherine, over a thousand kilometres away. The matron's advice was hot baths, hot fomentations, milk and salicylic acid, and total bed rest. At long last Doris started to recover.

Not all illnesses had happy outcomes. In July 1900, Thomas Bradshaw's younger brother, Ernie, arrived at the telegraph station. Ernie, a bookkeeper by profession, was suffering from tuberculosis, and had come from Melbourne to live with the Bradshaws, hoping the dry climate of Alice Springs might improve his condition and that Atlanta could nurse him back to health. But the tuberculosis slowly ravaged him and he became thinner and thinner.

At the time Atlanta was pregnant once again and in the scorching heat it became more and more difficult for her to run the household and care for Ernie. On 15 November 1900, a few months after Ernie's arrival, the Bradshaws' fifth child was born. They christened him Stuart MacDonnell Bradshaw, after the nearby township of Stuart.

There had been no time to take the long buggy journey to Hermannsburg Mission to seek Frieda Strehlow's services as a midwife. Young Annie Meyer, with no experience in midwifery except giving birth herself, helped deliver baby Stuart. Atlanta's eldest daughter, Doris later wrote in her memoirs that lack of proper obstetric and medical care resulted in her mother developing gynaecological problems.

Just as Atlanta was recovering from the birth of Stuart, Ernie's condition deteriorated sharply and he started to cough up blood and died. The Bradshaws were desolate. Due to the heat they had to bury the young man the following day. He was laid to rest in the tiny cemetery at the telegraph station, beside the late Superintendent Ernest Flint.[16]

❦ ❦ ❦

The annual arrival of the camel train at the Alice Springs Telegraph Station must have been quite a sight. Haughty-looking camels were linked to each other by ropes attached to a nose peg made of bone or ivory. The Afghan drivers made the camels lie down — grunting or squealing as they did so, folding their bony legs as they sank to the ground. Then the ropes holding the great packs and baskets, some weighing over 200 kilograms, were unfastened.

The station master was given a 'free allowance' of freight as part of his salary (which was not a large one). If he exceeded this he would have to pay for any items he shipped to or from Alice Springs — quite an expense. Thomas and Atlanta kept a running list of everything that needed replacing, from household crockery to the men's work boots, shirts and trousers. Also included were bolts of cloth from which Atlanta would sew clothes for the children and her house girls.

When the stores arrived, the children and telegraph staff rushed out to see them, and the Arrernte hurried up from the creek. Everyone would be shouting and gesticulating in excitement. They would all help carry the goods into the storeroom, which adjoined the buggy room. For the Arrernte, the arrival of rations meant less work for them hunting and gathering food.

While the Arrernte men were the hunters, it was women's work to harvest fruits like bush onions, desert raisins and shiny red *quandongs* about the size of a small plum. They would carry the fruit back to the camp in *coolamons* (oval wooden dishes). The women also went out with their digging sticks to look for witchetty grubs, which they knew nested in the roots of cassia trees, several kinds of acacia and prickly wattle. They used their long *kurupa* (digging sticks) like crowbars to break up roots and find the fat witchetty grubs, which were very rich and tasted something like scrambled egg when roasted. The Bradshaw children also loved to eat them.[17]

Gathering seeds was far more laborious. When times were good, the Arrernte women gathered and cooked the tiny seeds of woollybutt grass, native millet and seeds from a tree they called *ngalta*. The seeds were lightly singed over a fire of cassia twigs, winnowed and then ground to a fine powder on a grindstone. Once they were pulverised, the resulting fine meal was patted into little cakes, bonded together with animal fat and baked in the ashes of the fire.

The Arrernte women much preferred to use the flour Atlanta gave them, as making a paste from flour and water was far quicker than pounding seeds to a paste. Each Saturday rations of tea, flour, sugar and fresh meat were given out from the storeroom to the Arrernte, regardless of whether they worked for the telegraph station or not. The handout of rations was especially welcome in times of drought when the seeds and berries were scarce. For a special treat there were 'rice nights' when Atlanta and the house girls cooked up huge quantities of rice, just as they did in times of drought. The Arrernte loved this and came to collect the rice in old jam tins or other receptacles, sometimes with curried goat's meat as an additional treat. One elderly man, young Doris Bradshaw recalled in amusement, carried away a rice curry in his hat. Most of all they loved the special treats of treacle and small cakes. Atlanta would prepare such things on special days like Christmas and the Queen's Birthday.

Christmas Day, when Atlanta fed extensive numbers of Arrernte as well as her own children, was an exhausting day and no holiday

PHOTOGRAPHED BY JAKE DE VRIES FROM A DISPLAY AT THE OLD TELEGRAPH STATION MUSEUM.

Atlanta Bradshaw distributing Christmas pudding mix at the telegraph station camp.
Rungee stands behind her to the left in white.
Glass-plate photo by Thomas Bradshaw.

for Atlanta at all. Each Christmas Day she and Thomas rose early
and had a brief Anglican service with Christmas carols in the living
room. Then Atlanta retired to the kitchen to work over huge pots
on the wood-burning stove. This was the hottest time of the year
and the heat in the kitchen soon became oppressive. However, the
Bradshaws felt they had a responsibility to carry on the tradition of
Amelia and Francis Gillen and provide at least 200 of the Arrernte
with a lunchtime feast of curry, rice and Christmas pudding —
which Atlanta served uncooked from a huge metal wash tub.

An undated glass-plate photograph shows Atlanta, flanked by the
faithful Rungee, down at the Arrernte camp. Atlanta is wearing a
hat, a white blouse and a long black skirt. Tousle-headed children in
long dresses help themselves to pannikins of the uncooked
Christmas pudding stiff with fruit in the wash tub. The Arrernte
women, also wearing long dresses (possibly made by Atlanta), wait
patiently in line to take some of the mix once the children have
finished. Atlanta does, indeed, look rather tired.

In her book, Doris Bradshaw recorded that in order to give the Arrernte a happy day, the Bradshaws always postponed their own Christmas meal of bush turkey, plum pudding and Christmas cake until the evening, by which time Atlanta was usually exhausted.

꘏ ꘏ ꘏

Washing and ironing for a large family, in which more often than not there was a new baby, was endless. The red earth around Alice Springs stained clothes very badly and it was difficult to get them white again. A great deal of Reckitt's Blue had to be used, specially imported on the annual camel train.

Soiled clothes and nappies were boiled in a copper beside the kitchen, lifted out with a stick and placed in the wash tub where they were pounded with a wooden paddle called a 'wash dolly'. Bad stains were removed by hand on the corrugated washboard. The wet clothes were rolled through a hand mangle, and the squeezed-out water used for watering the garden, since all water was precious. The washing was then pegged out by the house girls. In the heat it dried very quickly.

Atlanta had to keep an eye on everything, including the ironing which was done with heavy flat irons heated over the stove and, unlike modern electric irons, had no temperature controls.

At night, the Bradshaws made their own entertainment. Bertha Easom, and the governesses who later replaced her, would play the piano by candlelight. Bertha gave Doris music lessons and taught her to play light classical pieces and to accompany songs. With no radios or televisions for entertainment, musical ability was seen as an essential attribute of any properly educated young lady in those days. Doris also undertook a drawing course with lessons sent out to her by the Adelaide School of Art.

After the family meal, sometimes they all gathered in the sitting room round the piano for a family sing-song. But most nights, while Atlanta and the governess sewed by the light of the lamp and mended the children's clothes, Thomas retired to his book-lined study, wrote up his diary and studied the Arrernte language. He also noted down the judgements he had made in court.

As officer in charge of the telegraph station, Thomas Bradshaw also functioned as special magistrate. The Alice Springs court was held in the men's dining room at the telegraph station. At these initial hearings, Thomas had to deal with cases ranging from murder to gold miners' claims and disputes, petty pilfering and maltreatment of animals. Thomas had to send cases of arson, murder or rape on to Port Augusta, so only relatively minor offenders were sentenced at the telegraph station. Although he had no legal training whatsoever, Thomas would sit in a high-backed chair at the dining table to dispense justice as he thought fit. He was referred to as 'Your Honour' by Constable Brookes of neighbouring Heavitree Gap.

An entry in Thomas's diary refers to an Aborigine who 'broke into a store, stole 15 lb flour, 1 lb tea, butcher's knife, sugar, etc. I got the goods back, so gave him 5 lb of flour and cleared him off to Barrow Creek [further north on the telegraph line].'[18]

Doris later observed in her memoir that Thomas 'even tried to extend justice to the aborigines and temper it with mercy; at the turn of the century in Central Australia that was not at all an everyday occurrence . . . any white man who demonstrated impartiality in affairs affecting the aborigines was in danger of being branded as a radical.'[19]

This was a rough, tough era and cruelty in the bush was endemic. Europeans were brutal to Aborigines, many of whom were brought to court chained by the neck. Frequently, the native constables, who were usually from different tribes, were the most brutal of all. Both the European and native police claimed the Aborigines would run away and vanish into the desert if not chained by the neck to be brought into the courtroom. Gillen and Bradshaw were outraged by this vile practice and did their best to stop it.

Thomas was also called upon to try cases of severe cruelty on the part of Aboriginal men who, on occasion, had savagely beaten their wives. Some of these cases were uncomfortably close to home. Their own servant Rungee, for example, had to suffer at the hands of her selfish husband who, according to Doris, 'regarded her as nothing more than a chattel'.[20]

Also appearing in Thomas's courtroom were Europeans and Chinese who had been brought to Australia as indentured labourers. Others on trial were drifters from the south, absconders from justice or from 'nagging wives'. In October 1905, Thomas recorded: 'White men Lennon and Gregory fined seven shillings and six pence each camel — for cruelty. Worked camels with sore backs.'[21]

⚜ ⚜ ⚜

As the Bradshaws came to know more about their new environment, they found their interest in the local Aboriginal people deepening. Each day it seemed a new practice or belief was revealed. On one occasion, Atlanta was asked to take some special food to Tom, a horse tailer and groom, who tended the sixty horses belonging to the telegraph station. Tom was a full-blood Arrernte and had had one front tooth knocked out, a sign that he had been initiated and circumcised. He had also been a special protege of Francis Gillen, who had photographed him and taught him some English.

Atlanta and her daughter Doris went to the camp by the riverbed and found poor Tom lying on a bed of rags in a shelter by the river, looking very ill indeed. No one had been able to diagnose Tom's illness except the medicine man, who was standing over the patient, looking pleased with himself. According to Doris, in spite of his filthy appearance the medicine man had the ponderous gravity of a Harley Street specialist. He turned to Atlanta and announced that he had succeeded in solving the problem. Tom was cured.

With a theatrical gesture, the medicine man pointed to a pile of pebbles and pieces of wood and told Atlanta he had sucked them out of different parts of Tom's anatomy, where they had been poisoning him. Tom, whom Gillen had found to be a most intelligent man, seemed equally confident that the cause of his illness had been discovered and truly grateful to the medicine man. He was convinced he was cured.

But Atlanta was still very worried. In an effort to impress her, the medicine man leaned over, sucked Tom's arm and triumphantly produced a small piece of broken glass which he held out to her. When Atlanta seemed disinclined to believe that the glass had come from inside Tom's body the medicine man looked most offended.

Tom seemed both shocked and embarrassed, and assured Atlanta he was feeling much better and would soon be able to attend to the horses again. He claimed not to have any appetite for food but promised 'Quei' he would eat later. She left the food beside him and since there was nothing more they could do, she and Doris returned to the telegraph station. They knew that the medicine man did have extraordinary powers of auto-suggestion and could effect cures. He could also 'sing' a man to death by pointing the sacred bone at him. So, Doris thought, this time faith in his 'treatment' would cure Tom.

Two days later a grieving Rungee informed Atlanta that Tom was dead. According to Aboriginal custom the name of a dead person cannot be mentioned for some time so his spirit can find rest and refrain from haunting his relatives. Rungee did not actually use Tom's name, but simply implied that he was 'dead feller'.

Francis Gillen had given the Bradshaws a copy of his and Professor Spencer's *The Native Tribes of Central Australia* when it was published, and through reading this classic book Thomas and Atlanta came to know a great deal about the Arrernte's beliefs in Dreamtime spirits and totemism. They also learned much from Hermannsburg mission leader Carl Strehlow and his wife. Like the Gillens and the Bradshaws, Strehlow did not want the Arrernte to forsake their tribal life — contrary to the philosophy of most other missionaries. Strehlow was very interested in the legends and beliefs of the Arrernte who were animists. The Rainbow Serpent and the Yeperenye (the Sacred Caterpillar), their Dreamtime spirit ancestors, inspired many fine rock carvings as well as their most sacred legends and dances. Strehlow and Thomas Bradshaw recognised the Arrernte's complex system of kinship and their feeling for their land were vital to their survival.[22]

Thomas and Atlanta became good friends with Carl and Frieda Strehlow and there was frequent transit between the mission and the telegraph station. Letters held in the Strehlow Research Centre at Alice Springs addressed to Pastor Strehlow's wife, dated between 1902 and 1906, attest to the friendship between the two outback women. Attie would write to Frieda recommending a certain type of medicine for one child's cough or an ointment for skin rash for another, and Frieda would provide support and encouragement during Atlanta's uncomfortable and difficult pregnancies.

On 29 September 1902, Thomas wrote to Pastor Strehlow thanking him for the gift of some emu eggs which Thomas wanted to send to relatives in England. In his letter he also asked Frieda to call in at their house to see Attie when she next came over for the mail. Each Christmas and New Year the families exchanged greetings and small presents.

The last letter from the Bradshaws in the Strehlow Collection is dated 26 November 1906. In it Atlanta wrote to say she had sent the Strehlows a present of some home-grown tomatoes and a basket of fruit for one of their children who was sick. The fruit had been grown and packed by the Bradshaws' Chinese gardener (a new arrival at the telegraph station). Atlanta sounded very concerned for the sick boy, expressing her hopes that he would recover soon. She signed her letter, 'Your loving friend, Attie Bradshaw'.

While the Bradshaws respected the Aborigines' beliefs and rarely sought to challenge them, one thing Atlanta did insist on was gathering the house girls together with the family for religious instruction on a Sunday morning. Attending morning service was compulsory for all telegraph employees and the Bradshaw children.

Doris recorded how her mother would use illustrated Bibles to instruct the house girls. Rungee, probably trying to please the mistress she served so faithfully, became imbued with her own special blend of Christianity and animism. Knowing she was dying after she was struck with flu during the 1919 epidemic, Rungee sent a message to Atlanta who had long since left the telegraph station, via Atlanta's brother, Ernest Allchurch. 'You tell'im Quei me go alonga Jesus,' Rungee said.[23]

⁂

On 27 December 1902, after a long and difficult labour, Atlanta brought another daughter into the world. The baby, once again delivered by Annie Meyer, was called Edna. She was Atlanta's sixth child.

With six children to mother, a staff of telegraph operators, station workers and camp Aborigines to nurse and cook for, and a store and home to keep in order, Atlanta was occupied day and very often night. However, she still made time for excursions with her children.

The main amusement for the Bradshaw children in these years was riding their horses and going on picnics. Like most outback children, Doris and her siblings excelled at riding and whenever possible would ride out to picnics together on their favourite horses. Thomas rarely came on these family outings, preferring to remain in his study with his beloved books, unless he wanted to take photographs of a particular place.

The birth of Edna meant there were now six little Bradshaws, plus their governess, Atlanta and Harry Kunoth the driver to cram into the buggy on outings to local beauty spots. It was fortunate then that Frank Gillen and Baldwin Spencer had called in on their return from a long and hazardous journey in central Australia (begun in 1901), researching for a sequel to their book. For such an arduous trip they had purchased a large and exceptionally sturdy buggy, a 'Rolls-Royce' of buggies in fact. It had been specially made for the former Governor of Australia, Lord Kintore, who had driven it on a journey between Darwin and Adelaide in 1891. After using the buggy to tour the centre of Australia, taking photographs and making notes, Spencer and Gillen returned to stay with the Bradshaws and Thomas agreed to purchase the large well-sprung vehicle. The Bradshaw children and Atlanta were delighted. Now they would be able to visit gorges and waterholes even further away.

Eventually there were seven Bradshaw children at the telegraph station.

That winter the children enjoyed many excursions by horse and buggy. But try as she might, Atlanta could not disguise the fact she was in considerable discomfort following Edna's birth. In September 1904, Atlanta finally decided she wanted to see a doctor.[24] She also needed some respite from blazing heat, sandstorms, flies, hard work, responsibility for nursing the sick and isolation. And of course she longed to see old friends, her parents and family, and breathe the sea air at Glenelg.

Atlanta convinced Thomas she must go back to Adelaide to consult a gynaecologist and suggested he could take leave and join her there. He agreed and they arranged to rent a house at Glenelg so the family would have a holiday at the beach. In spite of the pain she was in, Atlanta worked for weeks at the sewing machine to make the children smart new 'city clothes' so that she and their grandparents could be proud of them.

Their journey to Oodnadatta would take an estimated twelve to eighteen days by horse and buggy. The old unsprung buckboard would take the trunks, tents, blankets and food and any excess children. There were no shops en route but it would be possible to buy freshly killed meat from cattle stations and barbecue it beside their tents. Atlanta had to plan ahead for meals for a very large party.

There were her own six hungry children; three Aboriginal grooms; a former governess; Vernon South, the young son of the new owners of the Stuart Arms hotel, who was travelling to Adelaide for medical treatment; the present governess; Harry Kunoth; and another driver.

Mrs McFeat, the former governess, was near full term of her first pregnancy. Edna was almost three by now, Stuart, known as Donnell, nearly five. The older children, Consie, Jack, Mort and Doris, were now mature enough to take care of themselves most of the time.

Harry Kunoth was a superb bushman and one afternoon when a sudden storm blew up managed to locate a pitched tent that had been left behind by some surveyors and in which they could now shelter overnight. It was a miserable camp. The water seeped into the tent and the children squealed and squabbled among themselves and complained of aches and pains until Atlanta dosed them all with camphor sprinkled on a sugar lump as a prophylactic against catching chills.

One evening the buckboard, with Doris, Mort and young Vernon South on board, had problems crossing a creekbed. The tired horses refused to move on and the driver whipped them frenziedly. In frustration he threw himself down to the ground. It was then he heard the distant rumble of floodwaters on their way down the creek. Redoubling his efforts with the horses brought more disaster. The lead horse reared up and badly tore the flesh on its rump. There was nothing to do but turn it loose. Doris, Mort and Vernon realised they had to get out quickly. They struggled to the far side of the bank. The horses suddenly became compliant and moved up also.

Atlanta, unaware of the near danger, had hurried on to prepare a worker's hut she had been invited to stay in overnight. When the others didn't arrive, she sent the Aboriginal grooms back to find them. The shaken children were relieved to meet the grooms and reach the safety of their mother in the hut.

Their next hazard was the flooded Alberga Creek. First the Aboriginal grooms found the shallowest place to cross. Once the packhorses were through, Atlanta had to cross in the buggy with most of the children and the two other women. Then came the much lower buckboard with Doris and Mort. Water surged over the back and sides of the buckboard and soaked the stores. Atlanta looked on grimly, as her two eldest children stood on the seat trying to keep dry. Two of the horses began to swim but the other two remained on their feet. Finally the buckboard was through and Atlanta heaved a sigh of relief.

The horses were by then exhausted, so fresh ones were sent out from Oodnadatta. The speed of the new horses led to the kind of accident Atlanta had always feared. Holding baby Edna on her lap she leaned forward on the high front seat of the buggy to admire the new horses, just as the iron-rimmed wheel struck a hidden rock. The buggy lurched violently. Atlanta, with Edna in her arms, was thrown headfirst out of the moving vehicle. As she fell, she threw Edna to one side to prevent her being trampled.

Harry pulled the horses to a halt and jumped down from the driver's seat. Edna was examined from top to toe but there were no signs of injury. As her sobs died away it was obvious that she had only been frightened. In fact it was Atlanta who had suffered most. Her knees and calves were badly bruised and would turn black, green and blue. But at least she had saved her baby. It took several months before the livid colour of Atlanta's bruises died away. Damage to her kneecaps would plague her for the rest of her life and make walking difficult in her old age.

Finally, after two weeks' travelling on the buggy and buckboard, they arrived at Oodnadatta. After a night's rest they boarded the old steam train to Adelaide. Stopping overnight at Hergott Springs (Marree) then Quorn, the train seemed luxurious after the bumpy buggy, particularly to the bruised and injured Atlanta. Her brood of children were fascinated with the novelty of the long, powerful train. By now they were all filthy, covered in smuts from the steam engine. As they neared Adelaide, Atlanta cleaned and brushed up the children, ready to meet their relatives.

Atlanta was overjoyed to see her parents and her sister Emily. The family spent nine months beside the ocean in a rented house at Glenelg, Thomas joining them for a holiday in January 1905. By the end of February the Bradshaw family set off for the long haul back, bringing with them a new governess.

≈ ≈ ≈

During Thomas's absence, Atlanta's brother, Ernest Allchurch, had acted as locum to run the station affairs. Ernest had previously lived in the men's barracks but moved into a small thatched cottage in the grounds when he married Elizabeth Williams, Annie Meyer's younger sister. The marriage had taken place in the tiny church at Hermannsburg Mission, the only church at that time between Lake Eyre in southern Australia and the tropical north.

The Bradshaw children were overjoyed that Uncle Ernest Allchurch had married and set up home in the grounds of the telegraph station. For them it meant new people to talk to and another household where they were welcome. The marriage of their siblings drew Atlanta and Annie Meyer even closer.

By now Doris was old enough to sympathise with her mother, watching how hard she had to work to run the household, keep six children in clean clothes and cook meals for them all. On top of this Atlanta still tended sick Aborigines and looked after travellers — all without the benefit of running water or any of the labour-saving devices that we find indispensable today.

Although Atlanta had the assistance of her Arrernte house girls, they were sometimes more of a hindrance. Not long after Edna's birth, one particular fifteen-year-old Arrernte house girl called Katie had been foisted on Atlanta by Katie's much older husband. His eagerness to get rid of Katie should have warned Atlanta something was wrong. Later it was revealed the husband had tired of Katie's irrational behaviour and her constant, foolish giggle. The poor girl, it seemed, was retarded. Katie's husband already had another wife and family (since the Arrernte were traditionally polygamous) and he wanted nothing more to do with Katie.

Atlanta was initially wary about employing Katie, who spoke very little English. But her husband pushed her inside the house and departed. As far as he was concerned, Katie was now the Bradshaws' responsibility.

Poor Katie did not mean to but she seemed to create havoc wherever she went. One evening, not long after her arrival, the family were at dinner. Baby Edna was heard crying in the bedroom. Atlanta was busy doling out the food and asked Katie to fetch the baby. There was a long wait while the baby continued to howl. Then came the sound of bumping and thumping along the veranda and finally Katie appeared tugging a large cast-iron boiler across the floor. Boiler, it seemed, was the only English word Katie understood that began with 'b'.

The next day Katie discovered that cupboards and drawers contained interesting things. In one drawer she found a pair of scissors, something she had never seen before. Unfortunately the children showed her how to use them. The following day, while Atlanta was busy cooking, Katie tried out the scissors, cutting a ragged fringe around a good tablecloth and shortening the brand-new curtains considerably. The damage was bad enough but the worst of it was that it was impossible to obtain replacements until the next camel train arrived six months later. Not long after this incident, Katie had to leave those fascinating scissors behind and return to her husband in disgrace.

A total contrast to poor Katie was the devoted, reliable and highly efficient Rungee, who stayed with the Bradshaws for the full nine years they spent at Alice Springs. Rungee was locked into an unhappy arranged marriage with a man much older than herself, infant betrothal of girls to older men being an Aboriginal tradition. Rungee lived with her husband's family, who were very unkind to her as she was childless. She poured out her love and affection on Atlanta and treated the Bradshaw children as lovingly as though they were her own. Whenever Atlanta was feeling unwell, Rungee would put a protective arm around her and say, 'You go longa bed, Quei; me shepherd'em piccaninnies.' Doris remembered she shepherded them as gently as any loving mother or auntie.[25]

Although Rungee and Atlanta had a close, warm relationship, occasionally there were misunderstandings since their two cultures had such widely differing sensitivities regarding nudity. One night, Rungee, proud of her dancing and body-painting skills and keen to demonstrate them to her adored Quei, invited Atlanta to attend a women's corroboree. Most women's corroborees were secret affairs which men were not allowed to witness, just as the men's corroborees were taboo for women on pain of death. However this corroboree, Rungee said, was different, not secret at all, so anyone could watch.

Atlanta, who had already been invited to one corroboree where the women danced stark naked, declined. 'No, Rungee . . . That other time I go you give me big-feller shame — all those girls with nothing clothes . . .'

'You come tonight, Quei, me tell'im allabout must wear shirt,' Rungee insisted.[26]

Not wanting to hurt Rungee's feelings by refusing the invitation, Atlanta agreed.

Thomas was away dispensing justice at Barrow Creek so Atlanta invited Doris, Mabel Taylor the new governess and Leslie Spicer, a telegraph operator, to witness the spectacle which Europeans rarely saw. At the corroboree place, the four of them sat and waited for the rhythmical clicking of the oval clapping sticks to start and the women to commence chanting.

Finally the women appeared in a long line, shuffling and stamping their feet in time to the beat of the clapping sticks. Their faces were painted with mask-like designs in white, yellow and red ochre, their dark eyes gleaming against the vivid colours. But, in spite of all Rungee's promises, the women were naked. As they danced, their naked breasts bobbed and bounced about, their thighs outlined by strong designs in ochres and white pipe clay which stood out vividly against their dark skins. In a crowning irony, faithful to Rungee's promise, each lady had tied her shirt around her neck by the sleeves ensuring it covered her back.

The next day when Atlanta told Rungee that she and the new governess had been embarrassed in front of the young man, Rungee was bewildered. Had she not followed Quei's instructions? Had the women not *worn* their shirts?

Women's ceremonial designs for a corroboree.

Education for their children became a problem for the Bradshaws once they were back at Alice Springs. Mabel Taylor completed a term of two years but the Bradshaws found it impossible to find a new governess in Adelaide for the kind of wages Thomas could afford to pay. So sixteen-year-old Doris, who now regarded herself as a 'young lady' and rode side-saddle, taught her younger siblings in the schoolroom, something she did not always enjoy, feeling that her girlhood years had been curtailed.

Meanwhile there seemed to be an increasing number of visitors to accommodate, and, as rushes continued on the nearby Arltunga and Winnecke gold fields, more disputes over claims for Thomas to settle. Gold fever had even infected Atlanta, who in 1902 was persuaded by a couple of speculators staying at the telegraph station to invest in a mining claim. Atlanta did so — on nothing more than their recommendation — and lost her savings. Despite having shown them hospitality, Atlanta refused to blame the men, who had presumably known their vein was small and got themselves out of the investment but had not told Atlanta, much to the disgust of the old bushmen of the area.

Late in March 1906, three exhausted government geologists, all relatively young fit men when they set out, arrived at the telegraph station suffering severe heat exhaustion, dehydration and flesh wounds from spear injuries. They had been on a mineral survey in the Petermann Ranges and had run out of water. Although they had done nothing to upset the Luritja, they had been attacked while sleeping by men of the Luritja clan who had previously been badly treated by gold prospectors and hated all Europeans.

The leader of this small geological survey party, Frederick George, had managed to find water and care for the two wounded men, one of whom had been speared through the eye and another through his leg and chest. He had removed the spear points and nursed both men until they were well enough to travel back to the telegraph station and be placed under Atlanta's care. Frederick George himself was also ill having contracted dysentery from a well that had been polluted by a dead animal.

In spite of Atlanta's devoted care and consultations with nurses and doctors over the line, Frederick George died at the telegraph station early on the morning of 4 April, aged only thirty-two. He was buried in the small cemetery beside Thomas's brother Ernest. Atlanta nursed the two other wounded geologists until they were well enough to undertake the gruelling journey back to Adelaide.

She also nursed gold miners during a typhoid outbreak at Arltunga gold fields.

In November 1907 Atlanta's seventh child was born. He was named Alan Todd Bradshaw after Charles Todd, Thomas's director of the Post and Telegraph Office. The stream of visitors continued. Only a month after Alan's birth Atlanta had to play hostess again. On a hot day in December 1907 the Bradshaw children and members of the Arrernte crowded around when the grazier Harry Dutton of Anlaby and his friend Murray Aunger

Doris Bradshaw (Blackwell) as a young woman.

arrived at the telegraph station. They turned up in a heavy open touring car, a 24-horsepower Talbot specially built and modified in England for desert conditions. The children had already seen cars before in Adelaide but for the Arrernte people and some of the telegraph operators it was as though two spacemen had arrived in a spacecraft from Mars.

The Talbot, which Dutton and Aunger had christened Angelina, had a canvas hood for protection and its heavy body was festooned with spare tyres, jerry cans, shovels, axes, rifles and water bags to undertake the journey. Dutton and Aunger's aim was to show that their motor car could penetrate places previously thought impossible for that type of vehicle. They intended to drive as far as Darwin to prove that the car could traverse vast distances of land without roads and even ford creeks — quite a journey. Young Ernest Allchurch was fascinated and hung over the engine for hours.

Dutton and Aunger were honoured guests at the telegraph station for a few days before setting off on a journey that would daunt most motorists in cars of today. Unfortunately, the weather was against them. Rain arrived early that year and they were held up at Barrow Creek Telegraph Station for four days. They set off again but before they had gone far bogged down, as the red soil turned to sticky mud and swamps. Angelina's transmission felt the strain and eventually the universal joint cracked. By now the Big Wet was upon them, which meant the end of their epic journey for that year.

Dutton and Aunger managed to obtain help through the telegraph line and a rescue party arrived, but the two men had to abandon Angelina. However, they made plans to return the following year and promised Atlanta's brother that he could make the trip with them.

Once the excitement of seeing a motor car died down, life went on with lots of riding for the children and picnics with their friends the Meyers. However, as Mortimer and Jack grew bigger and more boisterous it became harder for Doris to discipline them in the schoolroom and Atlanta became concerned.

❧ ❧ ❧

It had also become apparent that the children needed a proper teacher who had a deeper knowledge of mathematics and science than Doris. Thomas decided they must leave the outback and return to Adelaide. Atlanta was overjoyed at the thought of seeing her parents again but sad to leave her friends the Strehlows and the Meyers, and dear old Rungee and Amelia.

A month before the Bradshaws were due to depart, the intrepid Dutton and Aunger returned in a second Talbot car with enough spare parts to rescue Angelina. They kept their promise and took young Ernest Allchurch north with them, his skills as a telegraph operator being regarded as useful on a dangerous trip of this nature. They managed to fix Angelina and restart her engine, and both Talbot cars succeeded in reaching Port Darwin after a dangerous 3200-kilometre journey lasting forty-two days. Dutton and Aunger made history as the first team of motorists to cross Australia.

Having joined the two adventurers on their trip, Ernest also attained his moment of glory. When the trip was over he went to work at the telegraph office at Hergott Springs (Marree) for a few years. Many years later he was promoted to superintendent of Alice Springs, working from 1924 to 1932.

As the Bradshaws prepared to leave Alice for good, Atlanta knew there were things she would miss. She loved the wonderful sense of space, the beauty of massed wild flowers after winter rains — the yellow *Senecio* daisies, the mauve sprays of desert myrtle and the clumps of *ptilotus*, their vivid white contrasting with the deep red soil. The great white ghost gums around the telegraph station, the dark green cycads, relics of a prehistoric age, the old house where they had been so happy and their picnics to Standley Chasm and the Wigley Waterhole had become part of her life.

The Bradshaw children were unhappy to be leaving the freedom they had enjoyed in the outback and abandoning their beloved horses to live in Adelaide. 'We've been there once; we don't want to go again; we want to stay here,' were Doris's sentiments.[27]

Amelia and Rungee, as well as the other station Aborigines, were disturbed that the Bradshaws were leaving, particularly the three children who had been born there. They were leaving their country — 'Him bin grow'up longa this place,' they pleaded.[28] Rungee could not leave since her responsibilities lay with her husband and her people but Amelia burst into tears and begged Atlanta to take her with them to Adelaide. Atlanta considered this but decided it would be foolish and risky to take Amelia to the unknown, so far away from her people and her culture.

On the day of the Bradshaws' departure there were many last-minute farewells to make. The children waved a sad goodbye to the Aborigines, to their beloved horses, and to the townsfolk at Stuart, knowing that the last link with Alice would disappear the moment they crossed the plain.

The first day they did not get very far before making camp, and this was just as well. No sooner were the tents erected when one of the Aboriginal grooms arrived on horseback bearing a message that had come in over the wire. He gave it to Thomas to read. Thomas's face changed. Without saying a word to the children, he beckoned to Atlanta and took her aside. The children heard their father talking and their mother give a long despairing wail then burst into sobs while Thomas tried to comfort her. Their father came back and told the waiting children, 'Your grandmother died yesterday, just as we left.'[29]

All her pregnancies and deliveries without the help of a doctor or midwife had seriously affected Atlanta's health. Her complexion had been coarsened by the sun and her knee joints badly damaged when she and baby Edna were thrown from the buggy. The journey to Adelaide and the shock of her mother's sudden death now took a further toll on her.

Once back in Adelaide, where Thomas returned to his old job at the telegraph office, he and Atlanta settled down in a house they bought at Glenelg. At long last Atlanta was back near the sea.

Atlanta had one more child, Sheila Pont Bradshaw, born 10 August 1909, shortly after their return to Adelaide. Her damaged knees continued to give her a great deal of pain, and no doctor seemed able to come up with a cure.

Thomas and Atlanta Bradshaw.

Once Atlanta and her children had left the Northern Territory of South Australia (as it was then known), Annie Meyer found she could not stand the loneliness. The fact her husband, Charlie, was drinking heavily did not help matters. So Annie and her children left Alice Springs as well. They were driven in a buggy to Oodnadatta and caught the Ghan to Adelaide. Eventually, Annie returned to Alice Springs and opened a boarding house, where the famous anthropologist Olive Pink would stay before moving into a converted army hut.

Both Thomas and Atlanta were shocked when they heard from Frieda Strehlow in the early days of World War I that the Strehlows, being of German origin, might be removed from the mission into which they had poured so much time and money. Most of that money had been donated by Augustine, Frieda's wealthy aunt who lived in Germany. The Bradshaws and the other inhabitants of the area wrote to the Australian Government saying that removing them was ridiculous. They described Frieda and Carl Strehlow as patriotic Australians who had done nothing wrong and should not be imprisoned. Fortunately some notice was taken at high level of Thomas Bradshaw's letter and, as a result, the Strehlows, who had done so much for the Arrernte people and for the community in general, were left in peace for the rest of the war, although many other people of German origin were interned.[30]

Atlanta Bradshaw died in Adelaide on 12 August 1929 aged sixty-three, her life shortened by her time in the outback; Thomas Bradshaw survived her by five years and died on 28 August 1934.

In Atlanta's obituary the Adelaide *Advertiser* praised the contribution she had made to life in outback Australia.

The old telegraph station, surrounded by magnificent ghost gums, operated until 1932 when, in a dark period in its history, it became a home for part-Aboriginal children who had been removed from their mothers. This period is described in a book by one of these children, *Alec, A Living History of the Alice Springs Telegraph Station*.[31] By that time the actual telegraph station and post office had been moved to the old township of Stuart. (The road north, the Stuart Highway, still commemorates the name of explorer John McDouall Stuart.)

During World War II, the telegraph station was occupied by the Australian Army. In 1963 the Arrernte were moved from the old telegraph station to Amoonguna Settlement, south-east of Alice Springs, and the area was gazetted as the Alice Springs Telegraph National Park.

Today the station master's house, the men's barracks and the old telegraph office comprise a unique museum set up just as it was during the Bradshaws' period of residence. The battery room has the instruments on the table arranged as they would have been when an operator was on duty. The interior of the station master's house, with its thick stone walls, is decorated with furniture of the period and one can imagine Atlanta, Rungee and the younger children working and playing in the house.

Although the Bradshaws took their own furniture back with them to Adelaide, Doris Bradshaw (Blackwell) would later return to the telegraph station and explain exactly how it was furnished during her childhood so the correct period furniture could be purchased. Today's visitors can see the primitive kitchen where Atlanta cooked meals for her large family. A fascinating display of Thomas Bradshaw's photographs of life at the telegraph station at the start of the twentieth century, some of which are illustrated here, recreates the scene.

The picturesque setting of the telegraph station remains as it was when the Bradshaws lived there, shaded by those gigantic white ghost gums and the lilac and purple hills of the MacDonnell ranges on the skyline. This is one of the views that the famous Arrernte artist, Albert Namatjira, who grew up at the neighbouring Hermannsburg Mission, would immortalise in his watercolours.

Clearly the contributions of Overland Telegraph Station managers and their wives who had the commitment to providing medicine and nursing to the people around them has been underestimated in the story of Australia's outback pioneers. Atlanta Bradshaw and wives like her played an important and largely unsung role in the taming and development of that beautiful and fascinating area — the red centre of Australia.

CHAPTER 4

Jeannie Gunn, OBE
1870 – 1961

THE STORY BEHIND *WE OF THE NEVER-NEVER*

Early in 1902, when Australians were anticipating the coronation of King Edward VII, Jeannie Gunn, daughter of Melbourne journalist Thomas Taylor and granddaughter of a Baptist minister, arrived as a new bride in the Northern Territory of South Australia.

There were few European women in the Territory at that time. It was seen as a wild and lawless place, scarcely suitable for a station manager to take his wife. An undeclared 'war' was being waged by some pastoral companies and graziers against Aborigines who speared their cattle. For their part, Aborigines were dismayed to lose their traditional waterholes and see their supplies of game diminishing, and considered cattle to be a communal resource. When punished by Europeans on raids, the Willeroo, Mangarrayi and Yangman of inland areas retaliated by spearing stockmen and teamsters and leaving them to die or breaking their backs by throwing rocks down on them from high cliffs.

This was a frontier war with battles just as fierce as between the wagoners and native Americans (Red Indian tribes) along the Oregon Trail. Aeneas Gunn, Jeannie's husband, had gained first-hand experience of the violence of the frontier when he joined his cousins Joseph and Frederick Bradshaw in setting up the Marigui cattle run in the Kimberleys in the 1890s, and later what was known as Bradshaw's Run, south-west of Darwin. While at Marigui Station, both Joseph Bradshaw and Aeneas were injured by spears tipped with shards of glass during an attack on the isolated homestead.[1]

Aeneas had caught malaria while at the Prince Regent River, which forced him south to recuperate in Melbourne. There he took a two-year contract as acting resident librarian at Prahran Library, re-cataloguing its collection, a job he had just completed when he first met Jeannie Taylor.

Jeannie had typical Scottish colouring, pale skin that freckled in the sun, clear brown eyes, a firm chin and a mass of reddish-gold hair, usually worn in a knot on top of her head. She was petite (only 157 centimetres tall), and an excellent story teller with a sense of humour and an ability to laugh at herself.

Aeneas and Jeannie met by chance when Jeannie was going to a concert in a buggy with a woman friend who was driving a pair of frisky horses. As her friend reined them in outside the concert hall, Jeannie tried to climb down over the wheel, intending to hold the horses' heads and steady them so her friend could dismount, but she was hampered by her long skirts. Without warning, one of the horses shied, throwing Jeannie off the wheel rim and straight into the arms of Aeneas, who had gallantly hurried forward to hold the horses' heads.

From the moment they were thrown together by circumstance, Aeneas was fascinated by Jeannie's effervescent personality, her sense of humour and by the contrast between her small frame and strong spirit. After the concert, he obtained permission to visit her at her Melbourne home.

At the Taylors' comfortable house, Aeneas met Jeannie's journalist father. The Gunns, like Jeannie's family, were fiercely proud of their Scottish Presbyterian heritage. Aeneas, who also contributed articles to local newspapers, must have impressed the Taylors. With her father's approval, Aeneas started taking Jeannie out. Theirs was a whirlwind romance, and they married at the Scots Presbyterian Church on 31 December 1901.

Jeannie had grown up in the Melbourne suburb of Hawthorn. One of five children, she was used to the give and take of family life.

Aeneas Gunn on his wedding day.

She and her sister Carrie had run a small private school from the family home which they called 'Rolyat' (Taylor spelt backwards). Their English-born mother, Anna Lush, had also been a teacher and had taught her four daughters from home, providing them with an excellent education and encouraging Jeannie and Carrie to become teachers. Jeannie had gone on to study at the University of Melbourne.[2]

Having resisted the idea of marriage for years, Jeannie was now determined to follow her charismatic husband to the tropical north, then untamed and dangerous.

Elsey Station, where the Gunns were heading, was more than 100 kilometres south of Katherine and was one of the Northern Territory's largest cattle stations, covering a million and a quarter acres (500,000 hectares) of desert and scrub. It held 40,000 cattle, Arab horses and a large number of brumbies. It was the third-oldest station in the Territory, having been established in 1880 by Abraham Wallace, who drove 2728 head of cattle out to Elsey Creek, a tributary of the Roper River. Wallace had built a thatched timber house for the manager, and other outbuildings and storage sheds, before he sold the lease to J.W. Osmand and J.A. Panton.[3]

In 1902, following the death of Osmand, Elsey Station was up for sale and a consortium, which included Aeneas's brother Bob Gunn and Bob's business partner, a Dr Bennett, was raising money to buy it. The consortium planned to give Aeneas, who lacked capital, a share if he acted as manager.

Aeneas was not planning a long-term future in the outback. He was aiming to work hard and live cheaply at Elsey Station for a few years, to increase stock numbers, sell off the brumbies to the Indian Army and then, he hoped, the syndicate would sell the lease at auction profitably. With the proceeds of his share, Aeneas planned to take Jeannie, who had never been overseas, to Europe for a few years before returning to live in Melbourne.[4]

The outback country of the north, or the Never-Never, had a fearsome reputation. Friends and relatives warned Jeannie that she would be isolated and lonely. Nevertheless, they assumed that she would live in a handsome stone or brick mansion similar to those on pastoral stations in the western districts of Victoria. They did not realise that things were very different in the Northern Territory, where cyclones frequently destroyed the timber and tin buildings. They gave Jeannie highly unsuitable wedding presents, like fine china tea services, lace antimacassars and exquisitely embroidered hand towels, which Jeannie packed to take with her on their two-week steamer voyage from Port Melbourne to Port Darwin.

Doubtless married women friends also took her aside and warned her that she would have problems if she fell pregnant — the nearest doctor would be over 400 kilometres away. But Jeannie shrugged off their grim warnings. Among the Taylor clan, Jeannie's strong will and steely determination were legendary.

Aeneas Gunn must have had some qualms about taking his bride to the Elsey, especially as Mary Jane Bradshaw, wife of his cousin Joseph Bradshaw, had stayed a mere three months at the remote

Jeannie Gunn's home in Hawthorn, a leafy Melbourne suburb.

Kimberleys cattle station Marigui, and had endured the heat as well as attacks by Aborigines on the homestead. When she found a poisonous snake coiled around the legs of the piano organ, even courageous Mary Jane gave up and returned to Melbourne by ship.[5]

The newlyweds sailed north aboard the Eastern and Asiatic lines mail steamer *Guthrie*. The route hugged the coast of eastern and northern Australia. The couple took a short holiday in Port Darwin, then a very primitive settlement surrounding a magnificent harbour.

Concerned that Jeannie would be lonely, Aeneas had advertised for a maid or paid companion to accompany Jeannie to the Elsey. No matter how high the wages he offered, not one European woman applied for the post. Darwin people knew that several station homesteads had been attacked by Aborigines.[6]

The woman who kept the hotel in which the Gunns stayed knew the outback well. She warned Jeannie that she would be lucky to reach the Elsey Station alive, as the Wet was coming on; indeed heavy rains had already started. The hotel owner invited Jeannie to stay with her until the homestead on the Elsey had been restored. Jeannie politely declined the offer. It seemed everyone but the Gunns knew the homestead had been damaged in a cyclone — a fact the executors of the Osmand estate had failed to tell Aeneas. He only received the news when a telegram arrived in Darwin from stockman Jock McLennan, who was acting as temporary manager at the Elsey.

The telegram sent by Jock — or Mac, the Sanguine Scot, as Jeannie called him in *We of the Never-Never* — was one of many the Gunns received from him advising Jeannie not to come and giving a variety of lame excuses. While both of the Gunns were prepared for the danger and isolation of the outback, Jeannie, in particular, had not been prepared for the hostility of the stockmen towards her.

The station hands did not want Jeannie at the Elsey, fearing that if the boss brought his wife there she might make them dress for dinner and stop them cursing and swearing. She might also object to the custom of station hands temporarily taking a 'station gin'. 'Black velvet' was seen as one of the perks of the life of a single man in the outback.[7]

The Never-Never was a rough, tough, male-dominated place. Those who lived there cursed the Big Wet and the clouds of red dust that replaced it. What they loved was the sense of endless space in the outback, the beauty of its lily-fringed ponds, its thermal pools and swimming holes. Most men who worked on cattle stations in the Never-Never were bachelors or escaping from failed marriages; they had their own values of mateship and codes of behaviour.

In the restrictive post-Victorian era when Jeannie Gunn went to the outback, wives were still regarded as chattels of their husbands, and lacked access to bank accounts or loans. A white woman living in the outback was considered very daring indeed. Jeannie was already considered 'modern' for her times, an 'advanced' woman who had gone to university and had run her own school. (This may explain why Jeannie married at thirty, relatively late for a time when most women were married by twenty-one.) Jeannie must only have confirmed the impression of the 'modern' woman when, in anticipation of the tough travelling conditions ahead, she shortened her skirts. Instead of being an inch from the floor as was customary at that time, her skirts now offered a tantalising glimpse of ankle (trousers being considered quite improper for a woman).

Aboard the goods train they took from Port Darwin to Pine Creek, Jeannie told her husband she could live *anywhere* as long as she was with him. She *would* make friends with those hostile Elsey stockmen and get them to accept her.

The train zigzagged through forests and open plains, stopping frequently for the driver to chase kangaroos off the line, boil a billy for a cup of tea or greet a group of Aborigines and offer them hunks of watermelon. Eventually they arrived at Pine Creek, where they made their way to the hotel. As they waited for their tea in the saloon, where ladies were allowed to sit, an angry Scottish voice was heard through the partition that separated the saloon from the public bar, which was exclusively male. The voice proclaimed to all and sundry that the outback was not a fit place for a woman.

'The telegraphing bush-whacker', Jeannie said. 'Watch me defy him!'[8]

She slid down from her seat, put her small feet firmly on the floor and marched into the next room where she confronted a brawny Scotsman. Gingerly, she held out a firm hand towards the angry man.

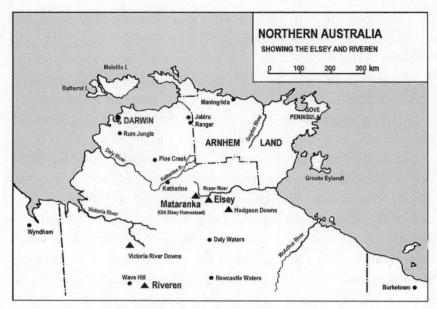

'How do you do?' she said, smiling up at him.

Mac's jaw dropped. So this petite woman was the dreaded ripsnorter! 'Quite well, thank you,' he responded, embarrassed that she had overheard him, and soon all three of them were grinning and talking away.

They had a job sorting out the luggage and picking what should be loaded onto packhorses and what had to be left behind until a team of bullock wagons could make the long journey out to the Elsey after the Wet. Jeannie said she could manage very well with just one bag of clothes for the trip, but became alarmed when Mac told her *everything* she needed had to fit in her swag. The rest could be loaded aboard the wagons when they made their annual trip bringing food and other supplies.

Jeannie could scarcely believe her ears. Wagons only went to the Never-Never *once a year*? The rest of her clothes and her household goods would only arrive at Elsey homestead in *five months time*! She stared in dismay at the one small bag she was allowed to take with her and at the pile of dresses, books and wedding gifts she was sure she could not possibly do without.

Mac said briskly, 'You'll have to cull your herd a bit, that's all.'

There was no room for books or needlework, or the pile of linen sheets, pillow cases, towels, cushion covers, lace doilies and antimacassars given by kind friends convinced that as the wife of a station owner-manager Jeannie would live in style.

'You won't need those anyway,' said Mac brutally, pointing at her pillow cases, 'for there's no pillows.' It seemed Jeannie might be condemned to use a folded jacket for a pillow, like the stockmen. 'A couple of changes of everything is stacks. There's heaps of soap and water at the station, and things dry before you can waltz around twice.'

Still anxious to please, Jeannie agreed to leave most of her clothes behind but did not realise that a couple of high-necked blouses, a cotton dress or two and a change of skirts would not be sufficient for five months' constant wash and wear. In the end, the pillow cases did go with her. By this time Mac was starting to feel sorry for Jeannie and assured her that 'all hands could be put on to pluck birds' for feather pillows as the Elsey was stiff with birds!

After a day of rain, the morning of their departure dawned bright and clear. The Elsey party decided to make a dash for the Fergusson River before the rains returned and made it impossible to reach the Elsey. Jeannie was riding side-saddle, wearing a long, cumbersome riding habit with divided skirts. The travelling was slow. In that wild country and with the Big Wet already started, they were lucky that the Cullen River, which could have been a roaring torrent, was only a stream and they forded it with ease. When they reached the Fergusson River, it was up to the top of its banks.

Mac suggested that if one of them swam a horse through the flood, the Missus could hang on to its tail. Unsurprisingly, it did not go down well with Jeannie. 'Anything but that!' she pleaded.[9]

Mac pointed to a thick wire rope stretched across the river from bank to bank. What about the flying fox? They sent mailbags and valuables on it when the river was in flood; why not send the Missus?

Jeannie felt sick at the thought of crossing swirling water holding onto a thin wire. But this was a test. She must not fail or the men would despise her. She nodded and managed a wan smile.

The crossing was put off until the morning and they made camp for the night, sleeping under nets, as the mosquitoes and sandflies were a torment. The next morning the Fergusson River was still rising.

'We'll have to bustle up and get across or the water'll be over the wire, and then we'll be done for,' Mac said.

Jeannie hurried, but getting across the river took a long time. It was an hour before Jackeroo, the part-Aboriginal stockman, managed to persuade Roper, the quietest and most reliable horse, to allow himself to be half dragged, half pushed through the flooding stream. With a good deal of urging, the rest of the horses also crossed. Then the hobbles were sent across on a pulley attached to the wire. The ever-smiling Jackeroo hobbled the horses again on the far side where he waited to take the swags and saddle bags sent over to him by Mac and Aeneas.

By the time they were across the river, it was after midday. Jeannie was still waiting, inwardly trembling but smiling so the men would not guess how scared she was. A surcingle, a long thick strap that keeps saddle bags in place on a packhorse, was buckled through the pulley. Aeneas crossed first, to test it. He was dragged through the water most of the way but called out to Jeannie that he was fine.

The surcingle came back across and Mac shortened the leather strap and reassured her, 'It's only a matter of holding on and keeping cool.' Jeannie stepped onto the strap and kept her eyes on her husband who was stationed on the other side hauling on the wire. 'Hang on like grim death,' he called out to her.

When Jeannie was halfway across, the wire began to sag and her long skirts trailed in the water, pulling her down. She feared she might be dragged under. Back on the bank Mac flung his weight on the wire making Jeannie shoot up in the air, a terrifying experience, but she was determined the men would not see her scared.

And suddenly she was on the other side in her husband's arms, relieved it was over. Jeannie looked back to the other bank, amused that Mac refused to trust the wire. He swam through the strong current.

They still had to cross the Edith River, twenty kilometres farther on. The weather had become swelteringly hot, the flies were maddening and travel was slow. By sundown they found themselves looking down at the flooded Katherine River. They had travelled a mere 100 kilometres in three days. From the far side of the deep red rocks that surrounded the area a voice hailed them. Tom Pearce (*We of the Never-Never*'s Mine Host), owner of Katherine's only hostelry, the Sportsman's Hotel, was assuring Jeannie he'd row them across in no time.

Katherine turned out to be a tiny outback settlement 'on the telegraph line' like Alice Springs. All around it, and stretching away on every side, were hundreds of thousands of hectares of what Jeannie's husband called the Never-Never, 'because in it you can Never-Never find a bally thing you want,' he said. Jeannie had her own interpretation of the term, saying that it was so named because those who go there never-never voluntarily leave it.[10]

Beside the rickety pub was Tom Pearce's house with wide verandas screened by scarlet poinciana trees. Here the Gunns would stay while the stockmen camped out in the bush. Some of Katherine's residents gave her things she would not find at the Elsey. Fresh tomatoes and a cucumber from Constable Kingston (the Wag); some eggs from Mr Little, superintendent of the telegraph line; a freshly baked cake from the policeman's wife. When Tom Pearce and his wife gave Jeannie a pile of potatoes and a flat iron she thanked them politely but was puzzled. She was too new to the outback to realise how precious potatoes were and thought taking a flat iron on such a short journey seemed odd.

'What's it for?' she asked.[11]

'To iron duds [trousers] with, of course,' replied the Wag. In Katherine its value lay in keeping the pub door open.

'But I won't *need* to iron any duds until we reach the homestead!'

'It's *for* the homestead. There will be nothing like that there,' her husband informed her.

Jeannie smiled a little uncertainly. Then Tom Pearce brought out a couple of china cups and put them with the baggage. Jeannie was delighted. She didn't know it then but the flat iron would become one of her most cherished possessions.

Jeannie was beginning to change her ideas about the kind of mansion she would be living in at Elsey. Mac decided to set her straight. The homestead on the Elsey is 'mostly verandahs and promises', he said, 'but one room is finished. *We* call it The House, but you'll probably call it a Hut, even though it has got doors and calico windows framed and on hinges.' But on the bright side, 'there's a looking-glass — goodness knows how it got there! You ought to be thankful for that and the wire mattress. You won't find many of them out bush.'

❦ ❦ ❦

With more rain expected and the flooded King River still to cross, the party was anxious to move on. When they had arrived at Katherine the Katherine River had been too swollen to take the horses across. After four days it had subsided enough for the difficult crossing to begin. Ten horses had to be dragged over the river behind a flat boat, the halter of each horse held by a man in the stern. It took a day to complete the task, but at sundown Mac nevertheless set out with the pack teams and horses. The next morning Jeannie and Aeneas climbed up onto a buckboard provided by Tom Pearce to begin the next leg.

They caught up to Mac and after a day's jolting over creek beds, successfully fording the roaring King River, and bouncing through forested country and long grass, at sundown they stopped. Aeneas and Mac bowed to Jeannie and said, 'Welcome Home!' They were at the Elsey 'front gate'. Another seventy kilometres and they would be at the front door of the homestead.

They camped the night by a wide sheet of water, Easter's Billabong. At supper, amazed to hear that Jeannie had never tasted Johnny cakes, Mac promised her some for breakfast. Producing flour, cream of tartar, soda and a mixing dish from his saddle bag, he set to work. Cutting off chunks of dough, he buried them in the ashes of the fire, cooking them until they were brown and crisp.

Rain was on the way and the mosquitoes were a torment for Jeannie's pale skin but she did not complain. They rigged their tents and Mac carried the Johnny cakes into his tent for safety, although he did not really expect the billabong to flood in the night. However, it did flood and he spent the night perched on a pyramid of pack-bags and saddles, the crisp Johnny cakes at the bottom of the pile. By breakfast time they had turned to wet, stodgy slabs, but there was no other kind of bread so they ate the crispest, crustiest bits and Jeannie fibbed that they were delicious.

That last full day, traversing the black soil flats, was the worst for Jeannie. The driving rain had turned the ground into slush. The springless buckboard bounced about like a rubber ball, Jeannie with it, as they skimmed between trees, swung through scrub, at one point avoiding a fallen tree and missing a boulder by inches. Mac pulled the buckboard up, at the right time, in exactly the right place, for their overnight camp at Bitter Springs, where Dan (Dave Suttee — the Head Stockman) and his faithful dog waited to greet them. Dan soon had a fire blazing and a billy boiling. To Jeannie's delight he also produced from a tea towel a crisp, freshly baked damper.

Dan was a shy, quiet old man, wary of women. He watched Jeannie closely as he asked her questions about the road and their journey. Jeannie knew that his shrewd hazel eyes were judging her. She wanted this kind old bushman to like her.

By the time supper was over, Dan had risked a mild joke or two and laughed loudly at the answers she gave to his questions on bushcraft. What they must do, Dan said, was to teach her some of the signs of water at hand, right off, 'in case she does get lost any time'.[12]

She was as determined as ever to win these men over. Used to finding her way about a city and sure she would soon get the hang of things in the bush, Jeannie replied confidently, 'You needn't bother about me. If I ever do get lost, I'll just catch a cow and milk it!'

This brought a roar of delight from all three men who knew how fierce the cattle could be. 'Missus! Missus! You'll need a deal of educating!' Aeneas said.

Over breakfast the next day Dan made the first joke. He was surprised, he said, really surprised, that Jeannie — the Missus — hadn't been out already to catch herself a milking cow. He had been looking forward to fresh milk for breakfast. Jeannie laughed at him, and at herself.

'She'll do for this place!' Dan declared. With all the experience of knowing eight or ten women in his forty years in the bush, he could pronounce that 'the one that could see jokes suited best'. Jeannie soon spoiled her previous good impression, however. Finding flies drowning in her mug of tea, she poured the liquid onto the ground. The waste of good tea upset Dan.

Aeneas quickly spoke up for his wife. 'She'll be fishing the flies out with the indifference of a Stoic in a week or two.'

As the jolting buckboard had no canopy, Jeannie was soon covered in a layer of reddish-brown dust. They had almost reached the Elsey when around a bend they came upon Jack McLeod (the Quiet Stockman of *We of the Never-Never*), a strong young man, who was herding out a mob of horses.

'Hallo there,' Mac shouted. 'This is the Missus, Jack!'

Another man shy of women, Jack moved uneasily in his saddle, not daring to look Jeannie in the face. Only that morning he had decided that he would not stay to meet that terrible ogre the Boss's wife. He would be gone before they arrived. Now he was embarrassed at seeing her. He couldn't stand women, always nattering about something or other and stopping a bloke doing what he wanted to.

Jeannie looked after his retreating figure, realising this man wanted to avoid her at *all* costs.

They continued their journey until Mac shouted, 'Eyes front!' and Jeannie craned her head to catch a glimpse of her new home. Mac was smiling as they bumped over the rough dirt track. He whipped up the horses and urged them through the slip-rails, past the stockyards, over the grassy homestead paddock, and they halted in front of a few down-at-heel wooden buildings.

Here at last, Jeannie thought. Descending the step, she found herself standing in the shadow of an unfinished timber building, surrounded by a mob of barking dogs. Was it a house or a hut, Mac was keen to know. 'A Betwixt and Between,' was Jeannie's opinion.

While station hands took charge of the buckboard and horses, Aeneas and Mac were greeted by Herb Bryant, the station bookkeeper-cum-drover, an educated and neatly attired man (known as The Dandy in *We of the Never-Never*). He was introduced to Jeannie and looked at her approvingly. 'I'm sure we're all real glad to see *you*,' he said.

One small victory, thought Jeannie.

Elsey Station turned out to be a group of ramshackle timber huts with dirt floors, some with thatched roofs, others with tin roofs. Jeannie was shown the cook's quarters, the kitchen, the men's quarters, a store where dry goods were kept, a meat house, a blacksmith's shop and a buggy or cart shed. In the centre was an immense wood pile. There was also a blacksmith's forge and a 'humpy' where some of the Yangman and Mangarrayi station hands lived. They were 160 kilometres from Katherine. One neighbour was 140 kilometres east, another 170 kilometres to the south and more neighbours were about 320 kilometres to the west.

Jeannie examined the manager's house and decided that Mac had been right. It *was* mostly verandas and promises. Back in 1897 a cyclone had wrecked the house. A travelling Chinese carpenter with grand ideas had arrived and started to rebuild but only one room had been completed; the second room was nothing but uprights and cross beams. The Chinese carpenter complained he had run out of wood, asked for his cheque and vanished, never to return. They would have to live in the undamaged room until the rest could be restored.

The Elsey in 1902. From left to right are the harness room, the meat house, the blacksmith's shop, the men's quarters with stockmen outside, and the Gunns' renovated homestead.

COURTESY JENNIE BLUNDELL.

The huge termite mounds of the Northern Territory impressed Jeannie Gunn as she rode among them.

The furniture in the livable room consisted of four chairs, a large dining table with one leg shorter than the others, a four-poster bed with a rusty wire mattress and a looking-glass spotted with damp. Jeannie tested a small side table made from an old packing case, the legs of which seemed solid enough, a washstand, which lacked a jug or washbasin, and an ancient, wobbly chest of drawers.

The walls were decorated with muddy footprints, as though the station dogs had pitter-pattered all over the timber as it lay in the yard. But as she looked at her home and its furniture Jeannie tried to appear cheerful. She was glad none of her old friends who had given her all those expensive presents were here. All around the house were hillocky tussocks of coarse grass, beaten down by dogs, goats and fowls. Along the banks of the stream or billabong was a scruffy vegetable garden. Beyond it were stockyards and the house paddock and on the surrounding plains Jeannie saw reddish-brown towers of dried earth which her husband told her had been built by ants.

The primitive sanitary arrangements were one reason for men not wanting women in the bush, and consisted of a deep pit often called the 'long drop', on which the lid of an empty 44-gallon petrol drum with a hole cut in it served as a seat.

In her autobiography, *Nothing Prepared Me*, describing the Kimberleys in the 1950s, Edna Quilty is more outspoken than most about problems faced by women pioneers, one of them being the communal latrine pit shared by stockmen and boss's wife — horrific by today's standards. She describes a huge pit some distance from her main homestead, three sides of which were screened by hessian flaps, with an open doorway, no lock and hence no privacy from stockmen for the boss's wife.

Quilty, brave in other respects, was terrified of falling into the pit until finally her husband took pity on her and had a smaller latrine pit dug for her use.

Jeannie had to contend with much the same toileting arrangement, but fifty years earlier could not write about such unladylike things, so there are no mentions of such topics in *We of the Never-Never*.

After the men had shown her around Mac said, 'Well! I said it wasn't a fit place for a woman, didn't I?'[13]

Dan argued with him, 'Any place is a fit place for a woman, provided the woman is fitted for the place.'

Jeannie fully intended to fit into the place as neatly as anyone else. But some changes were needed. 'A few able-bodied men could finish the dining room in a couple of days, and make a mansion of the rest of the building in a week or so,' she said.

'Steady! Go slow, Missus!' they protested.

'We begin at the very beginning of things in the Never-Never,' said her husband. 'Timber grows in trees in these parts and has to be coaxed out with a saw.'

Jeannie looked in dismay at the distant trees against the skyline but was reassured to hear there was a carpenter 'inside' (the continent's interior) they could call on. And remember, said Mac, that they were now in the 'Land of Plenty of Time!' And so it was. 'Little Johnny', the jobbing carpenter, kept disappearing off to the pub in Katherine so progress on the new dining room was slow.

As she settled in, Jeannie began taking notes and planning a book about her experiences. But she was not the only writer in the Gunn family. Her husband was also making notes (which would later be destroyed) and writing humorous letters to the *Northern Territory Times* about life at the Elsey.[14]

He was also writing letters home in which he told of his admiration for the way Jeannie had borne the journey. In a letter to his brother, Bob, Aeneas wrote proudly of how his wife had coped with 'a roaring torrent to cross, mosquitoes and sand flies, snakes, the noxious smelling stink bugs . . . she won everyone's admiration . . . 150 miles in five days in a buckboard is a satisfactory performance for any woman'.[15]

Jeannie admired her husband, too, and soon discovered he had a talent for settling disputes harmoniously. When Jack, the Quiet Stockman, returned with some stock and told the men he was quitting, Aeneas quietly spoke to him. Whatever he said was enough to make Jack change his mind about leaving. That night at dinner the normally taciturn Jack announced, 'I'm staying on,' but gave no reasons for his change of plan.[16]

'Going to give her a chance?' Dan asked with a grin.

There were so many new things to be learned. Jeannie thought Sam, the Chinese cook, seemed cheerful but she could never tell what was going on behind his exterior. The meals he produced were often nothing like those she had asked for and could be most unusual. One breakfast consisted of pumpkin pie with raisins and mince! She didn't know how to deal with him. Nor did she know how to handle the Aboriginal women, who always said 'Yes, Missus' and 'I do it, Missus', then rarely did as she asked. Jeannie complained that she would ask the women to scrub the kitchen floor, leave them at it and then they would go walkabout in the bush, complaining the work was too tiring. Her husband suggested she should make her orders clearer. She tried hard to do so and gentle Old Nellie, one of the Aboriginal women, helped round up the girls when they showed signs of slacking off or 'knocking up', as they called it in the outback.

Mac also offered to tackle the women. In half an hour the kitchen was clean and shining and Mac was pleased with himself. 'You'll need to rule them with a rod of iron,' he told Jeannie authoritatively, but the next morning only Old Nellie appeared. Apparently the other Aboriginal women had gone for an outing to the Warloch Ponds with friends, claiming they needed a day's rest after so much hard work!

A few days later Jeannie went to their camp to see if they would give her a language lesson. The visit was reckoned a great success, with Jeannie setting off gales of laughter when she tried to say a few words in their language. The next day there were so many helpers about the place that the work was finished quickly in order to leave time for more merry-making.

All the new helpers set Jeannie a new problem: clothing them. Luckily she found a bolt of material in the station store, and it seemed that all their problems were solved — except for that of Sam the cook. Fortunately Sam decided to leave of his own accord, saying that the Missus and the 'Maluka' — 'old man', as the station Aborigines called Aeneas — were too fussy. The Maluka even insisted that the food for the men's quarters should be as good as that for himself and his wife! This would never do.

Sam announced he was going to write away for a new station cook who would arrive in about six weeks. He would see his replacement settled and then depart. Then, as if to spite them, Sam started to cook such delicious meals that they were almost sorry he was going.

✿ ✿ ✿

Station life was quite different from what she had expected, but Jeannie was beginning to enjoy it. She had plenty of free time to go riding and did not have to face the toil and financial hardship that other women in this book — Georgiana Molloy, Evelyn Maunsell, Myrtle Rose White or even Atlanta Bradshaw — had to endure. Conditions at the Elsey were primitive, but Jeannie had companionship, adventure, support and a station cook to prepare meals.

Although the Elsey was remote from civilisation, a surprising number of visitors passed through. Being within six kilometres of the Overland Telegraph Line, scarcely a week passed without one or more visitors. They were cattle drovers and stockmen, station owners, swagmen down on their luck, telegraph operators and heads of government departments. Each one brought news of the outside world and possibly extra mail. Usually they stayed a day or two and Jeannie enjoyed their company. There was only one room in the homestead but accommodation was no problem because bush travellers routinely carried a bluey (rolled blanket) and a mosquito net in their swag.

These visitors and bushmen sat among the buzzing swarms of flies and chatted about cattle camps and stampedes, dangers and extreme hardship. As she listened, Jeannie began to understand the stoic but lighthearted way these men accepted their tough life in the outback.

Not long after the Gunns had settled into the Elsey, Mac left to run a bullock team and wagons delivering goods to the inside. They could expect to see him when he returned after the Wet with Jeannie's belongings. Mac took with him Bertie his 'boy' (as the Aboriginal men who assisted as stockmen and drovers were called) and Bertie's wife, Nellie. With Old Nellie reluctantly gone, for a while Jeannie had her hands full adjudicating between a roomful of women who rushed to take her place. Eventually two were chosen for the house with the compromise that any who wished could help outside, and Jeannie set about making these new girls some clothes.

Slowly improvements were being made to the homestead. Garden beds were built up, seeds planted and paths marked out. After a trip to Katherine, Dan returned with the welcome news that Johnny the carpenter was getting his 'tools together and would be along in no time' to finish the house.

As it turned out, Jeannie had to wait longer for her new rooms, when the demands of the outback took precedence and Johnny downed tools at the house to go out and fix a well instead. Aeneas decided to take the opportunity this provided to 'go bush' and show Jeannie the southern part of the Elsey run. The Yangman and Mangarrayi watched her depart. They could not understand why Jeannie rode side-saddle but to see the 'little Missus' mount a horse was good entertainment.

They camped overnight and the next day, on the way back to the homestead, Dan, who accompanied them, suggested that Jeannie might care to take a look at her future 'dining room'. So they turned into the tall trees on the edge of the Reach, riding on through the luxurious shade where Jeannie was delighted to see the timber for her dining room actually growing.

Jeannie made a theme of her outback education in *We of the Never-Never*. Besides teaching her to live simply, appreciate what she had, wait patiently and do it all in good humour, the men were always keen to put her instinct — or naivety — to the test. One day, when the horses were collected in the stockyard and everyone had gone to see them, Dan said, 'Let's see if she knows anything about horses. Show us your fancy in this lot, Missus.'[17]

Jeannie looked at the beautiful creatures. A magnificent brown colt, ears shot forward, nostrils quivering, watched every movement she made. She nodded at him. 'Talk of luck!' cried Dan. 'You've picked Jack's fancy.'

Jack, his voice suddenly warm and friendly, said, 'She's picked out the best in the whole mob,' before turning back to the horses again.

※ ※ ※

The station received eight mails a year, with an extra delivery now and then brought by kind travellers. Everyone found a job to do at the homestead when the mailman, Henry Peckham (the Fizzer), was due to call. Peckham had once worked as a manager on neighbouring Auvergne Station, some time after the previous station manager, Tom Hardy, was speared to death by members of the 'Wild Blacks', a tribe of the Willeroo.

One day, Peckham arrived at the Elsey 'fizzing over' with news. Wagons were on their way to the 'inside'.

'Your trunks'll be along in no time now, Missus. They've got 'em all aboard,' he said.[18]

Herb Bryant — the Dandy — calculated that at ten miles (sixteen kilometres) a day on good roads and no mishaps to the bullock team, Jeannie's trunks might be there in four weeks. But, in fact, late thunderstorms and swampy ground meant they took almost twice as long. The way to make sure that at least the stores would arrive more quickly was to send a wagon to Katherine and collect them. So Bryant set off to do so.

Meanwhile, Johnny the carpenter had returned. He went on hammering the curves out of sheets of corrugated iron with which to cap the timber piles to stop white ants entering the house, all the while promising it wouldn't take long. Jeannie tried to believe him but was not convinced.

ᴸᴸ ᴸᴸ ᴸᴸ

Sam had just announced dinner one evening when they looked up to see a cloud of dust along the horizon. The cloud turned into a fat, jovial Chinaman dressed in a black-and-gold robe. He dismounted, calling, 'Good day, Boss! Good day, Missus! Good day, all about.'

'You've struck Cheon,' said Johnny. 'Talk of luck! He's the jolliest old josser going.'

The 'jolliest old josser' waddled over to the assembled group, bowed low and introduced himself as the new cook. He explained that he knew all about cooking, gardening, milking, fishing and shooting wild duck, and was ready to start at once.

Next day Cheon was up at dawn, refusing any help from Sam, who, distinctly miffed, asked for his pay cheque, shook hands all around and departed, never to be seen again.

Cheon turned out to be a superb manager. Within a week he had everything under control. Everyone seemed happier and Jeannie wondered how she had ever coped without him. Cheon kept everyone, men and women, hard at work until he was satisfied. And if any of the girls had not washed hands and pail and cows' udders before sitting down to milk them, they soon toed the line.

Although Jeannie enjoyed the company of the house girls and other Aboriginal women — especially their larking about as they washed the clothes at the creek — and they seemed pleased to volunteer to work at the house, she was certain she could do the housework in less time than it took to tell her girls what to do. When she set them to work for Cheon, he only sent them back to her. The problem resolved itself when one of the Aboriginal stockmen named Larrikin returned to the property with a pleasant young wife named Rosy, who asked if she could work for the Missus. She assured Jeannie she knew how to scrub, sweep, wash and starch. Rosy was, according to Jeannie, 'so prettily jolly, clean, capable, and curly-headed' that Jeannie immediately made her head of domestic staff.[19]

'Great Scott!' Aeneas groaned. 'That makes four of them at it.' Jeannie said she was sure that Rosy would be excellent. She was right, and Rosy and Cheon worked together splendidly.

Cheon at the Elsey.

Before long, Herb Bryant was back from Katherine with some of the stores — rolls of unbleached calico, mosquito netting, matting for the floors, jugs and basins to wash in and more cups and saucers. Lacking a sewing machine, Jeannie had a mountain of needlework to do by hand. The calico was intended for false ceilings in the new rooms. But Jeannie's biggest task was to make a gigantic mosquito net for the dining room, to enclose the dining table, chairs and people from flies and mosquitoes.

All the while, the house was taking better shape. Rosy and the other girls scrubbed the muddy paw-prints from the old and new walls, which were made of sliced tree trunks dropped horizontally, one above the other, between grooved posts. Inset into every third panel was a window so the new house would stay cool in the heat of summer but, of course, having no electricity there could be no ceiling fans.

Huge sheets of bark were used as insulation between the rafters and the galvanised iron roof. These were to be covered with the calico panels Jeannie had sewn to create a false ceiling.

When she announced that the tent of mosquito netting for the dining room was finished, Johnny, Dan and Herb hung it from the beams using fencing wire. As Jeannie had intended, the long net curtains reached down to the floor and ended with deep hem pockets of calico which were weighted down so the netting would not move. Jeannie hoped that snakes would not hide in the pockets in the hem. Cheon was filled with admiration, assuring the boss that the Missus was 'plenty savey', before returning to his kitchen to prepare a celebration dinner which was to be eaten inside Jeannie's mosquito-proof tent.

When Aeneas came home from visiting a far-flung corner of the property and saw how good the place looked, he was so impressed he started to build bookshelves out of old packing cases. These were intended for the much-loved books he expected to arrive any time on Mac's wagons.

However, the wagons were taking a long time, and well before they arrived Jeannie faced another pressing problem — not a thing to wear. Due to their frequent washing in the creeks, where they were beaten on stones by the house girls, her clothes were falling apart, and soon she was left with only one dress that was wearable. There was nowhere to buy new clothes, so Jeannie set about making herself a new dress from the unbleached calico she had used for the ceiling. She hadn't got far when her husband arrived from the station's own store bearing a roll of deep pink, thick, shiny cotton intended for dresses for the house girls, and some white braid. Brilliant pink was not a colour that Jeannie liked or normally wore. But she set to with her needle and soon appeared in a bright pink blouse and skirt ornamented with white rickrack braid.

Jeannie found there was so much to do in the outback she was never bored, but she missed her parents, sisters and friends a great deal. Like everyone else, she was looking forward to the next mail call by Henry Peckham, the Fizzer. It had been six weeks since his last. At sundown he arrived, covered in red dust and leading a packhorse bearing mail bags. Everyone rushed to welcome him and watched eagerly as he broke the seals of the bags and tipped out the mail. Jeannie was thrilled to receive *thirty* letters.

The next day the Fizzer was up at dawn. He ate a hearty breakfast of chops and fried eggs and climbed into the saddle, calling out, 'So long, chaps. See you again, at half-past eleven, four weeks.'[20]

The station hands knew the Fizzer would, if humanly possible, be back on time with their mail. In extremely high temperatures and with no shade, he feared that he could die of thirst out there in the bleak waterless desert and the dingoes would gnaw at his body as he lay dying. In fact, his death was quite the opposite: in later life Jeannie would learn that the Fizzer drowned while crossing a river to deliver a letter from a sick woman who lived on a remote cattle property who was asking for help.[21]

With the Fizzer been and gone, Jeannie still had the arrival of Mac's wagons to look forward to. The Gunns were up at dawn to see Mac, Bertie and Nellie rumble in with the stores — and all those lovely things Jeannie had had to leave behind at Pine Creek. For Jeannie unpacking her trunks was truly wonderful, like receiving her wedding presents all over again.

Cheon admired the silver teapot and her big brass lamp. He looked at the photographs of her friends and relatives and thought one of Jeannie's girlfriends so good-looking that she would fetch a very good bride price indeed in China! He watched in amazement as Aeneas picked up one book after another, dipping into a page here, a page there. But what pleased Cheon most was the egg-beater. He bore it away in triumph to his kitchen and used it to produce sponge cakes light as a feather.

Jeannie and her husband spent the rest of the afternoon arranging the home which they had waited four months to enjoy. By evening the dining room was transformed with ornaments on small tables and shelves, pictures on the walls, much-loved faces in silver photograph frames, a folding armchair, flowered curtains in the doorway between the rooms. Inside the shimmering white mosquito-net tent was some blue and white matting on the floor, and on the dining table a crimson cloth topped by a flower bowl which Cheon insisted was silver, although Jeannie knew it was only plate. But what made Jeannie and her husband happiest were the rows and rows of books filling the new bookshelves Aeneas had made.

Some time before Mac had left to go delivering with his wagons, Jeannie, Aeneas and Mac had gone on an overnight camping expedition to the Roper River. Noticing tracks, they followed them and found a young part-Aboriginal girl trying to cook a piece of meat over a campfire. Naked and shivering, her long hair matted with dirt and with a bone pierced through her nose, she told Jeannie her name was Dolly and that she was the daughter of Katie Wooloomool (niece of Ebimil Wooloomool — Old Goggle Eye, an elder of the Elsey Yangman) and a Scottish telegraph linesman named Lewis Cummings, a secret Jeannie did not divulge in *The Little Black Princess*, the book she published in 1905 about Dolly.[22]

Dolly told Jeannie that the Yangman had been attacked by the Willeroo, a 'wild' tribe, who came from far away searching for women. They had already speared and killed several Yangman men and captured Yangman women, who were raped and then carried off. During this attack, Dolly's relatives fled. In the confusion Dolly fell in the water and hid there, preferring to risk death from a crocodile rather than be raped or killed. The little girl survived by standing on the roots of an old tree and managed to breathe under cover of the lily leaves. Creeping out a few hours

Dolly Cummings (Bett-Bett) with her spotted dog, Sue.

later, she found the camp deserted except for her little black and white dog, who was delighted to see her and licked her face.

Cold and hungry, Dolly rubbed two sticks to make fire. She huddled close and tried to cook a piece of goanna meat that had been overlooked in the raid.

Dolly was a bright little girl and said to Jeannie Gunn when they first met, in the pidgin English which most of the Yangman spoke, 'Me plenty savey Engliss, Missus!'[23]

The Gunns were worried about Dolly being so thin and cold and in a state of shock after spending a long time submerged in the river. They fed her damper and honey, which she loved. She was scared the Willeroo might return, so Jeannie invited her to sleep in the Gunns' camp and gave her a shirt to wear.

In *The Little Black Princess*, Jeannie described how the next day she invited Dolly (Bett-Bett) to come and live with her.[24] Dolly was pleased with the idea. Presumably, it was with the agreement of her relatives that Dolly continued to stay at the Elsey but Jeannie ignores this point.

Initially Dolly refused to sleep in a bed, and insisted on sleeping in a blanket roll on the bathroom floor with her dog beside her. She was free to go to the Yangman camp whenever she wanted but seemed to prefer life at the homestead and the company of Jeannie, whom she followed like a shadow.

One day when they were walking through the vegetable garden Goggle Eye passed close to Dolly and told Jeannie he was her 'little bit father' and that Dolly was 'promised' to Billy Muck, another rainmaker like himself. Under tribal kinship customs, Goggle Eye was forbidden to look at the little girl or speak to her and so was cross with Jeannie for bringing her to the garden. He worried the 'debil–debils' would get him if he caught sight of Dolly.

Jeannie was curious and asked Goggle Eye why he could speak to his sister but not to his niece. Goggle Eye replied that as his sister had been born before him he was allowed to talk to her but not to her daughters or any other nieces, including Dolly.

Jeannie grew fond of Dolly and described her as 'lovable, happy and affectionate and always constant in her affections'.[25] She made the little girl a blue dress and petticoats, which Dolly called 'shimmy shirts'. But having no concept of property Dolly gave away the blue dress to another girl and ran about naked. So Jeannie had to make her more dresses.

Dolly soon became 'bush hungry'. Jeannie realised that walkabouts were an important part of tribal life and that she had to let Dolly go, hoping she would return safely. The little girl adored Jeannie and gave her a greatly treasured possession — a sea shell — before she took off into the bush with her little dog.

Jeannie waited and worried. Three days later Dolly returned in good spirits. It is significant that she chose to return to Jeannie and the Elsey rather than to her natural mother or her aunt who 'looked out' for her.

Both Gunns wrote about Goggle Eye, an elder of the Yangman and the chief rainmaker. Jeannie described all the initiation scars on his body and called him 'a lovable old rogue'. He was forever asking her for extra 'chewbacca' or flour from the station store or a new clay pipe, and always enjoyed a joke. Aeneas referred to him in a letter to the *Northern Territory Times*:

> There is nothing substantial going on here . . . rain, though not urgently needed, would be very welcome . . . King Ebimil Wooloomool, alias 'Goggle Eye', the boss rainmaker of the Elsey, frankly confesses the inefficacy of his magic to compel the clouds to drop . . . he has been deposed by the tribe . . . Billy Muck and Big Charlie have been appointed rainmakers, and to ensure a plentiful supply, we have engaged their services. To make assurance doubly sure, we would beseech the prayers of the righteous, were there not a reasonable certainty that the natural process of the elements will in time perform their intrinsic functions . . . We have no present thoughts of building an ark.[26]

However, drought was regarded by the Yangman as a sign that the ancestral spirits were displeased. Unfortunately for Goggle Eye, as the drought continued and game became scarcer, the Yangman sought a scapegoat. According to Aeneas, this meant

Goggle Eye had to die in order to stop the ancestral spirits being angry with the Yangman, although Jeannie suggests it was because he was getting too autocratic in his old age. Goggle Eye knew he had had the bone pointed at him by someone and was resigned to the inevitable.

Aeneas became interested in the role of auto-suggestion in bone-pointing, and described how Goggle Eye was sung to death:

> so that he might waste away slowly. All possible food was sung so that it might not nourish him. His various organs were sung so that they might not perform their functions. The sun was sung so that it should not warm his wasted form. The night was sung that it might not let him sleep. The water that it might not quench his thirst. All other blackfellows were warned that if they gave him food or shelter or help they too, would be sung dead . . . Mrs Gunn disregarded her possible inclusion in the comprehensive curse if she gave Goggle Eye . . . porridge and arrowroot . . . [27]

Poor Goggle Eye, once so strong, dragged himself up to the homestead to appeal to the white folk to lift the curse from him. But Aeneas knew they were powerless against 'blackfellow magic', which had already done its work. The respected elder of the tribe who previously had been in good health and enjoyed life was now wasting away, unable to eat.

Jeannie tried to understand what was happening and described it as being 'faith dying rather than faith healing'. She went to his humpy with a bowl of porridge and treacle, which he had always loved, and some tea with sugar. The hut was dark and smelly with a dirt floor, nothing more than sheets of bark propped against a tree and she could understand why Dolly preferred a nice room all to herself at the homestead. She saw how the Yangman shunned Goggle Eye, knowing the bone had been pointed at him. He was gaunt and racked with pain, while outside the hut Jeannie heard the Yangman whispering that he would die the next morning at 'fowl sing out', as Cheon described morning.

Jeannie ordered them to be quiet, hoping this would give Goggle Eye a chance of survival but he died, as they had predicted, at dawn the following day. No one would stay in a place where a man had died, so new huts were built further upstream, and by tribal law his name (Ebimil Wooloomool) could no longer be mentioned or his spirit would haunt them. Whether Billy Muck (the man Dolly had been betrothed to since childhood without showing much interest in him), who became the new leader, was involved in the removal of Goggle Eye from his position Jeannie does not say.

❧ ❧ ❧

With her dog, Sue, at her side Dolly spent her time helping about the homestead and taking reading lessons from Jeannie. Sometimes Dolly, Jeannie, Old Nellie (after she returned), Kitty and the other women walked to the Long Reach waterhole or to the Stanley Billabong. Mindful of the crocodiles and the marauding Willeroos, who were led by a murderous man named Monkey who had already killed or raped several Yangman, Jeannie tucked a revolver into her belt whenever she went on these excursions.

With Dolly to take care of and sew for, the homestead to run, gardens and building to supervise, and a constant stream of guests, Jeannie had no time to be bored. There were also the camping trips around the property, which Jeannie loved to join. Having the reliable cook Cheon, and no children, Jeannie was free to participate in this side of station life. Her writings show how much she enjoyed the freedom and companionship of these occasions, the beauty of the scenery and a chance to be on horseback for hours at a time.

Just as the renovations to the homestead were almost ready, the Gunns left to go mustering with the stockmen. They camped at Bitter Springs, a long, looping chain of mirror-clear pools which provided a plentiful stock of freshly grilled fish for breakfast and dinner.

Many of the Aboriginal men had brought wives or partners with them, and there was also a group of Aboriginal boys Aeneas was training, so the camp was large. One small tent served as a dressing-room for Jeannie; while *gunyahs*, or shade houses, were dotted about for the Yangman. Another *gunyah* stored the supplies and a very large *gunyah*, cooler than a tent, was made for Jeannie to rest in.

Dan decided to teach Jeannie how to roast a bush turkey. Hanging from a string at the end of a sapling propped across a forked stick, the carcass twisted and turned over a glowing heap of ashes until it was roasted to perfection and still juicy inside. Accompanying it was an enormous boiled cabbage from the garden. Jeannie set about making the damper and was wrestling with the dough when a traveller rode into camp. He asked if there might be a bit of spare meat because his was fly-blown and smelled awful. Dan offered him slices of bush turkey and a plate of cabbage.

The traveller's eyes gleamed. 'Real cabbage! Gosh, ain't tasted cabbage for five years.'[28] He wolfed it down and confessed incidentally that nor had he seen a woman for five years. Jeannie commented wryly it seemed that the lack of cabbage meant more to him than the lack of a woman.

Jeannie accompanied the men on many musters and tours of the station during her year at the Elsey. In doing so she learned to respect the endurance and courage of the stockmen, and became sensitive to her surroundings. She had also 'educated' herself to the extent that 'thirty-three nights, or thereabouts, with the warm, bare ground for a bed, had made [her] indifferent to mattresses'![29]

These excursions also made her aware of the precarious nature of life in the outback. On one trip around the run, they arrived at a waterhole to find cattle — some dead, some alive — bogged deep in the mud and impossible to get out. Two poor animals stood up to their necks in mud, bellowing piteously and slowly starving to death. The only thing to do was to shoot the poor beasts and put them out of their misery.

This was not the only time Jeannie witnessed the cruelty of those outback waterholes. Taking their customary stroll while on an earlier muster, Jeannie and her husband had emerged from the bush to see a strange and terrifying sight. At their feet, protruding from the turf, was a grey head without a body — a horse's head — whinnying piteously.

The poor animal had been grazing on the turf near one of the Bitter Springs holes when the thin crust of earth it had been standing on had given way. The horse had slipped through the hole that formed and was now perched on the rocky bed of the underground river, only its head protruding. The horse was dying slowly from lack of food and water. The grass around the hole as far as its head could reach had been eaten bare, and although its feet were in water the horse's mouth could not reach any. While Aeneas went to get the 'boys', Jeannie brought handfuls of grass to the horse and used her husband's hat to bring it water.

When Aeneas returned with the men from the camp, it was hard work getting the exhausted animal out, but after an hour of digging and rope-pulling the poor horse was rescued.

⁂ ⁂ ⁂

Following an outbreak of summer influenza among the men, Jeannie developed a sore throat and a high temperature. Aeneas was worried as the nearest doctor was 500 kilometres away in Darwin, so he stayed home to help Cheon look after her, sending the stockmen out to find enough cattle to fill an order from an Asian cattle dealer.

Cheon was delighted to have Jeannie doing as she was told and staying in bed, and he brought her in a constant supply of all invalid food possible — chicken jelly, barley water, egg-flips and junket. Her husband said she must eat and drink *all* of it. Aeneas read to Jeannie, plumped up her pillows and straightened the bed clothes every time he came in, Cheon nodding approval from the doorway.

After three days of this treatment, Jeannie thought that she would become ill from overeating! On the fourth day, with visitors in the house, she wanted to get up, but when both men begged her not to, she agreed, albeit with some reluctance. At least she could watch and talk to the visitors through the cracks in the walls.

Just as these visitors were to depart, another party arrived which forced her to leave her sick bed. This new group included two women and a brood of children and Jeannie welcomed the opportunity to lend a hand. The tired travellers were leaving the inside after fifteen years, during which three children had been born and raised, never knowing anything other than the outback. During a comfortable afternoon with tea and dinner, Jeannie later reflected, 'the women-folk spoke of their life "out-back"; and listening, I knew that neither I nor the telegraph lady [at Katherine] had guessed what roughness means.'[30]

Lack of fresh vegetables, unreliable water supplies and isolation from all medical help were constant dangers faced by inhabitants and visitors to the Never-Never.

The Gunns had only been back a few days from one of their bush trips when a traveller rode up to their veranda in search of help. 'Me mate's sick; got a touch of fever,' he said. 'I've left him camped back there at the Warlochs.'[31]

The man accepted eggs, milk and brandy which Jeannie gave him from the kitchen. But when Aeneas and Jeannie offered to ride out and bring the mate back to the homestead to be nursed, the bushman backed away, saying, 'If you please, ma'am . . . me mate's dead set against a woman doing things for him. If you wouldn't mind not coming. He'd rather have me. Me and him's been mates this seven years. The boss'll understand.'

And of course the boss did understand. These lonely, independent bushmen hated to be a trouble to anyone and were alarmed at the thought of being nursed by a woman.[32]

So Jeannie's husband rode to see the man, who had malaria, and implored him to come back to the homestead. But the sick man's mate had lugged his friend some 80 kilometres along a rough track and the sick man explained, 'He'll stick to me till I peg out — nothing's too tough for him.' The mate thanked Aeneas and said he would be grateful for some broth, fresh milk and medicines but *he* would nurse his friend.

The sick man managed to whisper, 'A good mate's harder to find than a good wife.'

For three days the sick man improved but his friend was totally exhausted by lack of sleep. Then the sick man slipped back into unconsciousness again and the Gunns knew that he might die unless he came to the homestead. The sick man still refused all help,

Roper River telegraph linesman's camp, circa 1900.

even when Jeannie sent a message that she would stay away from him unless he asked for her.

Finally, Herb Bryant — the Dandy — always good in a crisis, drove across to the camp and within an hour the sick traveller was in bed at the station, but at the first stirring of dawn he died.

Arranging the man's funeral was a problem, as even after seven years together, his mate did not know the dead man's religion or much about his next of kin. His name was William Henry Neaves, born in Wollongong in New South Wales.

'He was always a reticent chap. He never wanted anyone but me about him,' his mate insisted.

The station hands and Jeannie stood by an open grave under the pinkish-red flowers of a bauhinia tree. Aeneas read the burial service from his prayer book in his strong clear voice. Jeannie felt proud of her husband. The men shovelled earth on the grave and left him in the Elsey's little cemetery beside the graves of stockmen who had worked on the station and died there, many also from malaria, which so often followed the Big Wet.

Later, after the man's mate had packed his friend's swag for the last time, he came to the homestead and gave Aeneas two gold sovereigns, which he could ill afford, as recompense for his food and care.

'I'll have to ask for tick [credit] for meself for a while,' he said. 'He was always independent and would never take charity.'

Aeneas returned the gold coins saying gently, 'We give no charity here; only hospitality to our guests. Surely no man would refuse that.' Tactful as ever, Aeneas Gunn had said the right thing.

The man put the coins in his pocket. 'Not from your sort, Boss.'

Weak from lack of sleep and stress, the sick man's friend became their next patient. A few days of rest and sympathy, Cheon's meals and Jeannie's egg-flips brought the man's strength back. When the telegraph line superintendent sent word to say there was a job for him with the line party, the man left Elsey Station happy with the thought of work waiting for him.

House visitors arrived again in the form of Overland Telegraph linesmen with unexpected but welcome mail. Jeannie was amused to find that in two of the letters from Melbourne, her women friends demanded, 'Whatever do you do with your time? The monotony would kill me.'[33]

✤ ✤ ✤

Another trip out along the Roper River made a pleasant working holiday for Jeannie and her husband. The dark, clear water of the lagoons was filled with lilies in flower. The blue and crimson blossoms clustered on long stalks above floating leaves. On either side of the Roper River were wading birds, cranes, jabirus and graceful brolgas.

As she rode back to the homestead, Jeannie realised the Dry was almost over and the monsoon season would soon start. It was baking hot. There was no grass within sight of the homestead and dust was everywhere. The air was oppressive and there were distant rumbles of thunder, and flashes of lightning lit up the sky which had turned the colour of pewter.

The mailman was due so Aeneas wrote to his brother, Bob, and told him how they were living very cheaply at the Elsey, no rent, free game and all the beef they could eat. Jeannie had become so fond of outback life that they had decided they no longer wanted to leave the place. Bob's wedding was taking place very soon and Aeneas wrote that he hoped that Bob and his future wife, Nellie, would be as happy as he and Jeannie were.[34]

By this time Jeannie had realised that Jack McLeod (the Quiet Stockman) could not read and used this period of hiatus in activities before the Wet to teach him. She used the same text book she had in her lessons with Dolly, who was not a very attentive pupil and preferred polishing the silver or going down to the creek with Jeannie and the other women to do the washing and play in the water. Jack, however, was determined to read, tackling the letters of the alphabet in the same energetic way he tackled the colts. When he finished the reading primer, Jeannie started him on Kipling's *Just So Stories*.

Right on time the Fizzer arrived with a mail bag containing fifty letters, sixty-nine papers, dozens of books and magazines, and parcels of cuttings for the garden Jeannie was expanding. He told them Mac would soon be back, fed up with 'bullock-punching' and anxious to get back to work with horses.

But the Dry continued and each day the water from the soakage shrank. The Elsey homestead, wreathed in creepers and set amid a green garden of melons, was a pleasant oasis in the desert of dust and glare. As it became hotter and drier, Cheon, who carefully tended his vegetable garden, and Billy Muck, Goggle Eye's successor as rainmaker of the Yangman, who had against all odds successfully cultivated watermelons for Jeannie, competed fiercely for precious water which was fast running out.

The billabong dried up; the soak became so low that its water had to be kept strictly for personal needs. Everyone gasped in the stifling air and waited for the rain. Two cows died of heat exhaustion in the yards. When a few cool, gusty puffs of wind finally blew up, Jeannie and her husband ran outside to enjoy them. They didn't have long before the first shower arrived. Rain swept over the homestead and away to the south-east. Then came the deluge which filled the waterholes to overflowing.

Soon grass, inches tall, was rippling around the homestead. Jack kept at his *Just So Stories*, finished the book and asked for more.

Jeannie was pleased to see that learning to read had given him more confidence and made him more talkative.

⁂ ⁂ ⁂

On 7 November 1902, Jeannie wrote Bob and Nellie Gunn a cheery Christmas letter telling them how happy she and her husband were together, and poignantly confided to her sister-in-law, 'I would like to grow old slowly together'.[35]

She and Cheon planned to make that Christmas a splendid one. It was decided that the homestead and the stockmen would eat Christmas dinner together on the eastern veranda, and that a vealer (an eight-month-old calf) would be provided for the meal. While they waited for the Dandy to return from Katherine with supplies, the Fizzer came and went again. He would have a merry Christmas, he said, with damper and beef served on a packsaddle!

Cheon had promised seven kinds of vegetables for Christmas dinner. But while the gardens had survived the Dry, he now witnessed them being destroyed by grasshoppers. Ever resourceful, Cheon helped himself to tins of vegetables put aside for the telegraph linesmen, donating them some fresh eggs in return.

Cheon's preparations were long and hard. On Christmas Eve he spent the night watching a huge Christmas pudding with silver threepenny bits hidden in it. Jeannie and Aeneas offered to share the watch but Cheon refused. Everyone, he insisted, must have a good sleep that night so they would be able to appreciate his beautiful dinner. Besides, he still had to make mince pies, hop beer and another big plum pudding for the Yangman camp.

On Christmas morning, when the boss and his wife went into the kitchen to be wished a merry Christmas by Cheon, they were immediately given jobs to do. The vealer was to be slaughtered and cut up; six women were needed to pluck the young hens. Anyone else available was sent by Cheon to bring in green branches and 'mistletoe' for decorating the house and kitchen.

A light breakfast of sausage without the skin was only the prelude to a superb Christmas dinner, the best they had known. Every seat on the run was retrieved, two tables were placed end to end under the decorations of greenery and covered with clean white cloths. The hop beer was set in canvas water bags to keep cool. A canvas awning was stretched from the veranda to the kitchen and more greenery was hung there, to make it a fit place for the promised procession of food.

In honour of Cheon's Christmas lunch, men who normally did not give a fig what they looked like had smartened up. They had cut each others' hair and shaved their stubbly chins. Jeannie could scarcely recognise some of them!

Aeneas, in a white shirt and white linen trousers with a red silk cummerbund and matching tie, looked even smarter than the Dandy. Jeannie wore one of her best Melbourne dresses, made of cream silk with a matching lace collar.

Then Cheon, grinning from ear to ear, rang a bullock bell to summon the guests, announcing: 'Dinner is served!' Young Nellie arrived with six chickens on a platter. Rosy carried the haunch of veal; while Bertie's Nellie brought in the ham. Dolly came last, proudly bearing the bread sauce. The higher their plates were piled and the sooner they were emptied, the happier Cheon was. And when a bottle of the hop beer he had just brewed popped its top and sent froth shooting everywhere, he beamed with joy.

Cheon went to the open-air kitchen and returned bearing a huge pudding ablaze with brandy and crowned with mistletoe. Normally Christmas Day in the Territory was hot and muggy but for some reason this was an unusually cool day, so they sat happily on the makeshift chairs and stools, telling jokes and chatting the afternoon away.

In the Yangman camp, there had also been a feast, the Aborigines deciding this Christmas dinner was the best thing the Maluka and Gadgerri (their name for Jeannie) had arranged for them. The Aborigines ate half the vealer and Cheon's plum pudding, and each of the men was given a new clay pipe as well as some plug tobacco.

At the homestead Cheon's Christmas was a triumph. Each of the 'guests' signed an autograph book for Jeannie and wrote her a special message. Only Dan was missing. He arrived two days later and pleased Cheon enormously by insisting that Christmas dinner at the Pine Creek Hotel had not been nearly as good as the one at the Elsey!

❦ ❦ ❦

Soon they reached the anniversary of the day on which the Gunns had first arrived from Darwin.

'A year today, Mac, since you sent those telegrams!' Aeneas teased Jock McLennan,[36] reminding him of his attempts to put off Jeannie's arrival. But arrived she had. And perhaps in thanks for the way she had fitted into station life and taught him to read, Jack McLeod offered Jeannie a New Year present of a beautiful chestnut filly he was breaking in. The idea of having her own horse thrilled Jeannie.

New Year 1903 brought more travellers to the Elsey but it also brought tropical rains and malarial dysentery, the scourge of the Big Wet. Some of the travellers recovered but two were very ill with high fever and, in spite of careful nursing, one died and was buried in the cemetery on the station. The other, a man of seventy, recovered and they watched him ride away again.

Jack took to the bush to train his colts. Mac and Dan went into Katherine to order supplies, while the Dandy remained at the Elsey and waited for the Wet to lift and the supply wagons to arrive.

For cheerful Jeannie, delighting in the outback and in love with her husband, life was full. She wrote to her new sister-in-law Nellie Gunn that there was a lot to discover about marriage. She joked that she had been 'led on shamelessly' for '[Aeneas] has led me to imagine I was the boss, until one day I suddenly found that I wasn't. Perhaps you have found out already there is a good deal of grim determination under a Gunn's tenderness!'[37]

As usual after the Wet, Aeneas went out mustering with the stockmen. She watched them leave the yard, the horses restive, the men enjoying it all.

A few days later, however, Aeneas was brought back to the Elsey. He was far too ill to sit on a horse, and was slumped across the front of the Dandy's saddle. Jeannie rushed out of the house and she and Herb Bryant lifted Aeneas down from the horse. They carried him into the homestead, his brow burning with fever and his lips cracked with thirst.

Herb volunteered to nurse Aeneas, as he knew all too well the terrible effects of dysentery and malaria and possibly blackwater fever caught from polluted water. Aeneas was suffering from diarrhoea, a high fever and an engorged and very painful spleen, but Jeannie would not hear of Herb nursing her husband. She took on the role of nurse, tried all the bush remedies she knew, brought cool drinks and cold compresses for his forehead, sat with him day and night and half slept beside him at night. But before the invention of antibiotics, nothing anyone could do would have lowered her husband's fever or abated the pain from his engorged spleen.

With the nearest doctor so far away, it became obvious to everyone Aeneas was getting weaker.

On 16 March 1903, Jeannie's beloved husband died with her at his side. They had been married for only fourteen months. Jeannie's grief was so intense she cried until the bones of her face ached and she lay on her bed exhausted, her head splitting with migraine.

Two days later she felt well enough to write letters to her father and sisters and to Bob Gunn telling them the terrible news. She told Bob that she had never heard strong men sob before and that knowing how fond everyone on the station had been of her husband was some comfort. The men in the Aboriginal camp had asked if they could draw the buggy carrying the coffin to the little cemetery on the hill. Aeneas had proved that treating the Aborigines like human beings had won their trust and affection, she wrote. She added that her sorrow was now too deep for tears and she must not cry any more as she needed to be composed enough to take part in the funeral ceremony.[38]

The Elsey was silent, everyone wrapped in grief. The stockmen cut down timber, made a coffin and dug a grave. The Aborigines pulled the buggy up to the small cemetery. They lowered the Maluka's coffin on ropes into the grave and piled red soil on top.

Most people present were weeping. Jeannie, however, managed somehow to control her tears and say a few words. It must have seemed incredible to Jeannie that the husband she loved was inside that wooden box. The pain of leaving the person she loved most in the world was so intense that she could write only briefly about it in her book:

> All unaware, that scourge of the Wet crept back to the
> homestead, and the great Shadow, closing in on us, flung
> wide those gates of Death, and turning, before passing
> through, beckoned to our Maluka to follow . . . A
> sobbing cry went up from the camp, as the tribe mourned
> for their beloved dead — their dead and ours — our
> Maluka, 'the best Boss ever a man struck'.[39]

The Yangman held a corroboree to mourn the loss of the Maluka and the stockmen repeated those words again and again that the Maluka had been 'the best Boss ever a man struck'.

For weeks Jeannie was in such a shocked, depressed and miserable state that she could not leave her room or eat and had difficulty sleeping. She sat there by herself, brooding on the death of Aeneas and recalling incidents from that brief but happy fourteen months of marriage. The stockmen were kind and understood her anguish and despair, which seemed as if it would never lift.

Her family were so worried about Jeannie that her sister, Carrie Taylor, sailed north to Darwin to meet her and bring her home, and so a grieving Jeannie returned with her sister to Melbourne.

◦◦◦◦◦◦

Over the next few years Jeannie worked on turning the notes she had made at the Elsey and the letters she had written to friends into two books.[40] The first, published in 1905 and designed for children, was a suitably sanitised version of Dolly's story — *The Little Black Princess* — in which Dolly was called 'Bett-Bett' by Jeannie. The other, published in 1908, was designed for adults and titled *We of the Never-Never*. It was a loving depiction of the time she had enjoyed with Aeneas. The fact that Jeannie lost the husband she adored after only fourteen months gives her second book its special poignancy.

Although modern critics have sometimes charged Jeannie with racism, both her books have become Australian classics, enjoyed by people all over the world. Jeannie's style was light and amusing but showed respect for the people she met during her year in the Never-Never. She wrote with empathy and understanding about the Aboriginal house girls and the fun they had together, and did this in an era when empathy and understanding was lacking among most Europeans in the Northern Territory. She has been called patronising, but she was a woman of her times. And it is significant that all her life Dolly had nothing but praise for Mrs Gunn, and never once complained that she had found her patronising.

While never conceding her position both as a white woman and an employer, Jeannie's descriptions of the Aboriginal customs and culture she encountered — the complex kinship systems, or the bone-pointing that led to the death of Goggle Eye, for example — showed tolerance for beliefs other than her own and appreciation for the survival skills of Aborigines.

She not only donated money to various Aboriginal causes but also quite explicitly defended the Aboriginal point of view with regard to taking their land and for allowing them to spear cattle without being punished rather than go hungry:

> The white man has taken the country from the black
> fellow, and with it his right to travel where he will for
> pleasure and food, and until he [the white man] is willing
> to make recompense by granting fair liberty of travel and
> a fair percentage of cattle or their equivalent in fair
> payment — openly and fairly giving them, and seeing
> that no man is unjustly treated or hungry within his
> borders — cattle killing, and, at times even man killing by
> blacks, will not be an offence against the white folk.[41]

How much Jeannie knew about the real purpose of 'surprise parties' against Aboriginal groups, which she mentioned in her writing, and the systematic measures taken by pastoralists to destroy them, is unclear. It was certainly part of the outback she came to feel so happy in. Aeneas was presumably well aware of such practices, and had himself participated in retributive hunts of Aborigines while he was at Marigui.[42] Jock McLennan was later accused of conducting, on behalf of the Eastern African and Cold Storage Company (owners of the Elsey), systematic killing raids on 'wild' Aborigines who threatened stock.[43]

Jeannie may have been protected from this most brutal side of outback life. In a reference in *We of the Never-Never* to 'outside blacks' advancing along the river 'inside' the property while they were out preparing for a muster, Jeannie wrote that her husband considered it too dangerous for her and sent his wife back to the homestead.[44] Nevertheless, Jeannie did give hints that she knew in theory what could occur. When she wrote about the 'surprise party' she participated in herself, she explained that it 'would only involve the captured with general discomfiture', but she conceded that 'emergencies were apt to occur "down the river" and we rode out of camp with rifles unslung and revolvers at hand'.[45]

If her views on the rights of Aborigines were ahead of her time, in other ways Jeannie was still very much part of pioneer society. References to 'nigger-hunting' have been removed from some later abridged editions of *We of the Never-Never*, but so, surprisingly, have some of her most supportive statements of Aborigines. It is hard to read her books without responding to the warmth and affection she felt for the Yangman and Mangarrayi of the Elsey — and her understanding of their plight:

> A black fellow kills cattle because he is hungry and must
> be fed with food, having been trained in a school that for
> generations has acknowledged 'catch who catch can'
> among its commandments; and until the long arm of the
> law interfered, white men killed the black fellow, because
> they were hungry with a hunger that must be fed with
> gold, having been trained in school that for generations
> acknowledged 'Thou shalt not kill' among its
> commandments; and yet men speak of the 'superiority' of
> the white race, and, speaking, forget to ask who of us
> would go hungry if the situation were reversed . . .[46]

Once her royalties started to accrue, Jeannie took practical measures to help Aborigines, often anonymously. One gift that is recorded was her donation of autographed books to help raise money to build a pipeline to bring a supply of pure water to the Hermannsburg Mission in central Australia, run by Carl and Frieda Strehlow.

Jeannie's affection for the Elsey stockmen, who were so kind to her after the death of her husband, led her to protect their reputations in her books. She was careful to mask the identities of her characters by using stylised names such as 'the Dandy', 'the Sanguine Scot', 'the Quiet Stockman', as well as protecting Dolly by calling her 'Bett-Bett'.

One highly significant letter among Jeannie's papers in the National Library of Australia was written by Jock McLennan, the Sanguine Scot, dated 5 July 1906. Mac thanked Mrs Gunn for sending him a copy of *The Little Black Princess*, which he described as 'A good book written by a good woman'. He added, 'I know you could have written a slightly different tale and still have been close to the truth. I know your aim is not to give pain to anyone.'[47] Jeannie told McLennan that she aimed to present the beauty of the outback and the loyalty of bushmen, rather than showing life in the bush as 'a pandemonium of drunken orgies, black women, remorse and suicide'.[48]

The men of Elsey Station had grown very fond of Jeannie and continued to send her Christmas cards. Some, like Herb Bryant (the Dandy), the best educated of the group, wrote her letters. Jeannie also continued to correspond with Dave Suttee (Dan, the Head Stockman), who took over as joint manager with Bryant after Aeneas's death.

Jack McLeod, the Quiet Stockman, would always be grateful that Jeannie had taught him to read. He left the Elsey when it was sold, returned to Adelaide, and eventually worked for the Goldsborough Mort pastoral company, before adapting to the motor age and starting a service station at Angaston. Jack had six children, including a daughter he named Jeannie Gunn McLeod. He also included 'Gunn' in the names of another two children.

≈ ≈ ≈

In its day Jeannie's book for children *The Little Black Princess* was considered the first sympathetic story about northern Aborigines in the outback, at a time when most white people feared them.

Jeannie had had to pay half the cost of publication of her first book but managed to recoup this in sales. She was urged to write a second book about the outback, this time for adults. However, getting an adult book published as a woman in a male-dominated world was hard. Several publishers rejected Jeannie's manuscript before a London publisher accepted it, but for a low 'colonial royalty', claiming that freighting the books to Australia would be expensive.

Jeannie Gunn in later life.

Ironically, in view of the fact that six publishers had rejected the manuscript of *We of the Never-Never*, fearing they might lose money, Jeannie's second book about the outback became a bestseller and one of Australia's most loved stories. It sold well in England, and was translated into German and French. In a poll conducted by the Melbourne *Herald* in 1931, Mrs Aeneas Gunn was named one of Australia's most popular authors.

Following the death of her father in 1909, Jeannie fulfilled the dream she had nurtured with her late husband to make an extended visit to Britain and Europe. After spending almost three years overseas she returned to Melbourne and planned to write a book about Aboriginal lore as retold by John Terrick, son of one of the last Victorian Aboriginal chiefs, and incorporating Aboriginal lore she had learned from the Yangman and Mangarrayi.

The writing of her first two books had been hard, as Jeannie had had to deal with powerful emotions of grief and loss, especially while writing *We of the Never-Never* in which her husband is a strong and humorous figure. She also found it difficult to write about the bush while living in the city, and periodically stayed with friends in the more tranquil atmosphere of Monbulk, a picturesque wooded area where pioneers were struggling to establish themselves on small selections and where her father had owned a block of bushland.[49] Unfortunately, as she became caught up in work for soldiers during World War I and the Returned Services League (RSL) afterwards,

Jeannie found she had come to her project with John Terrick too late, after Terrick's memory had faded, so she had to abandon the idea. Terrick died in 1921. She would nevertheless continue to regard Monbulk as a refuge for the rest of her life.

From 1914 onwards Jeannie channelled her energies into fundraising efforts for wounded Anzacs. During the war she packed gift parcels of soap, hand-knitted socks, balaclava helmets and candles, all badly needed in the freezing cold winters in the trenches of France and Gallipoli. When she was in Melbourne she saw newly enlisted men off on their tours. She wrote letters to 'her boys' in the trenches, kept open house for them and placed their photographs on her mantelpiece and walls. No soldier in uniform was ever turned away from her home without a good meal. Even if returned soldiers arrived drunk at her house, the maid had instructions to give them plenty of strong black coffee and sober them up.[50]

After the Great War many war widows and their children suffered extreme hardship. Jeannie did what she could to comfort and assist them. She also visited limbless or blind men in rehabilitation centres, and became an unpaid and unofficial liaison worker between them and the inept bureaucracy of various government departments, and when necessary fought for the entitlements of 'her boys'. In 1925 she became patron of the Tubercular Sailors' and Soldiers' Relief Fund in Monbulk.

As a former teacher Jeannie was horrified to discover that the people of Monbulk had no books they could borrow — not even an atlas. She spent ten years of her life and her own money building up a lending library in the Monbulk RSL clubhouse for returned war veterans who could not afford to go to libraries in Melbourne and borrow books. She donated the bookshelves and wrote personally to many authors to request donations of books.

In 1939 Jeannie was given an Order of the British Empire in recognition not only of her services to Australian literature but also of her work with disabled soldiers and their dependents.

Her final book — never published in her lifetime — was to have been called *The Making of Monbulk*. It told the story of the men of Monbulk who served in the Australian Imperial Force (AIF) and of the Monbulk RSL of which she would become a generous patron. It was published in 2000 as *My Boys: A Book of Remembrance*.

In 1951 Jeannie was invited to lay the foundation stone for new clubrooms for the Monbulk RSL and unveil a memorial tablet to those who had died in war. The president of the RSL described how:

> Mrs Gunn had been the friend of every serviceman from
> the district in two wars, sending parcel, comforts and
> news from home. She had been their guide and
> counsellor in many personal circumstances and a
> consolation to those who were bereaved.[51]

Jeannie died in Melbourne on 9 June 1961, aged ninety-one. Her funeral was crowded with people who had loved her books and loved her. Generous to the last, her estate was divided among the many charities and humanitarian causes she had supported.

Perhaps the last word on Jeannie Gunn should come from the eulogy at her funeral, held at the Scots Church in Melbourne's Collins Street. The Reverend A. Crichton-Barr, who had known her well, told a large group of mourners from many different walks of life who crowded the church:

> Mrs Aeneas Gunn was a modest, gentle and courageous
> lady. Some people will remember her for her books and
> others for her unremitting service to those who fought
> for Australia. She will be remembered by many people
> with gratitude and affection.

'THE LITTLE BLACK PRINCESS'

Much more might have been learned about Dolly, 'the Little Black Princess', had the correspondence and diaries of Aeneas Gunn for the year he and Jeannie spent at the Elsey not been destroyed by the new owners. However, later in her life Dolly revealed some details to H. T. Linklater and Helen Frizell and made a recording about her life, a transcript of which is in the Northern Territory Archives.[52]

In her recorded interview, Dolly revealed that her father was Lewis Cummings, the telegraph repair linesman from Glasgow, who had migrated to Adelaide and then found work in a camp on the Roper River for the Overland Telegraph Line where Dolly was born.

Dolly disclosed that she spent her first months of life in the linesmen's camp close to Elsey Station. Her mother, Katie, had wanted to call her Katherine after the town of Katherine, but her father insisted she be named Dolly, because she was so pretty, 'like a little doll'. After Katie and Lewis fought over some rice Katie had burned, Katie ran away with her daughter back to the Aboriginal camp on Elsey Creek. Cummings eventually returned to Adelaide and married a European woman.

In the camp Dolly was looked after by her Aunt Judy (it is unclear what happened to Katie)[53] until she went to live at Elsey homestead with the Gunns. Dolly was free to come and go from the homestead to the camp as she pleased. From what she said when interviewed for an article in the *Sydney Morning Herald*[54] and the letters she wrote to Jeannie, Dolly was grateful for the year she spent with Jeannie at the Elsey, bridging black and white cultures, and had few regrets at leaving the Aboriginal camp.

A month after Jeannie left the Elsey, Mr Little, Superintendent of the Telegraph Office in Katherine and Protector of Aborigines, took Dolly Cummings to Darwin, where he placed her with the family of the governor of Fanny Bay gaol, as resident nursemaid to the governor's young children. From there Dolly wrote to Jeannie telling her that she was very happy. Fortunately, through living with the children of the gaol governor — who doubtless had a governess — Dolly was taught to read and write.

Eventually Dolly's charges grew up and no longer needed a nursemaid. The governor accepted a posting elsewhere and Dolly was placed with the Ward family, whose father also worked for the telegraph line. Dolly reported that her father visited her once while she was there, bringing her a doll and promising to return the following year, but she never heard from him again, which made her very sad.

*Dolly Cummings aged
about twelve.*

COURTESY STATE LIBRARY OF VICTORIA.

In April 1907 Mrs Ward took her children and Dolly to Melbourne, where she met Jeannie at the Spencer Street railway station. Jeannie took her back to her house at Creswick Street, Hawthorn, which she shared with her sister.

Dolly was now twelve years old.[55] Years later in Melbourne *The Age* would print a photograph that Jeannie took of Dolly when she visited Jeannie's home. Dolly was wearing a white dress and had a white bow in her long hair.

Dolly had never forgotten Jeannie and her days of fun and mischief at the Elsey homestead. She remained devoted to 'the little Missus', as she always called Jeannie. Many years later Jeannie revealed that Dolly had wanted to stay with her in Melbourne rather than return with the Ward family. It was a big decision but Jeannie decided against keeping Dolly in Melbourne with her. Jeannie later wrote that 'I was afraid of the climate and all the difficulties here [in Melbourne] for her upbringing, and her future.'[56]

Dolly returned to Darwin with the Wards, where she remained as housemaid until transferring to another home where she was unhappy.

It appears from Dolly's recorded transcript that she did not feel patronised or forced into anything by Jeannie and insisted that she would always be extremely grateful for everything Jeannie had done for her.

Through the intervention of Jeannie's friend Irene Pickersgill, Dolly became a resident ward maid at the Darwin hospital and was given a room in the staff quarters. Dolly had a loving and warm personality, was very popular with patients and fellow staff members, and got on well with Matron Pickersgill.

Two years after starting work at Darwin Hospital, and by now a very attractive and vivacious young woman, Dolly met tall English-born William Bonson on the beach at Fanny Bay, where she had gone to swim with friends from the hospital. She and William fell in love and since he had a steady job at Vestey Meatworks, he and Dolly were able to marry. He promised to build a house for them in Darwin.

The matron of Darwin hospital was Dolly's matron of honour, while a Melbourne friend of Jeannie's, at that time residing in Darwin, acted as hostess at the reception. Jeannie, who had always kept in touch with Dolly, sent a handsome wedding gift but did not attend. She and Dolly would correspond for fifty years but Jeannie never returned to the Northern Territory, possibly because it brought back sad memories.

William Bonson kept his promise to Dolly and built them a home. She and her husband had three sons and two daughters — and a share of life's ups and downs. Like many people in Darwin, Dolly's husband lost his job when the huge Vestey Meatworks closed. However, he was a hard worker and tried his hand at many different occupations, including working on the Darwin docks and owning a small banana farm at Humpty Doo, near Darwin.

During World War II, Darwin was bombed by Japanese planes and many people were killed. Dolly and her younger children were evacuated to Mildura. From there Dolly's eldest daughter travelled to see Jeannie, who was now in her seventies and living at Hawthorn. Another visitor was Dolly's eldest son who had enlisted and was for a while stationed in Melbourne. At the end of World War II, Dolly and her children moved back to Darwin.

In 1955 Jeannie publicly defended Dolly in the Melbourne *Age* against scurrilous rumours that 'little Bett-Bett' was destitute and living on the streets of Darwin, which were totally untrue.[57] Dolly was in Darwin for the arrival of Cyclone Tracy, which destroyed the city in 1974. By then eighty-two, she bravely endured a terrifying experience. The wind howled all around and there was a terrible sound of corrugated-iron sheets being dragged over the ground as whole houses were swept away. Dolly and her son Joe, a well-known footballer, sheltered under a bed while their house disintegrated around them. At length, the Bonsons were rescued and flown south to Melbourne to stay with a granddaughter who worked in a bank.

By this time Jeannie Gunn was dead, but her nephew and niece, the late Alfred and Dorothy Derham, invited Dolly to their home.

The replica of the Elsey homestead made for the movie We of the Never-Never.

They described how Dolly was taking the loss of her house with courage and dignity but, like most people who have lived through cyclones or floods, she grieved for the loss of photographs and possessions.[58] Dolly and her family were given aid by the government and eventually they had their home rebuilt and were able to return to Darwin.

Dolly died on 8 March 1988 in Darwin, at her daughter's home, having achieved a great deal. Today the Bonson family are well known and respected in Darwin, and several Bonson boys have distinguished themselves on the football field. Dolly's grandson, Matthew Bonson, a former lawyer, is now a member of the Legislative Assembly (MLA) in the Northern Territory.

&& && &&

In 1982 a film of *We of the Never-Never* was released, funded by the West Australian Film Corporation and Adams–Packer films, and was enjoyed on screen, video and television by a huge audience in Australia and overseas. A few years before her death, Dolly saw the movie and enjoyed it, according to her interview transcript. The movie made 'the little Missus', 'Bett–Bett' and 'the Maluka' famous to a new generation. The replica of Elsey homestead specially created for the movie is now open to the public at Mataranka Resort, 100 kilometres south of Katherine.

AFTERWORD

After the original wooden homestead near the Warloch Ponds where Aeneas and Jeannie Gunn lived was eaten by white ants, the Yangman and Mangarrayi carried galvanised iron and other building materials from Warloch Ponds to the Red Lily Lagoons in Mangarrayi country to rebuild it. But as malarial mosquitoes were a constant problem at Red Lily Lagoons, the site of the Elsey homestead was moved again and a new brick house erected at a place marked as McMinns Bar on local maps.

In 1968, following a decision of the Conciliation and Arbitration Commission, a minimum wage for all those working in the pastoral industry was instituted. In 1974 the Yangman and Mangarrayi moved to Jilkminggan, the site they occupy today.

In February 2000, Elsey Station was handed back to the traditional owners, the Mangarrayi and the Yangman, who had initially lodged their claim through the Northern Land Council in 1991, after buying the pastoral lease for the Elsey that same year.[59]

Elsey cemetery, which lies near the Stuart Highway to the south of Mataranka, contains the grave of Aeneas Gunn. A bronze plaque bears the arms of the Gunn family and an inscription 'In loving memory of the "Maluka"'. The cemetery also contains the graves of William H. Neaves, Jock McLennan, Tom Pearce, and Henry Peckham (the Fizzer), who drowned in Campbell's Creek delivering mail, and was reburied at the Elsey.

Beside the grave of Aeneas Gunn stands a smaller stone engraved 'In loving Memory of the "Little Missus", a tribute from descendants of the men whose stories Jeannie told'. Near it is a small memorial to Bett–Bett, who was buried in Darwin under her married name of Dolly Bonson.

CHAPTER 5

Evelyn Maunsell

1888 – 1977

AN ENGLISH ROSE IN THE OUTBACK

In 1912 when Evelyn Maunsell arrived at Mount Mulgrave cattle station on Queensland's Cape York, she brought with her a trunk filled with new clothes, a dinner service and two rolls of floral-printed upholstery material — a present from her bridesmaid, Paulina Fox, owner of the Imperial Hotel, Cairns. Evelyn, head over heels in love with Charlie Maunsell, the new manager on Mount Mulgrave, had been expecting to live in a gracious Queensland homestead, with wide verandas surrounded by tropical flowers and green lawns. She received a shock when she saw the tin shed that was to be their home.[1]

Mount Mulgrave Station had been owned by Paddy Callaghan, a wealthy bachelor cattle baron whose main preoccupations had been beef and beer. The 'homestead' had clearly been built by a man with no interest in homemaking. Its walls were unlined, the roof was made from sheets of galvanised iron and the floor was concrete so it could be hosed down after a drinking session. The only attempt at comfort was a wooden veranda tacked around it as an afterthought.

Evelyn peered cautiously round the back of the house and saw a big galvanised-iron water tank and a sagging clothesline. A separate shed, home to huge, hairy spiders, was fitted with a canvas-bag shower. Worst of all was the ten-metre-deep smelly latrine pit surrounded by sheets of corrugated iron. She was expected to share this with the stockmen until an outside 'dunny' could be constructed for her.

There was a dark kitchen with an ant-bed floor, a chipped sink and a wood-fired stove. The kitchen was fitted with another veranda where stockmen, fencers and visitors — all men — had their meals. Tacked onto the kitchen were two cell-like guest rooms. One was occupied by elderly Rudolph Morisset, a former gold miner who had been a drinking mate of Pat Callaghan. Callaghan had let Morisset live there for free in return for milking the cows.

Beside the creek was a gone-to-seed vegetable garden. There were no fruit trees and no green lawns, only gigantic gum trees. Evelyn's new abode was scarcely the tropical paradise she had dreamed of as her matrimonial home.

⚜ ⚜ ⚜

Evelyn had grown up in a large, well-furnished home at Ilford near London, with comforts such as carpets, paintings, a music room, central heating, running hot water and well-trained servants. Her father, Frank Evans, owned his own import-export business in the City of London. He was an alderman and also a Freeman of the City of London.

The Evans children took after their father — they were hard-working and adventurous in spirit. Two of Evelyn's brothers were army officers, hoping for postings to Australia. The eldest, Rupert, did go to Australia as a civilian, eventually working on a station in northern New South Wales.

Sweet-faced, elegant Evelyn, known as Evie in the family, had always longed to travel, and when she turned twenty-one the opportunity arose to go out to Australia also. Her round-the-world ticket had come about through a friend of her aunt, a Mrs Dean, recently widowed, who was about to take a world cruise to visit her married daughters, in Australia, New Zealand and South America. Mrs Dean wanted a paid companion, it being considered quite improper for ladies to travel alone. Evelyn jumped at the chance to see her brother and persuaded her parents to let her accompany Mrs Dean. It was a daunting journey, at a time when there were no aeroplanes and most British people travelled no further than Europe.

In Australia, Rupert Evans had made friends with the family of Thomas Hall, chief accountant of New South Wales Railways. As Rupert would not be in Sydney when she arrived, Evelyn wrote to young Harry Hall asking him to meet her when the ship came in.

Evelyn had had many admirers but hoped she might meet the man of her dreams on board ship. If she did not, she could always come home and marry nice, kind Reggie Grimwood, a friend of one of her brothers, who had loved Evie since they were children.

So, three years before the start of World War I, Evelyn and Mrs Dean were booked aboard an ocean liner from Marseilles to Sydney and allocated pleasant first-class cabins. Mrs Dean planned to spend four days sightseeing in Paris en route so she could shop for clothes in the fashion houses. She found Evie sweet and helpful and with a good sense of humour, and treated her like a long-lost daughter. In Paris she bought her a beautiful silk dress as a present. The two women went by train from the Gare de Lyon to Marseilles, where they boarded the SS *Osterley* for the six-week voyage to Sydney. But there was no shipboard romance. The male passengers were either married or elderly — and Evelyn resisted the romantic attentions of the ship's officers.

They arrived in Sydney on the Thursday before the Easter weekend. At Circular Quay, Mrs Dean was met by her daughter and Evie was met by Harry Hall and his wife, Maude. Harry, Maude and Evie drove in a horse-drawn buggy to Thornleigh, where Harry and his brother Arthur had homes on their father's property. Staying with Arthur Hall and his wife, Frances, were Frances's widowed mother, Jane Maunsell, and her sister, Phoebe.

Evie stayed on and off with the Halls for the remainder of the year, during which time she was reunited with her brother Aubrey (later to be renamed the less formal 'Tim' by Evelyn's future husband). Tim had quickly followed Evie out to Australia and was given a job by Thomas Hall in his orchards. In due course Rupert

Evans also arrived back in Sydney from his stint in the bush. Love blossomed at Thornleigh and Evelyn was pleased when Rupert and Phoebe Maunsell announced their engagement.

Evelyn frequently met up with Phoebe Maunsell and Frances Hall, who spoke with pride about their elder brother, Charlie. Charlie had just been appointed manager of Mount Mulgrave Station on Cape York Peninsula and was coming south by train to spend a week with them. Both Maunsell sisters were very attractive, tall and blonde, and Evie hoped their brother was as good looking too.

Her first impression of Charlie, however, was a disappointment. She saw him when he arrived from the railway station — a dusty-looking travel-stained figure, his face shaded by a battered hat. Oh dear, was this Charlie Maunsell, she thought.

That evening they met at Arthur Hall's home and Evelyn found herself confronted by a tall, handsome young man. Surprise, surprise, it was Charlie Maunsell. After a refreshing bath he had brushed his blond hair until it gleamed and then changed into a well-cut suit. When Evelyn started a conversation with him, she found that he had a sense of humour very similar to her own. He made life in the outbck sound like an adventure, but he was still very much a gentleman.

The more Charlie talked, the more Evelyn realised why his mother and sisters were so proud of him. He was the sort of man she had dreamed of meeting on board ship, and just as good looking as his sisters.

Charlie had only a week's holiday before taking up his new position. During that time he and Evelyn were scarcely apart. She felt very at ease with him; it was as though they had known each other for years. And not only was Charlie the most attractive man she had ever met, but he treated her like a princess. Having found him and being so much in love, how could she bear to go back to England and staid old Reggie Grimwood?

As his week's holiday drew to a close, Charlie realised that he, too, had found the girl he wanted to marry. As cattle mustering was scheduled on Mount Mulgrave, it was impossible for him to extend his visit. He knew he must act quickly and propose before Evie left Australia. If he did not do so now, she would leave with Mrs Dean for South America and he would never see her again. It was now or never.

Fired by love and admiration, and encouraged by his sisters, after dinner one night Charlie took Evie into the rose garden. He told her that he loved her and wanted to marry her. He also confessed that they would have to wait. Charlie was very honest with Evelyn and told her that although he knew a great deal about cattle and horses he had nothing in the bank. All he had inherited from his father was a crumbling old house in distant County Limerick, an estate that made no money and was unsaleable.

The Maunsells were Anglo-Irish landowners, with a pedigree going back to the Normans. Charlie's grandfather had been a kind and compassionate landlord to his tenants during the Irish famine of the 1840s when the potato crop had been attacked by blight, foregoing rents from the estate's tenants. Unlike many other landlords who evicted their tenants, Charlie's grandparents had funded soup kitchens. Being left deep in debt, they emigrated to Australia and settled in the Manning River district.

Charlie's father had grown up in Australia but was proud of his Anglo-Irish heritage. When he died, Charlie had been only sixteen, but had had to assume financial responsibility for his mother and sisters. He took a well-paid but boring job in a bank, paid his sisters' school fees and did his best to replace his father as the breadwinner. When Frances married wealthy young Arthur Hall, his mother and other sister were able to take up residence as long-term visitors with the Halls, and Charlie had been able to return to the land. For more than ten years now he had worked on properties in Queensland, including Paddy Callaghan's Mount Mulgrave Station. Following Callaghan's sudden death in a shooting accident, the executors offered Charlie the job of getting the property into shape and listing all the stock in order to sell it for a good price.

What if she were to rough it with him, Evelyn proposed. Could they manage on his salary? Charlie was delighted.

When Evie told Tim and Rupert that Charlie had asked her to marry him, she expected them to advise her to return home and think it over. But no — her brothers liked and admired Charlie and thought he was the right man for her. Rupert pointed out that a young man who was such a devoted son and brother would make an excellent husband.

Mrs Maunsell and her daughters were also very keen that Charlie should marry Evelyn. They felt she had the necessary strength of character and sense of adventure to face the hardships of pioneering.

Charlie wrote to Evelyn's father asking for his consent. Evelyn also wrote a letter, filled with praise of the Maunsell family and about New South Wales, which was all she had yet seen of Australia. She described Charlie's widowed mother as 'very ladylike' but with 'the saddest face [she] had ever seen'.[2] Jane Maunsell had lost her parents in the Indian Mutiny, then buried two children of her own who had died of dysentery, and finally lost her husband.

Once the week was over, Charlie headed north to his new job on Mount Mulgrave. Evelyn longed to go with him but cared enough about her family in England to wait for their response. In the meantime her brother Rupert had secured a job in Mitchell, Queensland, and left to find a home there for Phoebe and himself, as well as Mrs Maunsell, who would now live with them.

While waiting for a reply from her parents, Evelyn decided to take up an invitation from Rupert to stay with him and help prepare the house.

While Evelyn had written to her mother explaining she was in love and wanted to go and live with Charlie on a Queensland cattle station, she had said nothing of Charlie's finances. Nor had she mentioned the fact that Queensland was known as a place of tropical disease where Charlie's two brothers had died of malaria and where the wet season lasted for months.

There were other dangers too. Far north Queensland in 1911 was the scene of some of the bloodiest fighting in Australia between Europeans and Aborigines. It was hardly the place for a delicately reared girl to live. But Evelyn was certain that she wanted to marry Charlie. Once she received her parents' approval, she began the long journey north to begin her life with him.

From Mitchell, Evelyn travelled to Brisbane then took a steamer to tropical Cairns, at that time a small, rather ramshackle port largely surrounded by rainforest. A crowd of men waited at the quay. Just as tall and handsome as she remembered him, Charlie was there among them. With a lump in her throat and fighting back tears of joy and excitement at seeing him again, Evie walked down the gangplank and fell into her fiance's arms. Two days later, on 21 July 1912, they were married.

For years afterwards Charlie would tease Evelyn about having to pay half a week's wages to obtain a special licence so they could get married immediately in St John's Anglican Church, thus avoiding the delay of calling the bans in church. Evie was totally unused to the tropical heat and high humidity. Although she looked elegant, she felt hot and uncomfortable during the noisy wedding reception. There were no relatives present but Charlie's racing friends and Queensland cattle barons, as well as most of the hotel residents, attended. It seemed to her that almost everyone in Cairns knew Charlie and wanted to wish him luck.

She heard some guests at the wedding reception talking about Mount Mulgrave Station as though Evie was off to Mars, which she found rather alarming. Some of them seemed convinced that Charlie Maunsell was crazy to take her to the wilds. 'That English girl will never stick it out,' said one of Charlie's friends to Dick McManus, who had worked as a station hand on Mount Mulgrave before becoming its purchasing agent in Cairns. Dick knew how tough it was out at the station, and how dangerous, but said nothing about that to Evie.

The wedding guests had underestimated Evelyn Evans — she was much tougher than she looked. Despite the primitive conditions and isolation Evelyn faced on her arrival at Mount Mulgrave Station, she was determined to stay there and make a success of the property — and her marriage.

✿ ✿ ✿

They arrived at Mount Mulgrave after a 400-kilometre journey by train, buckboard and buggy. Evelyn was exhausted but Charlie went

The buckboard which carried Evelyn on her honeymoon.

straight to the stockmen's quarters to find out what was going on and left it to old Maggie to show Evelyn around. Evelyn found it unnerving watching Maggie, a Palmer River Aborigine, smoke a pipe. Maggie showed her to the main bedroom which had galvanised-iron walls and roof, a concrete floor, no ceiling and exposed rafters. The room lacked a wardrobe or a chest of drawers. All Evie found there was a small, cracked toilet mirror, a few wooden pegs on which to hang clothes and an iron bedstead with a lumpy horsehair mattress.

On isolated Mount Mulgrave Station, whose cattle runs and outstations made it one of the largest properties in Queensland, Evelyn was amazed to realise how frugally Paddy Callaghan had lived. In England, possession or management of broad acres automatically included a handsome home with all amenities and perhaps an art collection and a library of leather-bound books. Mount Mulgrave Station was stark and uncomfortable, the ceilings unlined so that without the protection of a mosquito net, spiders, bats, carpet snakes and even the odd small goanna fell from the ceiling onto the bed below. Floor-length windows in both the bedroom and sitting room led to the veranda; they were fitted with heavy wooden shutters with holes bored in them at eye-level so Callaghan could shoot at 'those damn myalls' (wild Aborigines) who might attack the station.

As Maggie showed Evelyn around, she told her about Mr Bowman, of the neighbouring Rutland Plains cattle station, who had recently been speared and left for dead by the 'myalls' — wild Palmer River people. Evelyn now realised that her new surroundings were not just primitive but also highly dangerous. Charlie had not told her anything about Mr Bowman's murder, although she had noticed the conversation had gone very quiet at the wedding reception whenever the Bowmans' names were mentioned.

That night after dinner, Charlie and his new wife went to their bedroom. Evelyn was horrified to find it full of fruit bats squeaking away in the rafters. Eventually the noise quietened as the bats flew out to their nocturnal feeding places, but it was soon replaced by the distant drone of a corroboree from the Aboriginal camp celebrating the arrival of 'new Missus belonga Boss'.[3]

It puzzled Evelyn that as soon as she had arrived, Mrs Lakeland, the station cook, had prepared to depart. Mrs Lakeland, whose

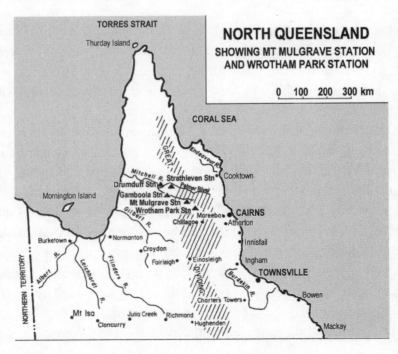

husband was a gold prospector, could shoot a gun as well as any man. As she was saddling up her horse Evie begged her to stay. Having come from London she knew nothing about outback cooking. But Mrs Lakeland refused, replying that it was nothing personal, but she just could not work with another woman in her kitchen. Her swag was packed and nothing Evie could say would change her mind.

Tom Graham, the odd job man, took pity on Evelyn who was now faced with running the domestic side of things. Tom taught Evie how to make damper and bread, staples of the station diet. Bread was made in an old wooden tub, covered with a blanket and placed close to the fire all night. The next morning the dough was kneaded, made into loaves and replaced in the tub until midday when, having risen, they were baked in a hot oven.

Evie channelled all her energies into trying to improve conditions on Mount Mulgrave: running the store, cooking, creating a garden and making the property a success.

She encountered none of the antagonism that had met Jeannie Gunn arriving at the Elsey. The stockmen on Mount Mulgrave were very polite and respectful. But apart from Tom Graham and old Rudolph Morisset, who both became good friends, she did not see a great deal of the other men, who ate in their own quarters.

One of the many jobs that Evelyn took on was overseeing the washing of not only her own and Charlie's clothes but the unmarried stockmen's as well. This was not a simple job. She had first to make cakes of soap rather than getting expensive loads brought in from Cairns. Making soap entailed dissolving caustic soda in water, then pouring in melted fat that had been strained through muslin. The mix was then boiled gently before being poured into trays. Once hard, it was cut into cakes.

One of the Aboriginal hands, Albert, turned out to be Evie's most loyal helper. Usually dressed in a white jacket and trousers, he was far better at doing the washing and ironing than the house girls Evie had to help her. Albert also did most of the heavy work around the house. Albert came from the Wide Bay district near Brisbane and had been trained as a doorman and driver by a local doctor who had later taken him to Cooktown. Albert's Wide Bay people were enemies of the Mitchell River people around Mount Mulgrave — he was so scared of them and their fearsome reputation that he refused to venture far from the manager's house.

Albert and Maggie told Evie that Aborigines from the Mitchell, Palmer and Coleman rivers hated Aborigines from other tribes entering their territory nearly as much as they hated the Europeans who had taken their land. Some years later, a Coleman River Aboriginal girl Evie named Mary came to work at Mount Mulgrave Station. Evie promised Albert he could marry Mary if he taught her to speak English. There were no kinship laws that prevented them from marrying, even though the Coleman River people were reputedly unfriendly with Albert's tribe. When they eventually did marry Charlie built them a separate house on the property and the couple would stay with the Maunsells for years.[4]

Evelyn's recollections in the book *S'pose I Die* reveal the warmth of her long-term relations with, among others, Maggie, Mary, Albert, and Finlay Callaghan who was believed to be Paddy's illegitimate son. These people served the Maunsells devotedly at Mount Mulgrave and later followed them to the Atherton Tableland. Charlie Maunsell had grown up on a cattle property where he had played with Aboriginal children as a boy, and he spoke several Aboriginal languages fluently. Although he had worked with both Paddy Callaghan and 'Terrible Jimmy Collins' of Koolburra Station,[5] both of whom had reputedly treated the Aboriginal people appallingly, Charlie did his best to treat indigenous people fairly. He followed the custom of the time of employing them as stockmen in return for the right to rations for themselves and their dependents and distant relatives. He saw that each Sunday Aborigines who lived on the property received rations of tea, sugar, meat and tobacco from the station store, and when necessary new clothes and work boots. The men also received a small wage, which was supposed to be kept in trust for them by the Queensland Government.[6]

While many of the stockmen at Mount Mulgrave Station were rough gold miners, Evie found to her surprise that Rudolph Morisset, who lived in a shack built onto the outside kitchen, was a highly educated man who had been to Sandhurst. He was the son of Lieutenant-Colonel J.T. Morisset, one-time commandant of the Norfolk Island convict settlement.

Morisset had once been a dashing officer in the Queensland Native Police Force. Despite living roughly for most of his life, he maintained gentlemanly habits and was a fount of local knowledge. Like many men who came to Cape York as gold miners and were now living in or around the property in ramshackle slab huts Morisset had gambled his money away. He still owned an impressive library of leather-bound books, kept up to date with gifts from his sister. One of Morisset's books was a copy of Jeannie Gunn's *We of the Never-Never*, published a few years earlier and then very popular. Morisset lent it to Evelyn but made her promise not to read the final chapter in which Mrs Gunn's husband dies of malarial dysentery (the same disease which had killed Charlie's brothers).

Over dinner Rudolph and Charlie would reflect on life at the station during its previous owner's reign. At meals old Paddy Callaghan, a giant of a man, had sat like an Irish chieftain at the head of a long trestle table, surrounded by his stockmen, including his part-Aboriginal son, Finlay.

Paddy, the rough, tough cattle baron who had started Mount Mulgrave, had arrived in Australia from the peat bogs of Ireland with the proverbial shilling in his pocket. He was a hard man who had worked in far north Queensland as a bullocky, carting telegraph poles for the telegraph line. Later he had gone into business for himself in partnership with a butcher to supply gold prospectors with meat. He had made more money doing that than the miners. When Paddy and his mates Jack Edwards, Tom Leslie the butcher, and Jack Duff had arrived at the river, they had encountered trouble from Aborigines, who rolled rocks down on them as they drove cattle up to the Palmer River. This was virtually unmapped country, and a war was going on between Aborigines and the white men who pushed north with their cattle. From then on Paddy and Jack Duff had carried guns everywhere and made a point of shooting as many Aborigines as possible.[7] Ruthlessness and cruelty made these men a great deal of money.

Paddy had bought leases on a number of properties to hold his stock, including Mount Mulgrave. Although he was a millionaire by the time he came to live on the station, he lived frugally. While some pastoral owners let the Aborigines take a few bullocks now and again, Paddy had been a man who felt outraged every time a beast was speared. He also had a reputation for kidnapping Aboriginal women and raping them.

The horrific stories Evelyn must have heard were hinted at in articles written by Jessie Litchfield, editor of the *Northern Territory Times* and one of the first women journalists in the north of Australia to write about the legacy of hatred the evil dealings of some white men had engendered. In her *Far-North Memories* Litchfield described how:

> fully nine out of every ten murders in the North have
> been due, directly or in part, to unauthorized interference
> with gins [a usual term for Aboriginal women at this
> time]. Not all the true facts ever get into print, of course,
> but those who have been privileged to peep behind the
> scenes know more than the general public can ever know,
> or ever want to know.[8]

Evelyn could understand why the Aborigines hated Callaghan and men like him and looked for opportunity to take revenge.

Paddy Callaghan lived and died by the gun. Fearing an attack by the Mitchell River people, he slept with a loaded revolver by his side. One morning as he was rolling up his swag the revolver accidentally discharged and killed him.

⚜ ⚜ ⚜

Besides Maggie, Albert, Mary and Finlay, Finlay's Aboriginal sister, aged about nine, also helped in the house. The European staff included Johnny Seibel, the head stockman, whose father had been a butcher on the Palmer River during the gold rush, and Tom Graham, who looked after fences, brought in the firewood and sometimes went out on the musters as cook.

Following Mrs Lakeland's departure, a new cook, Sin Sin Yu, arrived from Cairns, but proved very disappointing. He could not bake bread and had no idea what to do with dried and smoked salt beef — both standard fare in the outback. Fortunately, once again Tom Graham came to Evie's rescue. He taught her how to soak the beef overnight, change the water a few times to get rid of most of the salt and soften it up before making a beef stew.

Evelyn learned a great deal from her Aboriginal staff. Before the Aborigines at Mount Mulgrave became accustomed to European food or 'tucker', they supplemented the station diet of salt beef with other meat including roast crocodile. They also regularly caught fish in the river. The Aboriginal boys often caught young pigs and brought them in for fattening. Lizards, goannas and rock pythons, which looked like chicken when cooked, were wrapped in green leaves and covered with hot ashes in the camp fire.

The Aboriginal women on the station would sometimes take Evie with them when they went out hunting or to have a *bogey* (swim). Evie was fascinated to see they ate all kinds of food that were virtually unknown to white people, lily roots from the lagoons being one delicacy that they would dive for. They were excellent swimmers and never seemed to tire of frolicking among the blue lilies. The Mitchell River women collected seeds and fruit and wove intricate long fish-trap baskets from reeds. They also made a kind of bread from the nuts of the pandanus palm.

The women taught Evelyn how to make fire by spinning between her palms a firestick, which was inserted into a small hole cut in another stick and held firmly on the ground with one foot. As sparks appeared, grass was pushed down with the other foot. The spinning was kept up until there was enough smouldering grass to create a flame.

Despite their company, Evie was often lonely when Charlie was away on musters or other station work. She would eat her evening

A woman of the Mitchell River (Yir Yoront) people, painted and feathered for a corroboree.

meals alone, with time to reflect on the society she had once enjoyed in a life that now seemed so far away. She missed her large family dreadfully.

When Charlie returned she would be so glad to see him that she chattered away nineteen to the dozen about petty incidents and domestic concerns. Charlie rarely talked in the saddle except to issue orders and was not comfortable with such a flow of words. Without speaking, he would get up from the table and walk outside, preferring the silence of the outdoors.

This must have hurt Evie but she forgave him. Charlie was a good man and for Evie what mattered was her husband and her marriage. She was determined to stick it out and make things work. She knew how much Charlie wanted to make a success of this job and that he would hate to have to go to London with her and seek employment in an office.

Charlie was a thorough bushman, and like so many bushmen who had worked hard and endured tragedy, he was loath to show his emotions. He had never known his two elder brothers, who had died before he was born. Later, when his father died he had had to make the coffin and bury him.

To occupy herself while Charlie was away, Evie kept a journal. She was also kept busy with the store and garden, and tending to any crisis that developed.

As she was neat and methodical, Evie found she enjoyed the job of storekeeper. All dry goods and tools came out from Cairns by bullock wagon at six-monthly intervals. Evie ordered dry goods and clothing through Charlie's old friend Dick McManus, the man who had given her away at her wedding.

The six-monthly order to the station agent was always similar and included goods for her and Charlie, for the stockmen's kitchen and to sell in the store when travellers called in.[9] Evie also did the book-keeping and sewed dresses for the Aboriginal women who would otherwise have gone around half naked or in rags, as they had in Callaghan's day. She cared for the station Aborigines when they fell sick or injured themselves, relying on her limited medical knowledge and using her own small supply of medicines and bandages.

Nothing was ever wasted in the outback. Evelyn made pillowcases or tea towels from used calico flour bags, while smaller calico bags were used to hang salt beef. Evie used the jute bags from the coarse salt to line the walls of the tin house in an attempt to make it more 'homely'.

When she arrived at Mount Mulgrave Station, the only vegetable available was pigweed, which had spread over the damp ground where the kitchen waste was thrown away. People ate pigweed to avoid scurvy at a time when the bush diet consisted almost exclusively of salt beef and damper.

Evie was very keen to supplement the pigweed with crops from a vegetable garden. She had listened to Charlie's advice about what to plant in the fertile river flats after her first Big Wet. The Cape York Peninsula was known as a place where 'nine months [were] summer and three months Hell'.[10] The wettest months were January and February after which the rains eased off. April to October was largely dry with November seeing a build-up in humidity and the beginning of the Wet.

It became obvious during Evelyn's first Wet that while Pat Callaghan's corrugated iron house could resist white ants, he had built it too close to the river. As the rain fell the house became invaded by red–back spiders, scorpions and centipedes. Snakes also became a pest. There were snakes in the store, snakes in the saddle room, snakes in the blacksmith's shop, snakes in the kitchen, in the bedroom and behind the chintz curtain that covered Evelyn's dresses. On one occasion Evelyn was bitten by a scorpion and on another by a red–back spider; both bites were extremely painful. Charlie sterilised his penknife in the flame of a match, cut the bites, sucked out the poison and sterilised the wounds by pouring methylated spirits over them.[11]

Floodwater from the Little Mitchell, a tributary of the main river, joined the Mitchell River a quarter of a mile downstream from the house. Often it threatened to bank up the main stream and flood the house. If that happened, large canvas bags were hurriedly made in which to hang food. Old timber was carried to the base of the highest tree in case a platform had to be built in the branches as a last–ditch retreat should the river continue to rise.

During the first wet season Evelyn experienced, the water rose until it lapped the edge of the veranda, then the rain stopped, and slowly the water level receded. At least for that Wet the worst was over.

After April, once the waters had subsided and the ground was dry enough, Evie was keen to begin the garden. She spent many days down on the river flats supervising the ploughing and planting — maize, sweet potato, silverbeet, turnips, carrots, potatoes and more.

The subsiding waters had left stagnant pools — breeding grounds for *anopheles* mosquitoes, which plagued Evie. Unfortunately, the *anopheles* mosquito spreads malaria, but Evie was ignorant of this.

On the western end of the homestead veranda, Charlie also built a fernery for Evelyn. Evelyn loved the fernery and hosed it down each evening before dinner. She also ordered ornamental plants from catalogues and received cuttings from various neighbours. Before long the homestead was surrounded by a beautiful tropical garden.

Mango seedlings, a present from their neighbours at the much larger Wrotham Park Station, flourished as did the banana trees, pawpaws, custard apples, oranges and lemons which Charlie and Evelyn planted together with the help of Albert.

By the following November, Evie was pregnant. With heavy storms signalling the start of the next Wet, Charlie and the men set out to make their last trip around the property before Christmas.

Charlie had only been gone a few days when Evie was hit by malaria. Feverish and drenched in perspiration, she collapsed into her bed. The weather was extremely hot and humid, and without a generator there was neither refrigeration nor overhead fans. In an attempt to lower Evie's temperature, faithful Albert placed her on a wicker stretcher on the back veranda.

Malaria causes a painful enlargement of the spleen and total loss of appetite. Unable to eat and perspiring heavily Evelyn became delirious. At times she called out 'Charlie, Charlie' even though she knew that he was far away and could not hear her.

Before World War I and for many years after, the standard treatment for malaria was a teaspoon of quinine, made from *chinchona* bark (eventually replaced by far more effective anti-malarial drugs). Evie had already suffered mild bouts of malaria which she had treated herself. Quinine was extremely bitter to taste and was taken dissolved in hot water or alcohol (to make it act faster) and recommended to be taken twice daily. There was no doctor around to warn Evelyn that quinine was a toxic substance that all pregnant women should avoid.

Between bouts of fever, she dosed herself twice daily with quinine in water. The third dose of quinine brought on a show of blood, followed by a searing pain in her lower abdomen. Then the foetus came away from the womb.

Too weak to help herself, all Evelyn could do was to lie there bleeding, convinced she would die. The once white sheets and nightdress were dark with her blood, her long hair matted with perspiration. The bleeding would not stop, she had no anti-coagulants and no possibility of blood transfusions.

Her brow damp, Evelyn tried to collect her thoughts to speak to Albert. As she became weaker and drifted in and out of consciousness she was afraid that Charlie would return and be confronted by the terrible sight of her putrefying corpse, since Albert and Maggie would be too scared to bury her without Charlie's permission.

Charlie had been haunted by the memory of burying his father and Evelyn wished to spare him another harrowing experience. She wanted Albert to bury her as soon as she died. Charlie could read the funeral service over her grave later. Albert scarcely left her side but could do little to help, apart from trying to fan away the flies which gathered on her lips and around her eyes. The nearest doctor was five hours away on horseback. Rain had turned the surrounding country into a bog. Even had Albert been able to contact neighbours they would have been unable to come to Evelyn's rescue.

'Albert,' she whispered through cracked lips. 'S'pose I die, you dig a hole and put me in it, and cover me up, and tell Boss I bin lose em piccaninny.'

Albert looked horrified and pleaded, 'You no more die, Missus. You no more die.'[12]

The next day Albert asked her permission to borrow Charlie's gun. Although Charlie had told her never to let any of the Aborigines take a gun, Evelyn was too sick to care. She told Albert he could take the one which she kept loaded by the bed whenever Charlie was away.

Albert was gone for so long that Evelyn thought he must have tripped over and shot himself like Paddy Callaghan. Finally he returned driving a cow and her calf before him and holding a brolga's egg and two dead wild ducks. He told her he would make her something nice to eat. He milked the cow and baked a custard with the brolga's egg and brought them to her. Evelyn had not eaten for more than two weeks and felt nauseated by the custard but she allowed herself to be spoon-fed because she did not want to hurt Albert's feelings. He had steamed the duck and she managed to eat a little of the flesh and drink some duck broth, which gave her strength.

Evelyn knew the Mitchell River men would have speared or clubbed Albert to death had they caught him away from the homestead and on foreign ground. She was grateful he had risked his own life to save hers.

Finally Evelyn heard the clatter of hoofs that signalled Charlie and the stockmen were home. She tried to rise from her bed but was still so weak she fell over. The sight of his wife lying on the concrete floor, her long hair matted, her clothes stained with dried blood, gave Charlie a dreadful shock. He picked Evelyn up, her emaciated body light as a feather, and laid her on the bed inside. He stripped off the soiled sheets from the stretcher she had been lying on, dumped them in the tub in the laundry and told Albert to take the stretcher away.

Charlie returned to the bedroom with a bucket of warm water from the kitchen. Gently and tenderly he gave Evelyn the first wash she had had for three weeks. He combed her tangled hair, fetched clean sheets and a nightgown, propped her up with four clean pillows and gave her a shot of rum. The wash and the clean sheets made Evie feel better than she had done for weeks.

Once Evie was settled, Charlie went out on horseback and rounded up another cow. He came back, took Evelyn's temperature, which was still high, and gave her another dose of quinine in hot milk. He removed his spurs and revolver, had a shower outside and then sat beside her on the bed.

When Evelyn awoke Charlie was lying on his back, eyes wide open staring at the ceiling. 'What's the matter?' Evie inquired.

'I haven't been to sleep all night. I never thought you'd see it through,' Charlie admitted stroking her hair tenderly.[13]

The next morning Charlie killed one of the cattle. He went into the kitchen and made beef broth by boiling down a fresh shin-bone.[14] Evelyn reckoned Charlie looked after her far better than any paid nurse would have done. The contrast between the tender side of his character and his rugged masculinity never ceased to amaze her. Underneath his tough bushman's exterior, Charlie was the most gentle and considerate man she had ever known. It was clear he loved her deeply and would do anything in the world for her.

After four days of his loving care she felt strong enough to walk to the shower unassisted. Charlie found excuses to do small repair jobs around the house instead of going out on his horse, which was totally unlike him. Normally he was never happier than riding about with his men mustering cattle and Evie realised what a sacrifice he was making for her. From her window she could see that the wet season was approaching. She knew that her husband should have been supervising the moving of cattle away from woodland areas where the gums and cedars were huge and dead branches could fall on the cattle and kill them.

Whenever the weather was not too hot, Charlie would take a mattress out, put it under a shady tree and carry Evelyn to it so he could keep an eye on her while he worked. She was still skeletally thin, her once manicured hands were freckled claws. He would now joke that he had paid 'two pounds five shillings for just skin and bone', referring to the money he had spent on their special marriage licence in Cairns, half a week's wages at that time.[15]

In spite of Charlie's care, it became apparent that Evie was not recovering and needed treatment by a doctor. Christmas had come and gone. The Wet was at its height, and the ground so soggy that the sturdy buckboard would never get through. If they could get to the railhead at Mungana, Charlie said, she would be fine. Was it possible she could sit on a horse? The trip to the railhead 100 kilometres away — two days' journey in the buckboard — could easily take five days on horseback, especially if Evelyn had to rest for long intervals.

Evelyn had been telling her husband that she was not as sick as she really was in order not to worry him. But the idea of spending days in the saddle feeling as ill as she did horrified her. She was not a brilliant horsewoman. She liked riding quiet, gentle Biddy but the last thing she wanted was a long ride on horseback in her present condition. But there was no alternative. She would have to ride to the railhead or stay at Mount Mulgrave.

As if Charlie did not have enough to worry about, a letter arrived from Evie's brother Rupert saying that Charlie's mother, Jane Maunsell, had had a severe stroke and was unlikely to live longer than a few days. Since Charlie's mother could no longer recognise anyone, Rupert said that it was pointless for him to make the long journey to see her. Poor, poor Charlie, Evelyn thought, so much responsibility and I who want to help him have become an additional burden. Once again she felt she just had to get well soon for Charlie's sake. Eventually Evelyn gave in to Charlie's wish to travel to the railhead on horseback, as long as she could ride Biddy.

The heat and humidity were stifling and Evelyn was often barely conscious. When she felt as if she was going to faint she had to cling to the pommel of the saddle to stop herself falling while Charlie supported her. Evelyn was so weak that Charlie rode beside her, putting his arm round her and urging her to 'try and do another mile or two'.[16]

Even so, Evelyn had to dismount every so often to rest under a shady tree. Charlie would give her a nip of brandy from his flask and by the end of each day Evie felt light-headed.

After six days they reached Mungana. Charlie had to leave Evie and go straight back to work at Mount Mulgrave. He put her in a first-class compartment on the train for Cairns in the charge of the guard, phoned his old friend Dick McManus and asked him to meet the train.

Dick was distressed at the sight of the once elegant and beautiful Evie. He drove her to the Imperial Hotel where she was looked after by Paulina, who had been maid of honour at Evelyn's wedding and was now married to Dick. Dick had to admit people had been totally wrong in their estimation of Evelyn. 'The English girl' had grit and pluck; Charlie was very lucky indeed to have a wife like her.

At the hotel Dr Kerwin examined Evelyn. He sent her to hospital immediately, saying that she must have had a constitution of iron to have survived. After two weeks' bed rest and treatment, Dr Kerwin allowed her back to the care of her friend at the Imperial Hotel. By then Evelyn was feeling much better and desperate to return to Charlie. Without telling Dr Kerwin what she intended to do, she asked Dick to book her a seat on the train and wire Charlie that she was returning.

Charlie met her at Mungana railhead with a hired buckboard and a driver who took them as far as the Walsh River crossing. They crossed the river by boat and found Finlay waiting for them on the other side with the Mount Mulgrave buckboard and the billy on.

For the rest of that year Evelyn suffered recurring bouts of hot and cold sweats due to intermittent malarial fever. Gradually they decreased but her malaria would reappear at unexpected times for years.

ᵉ ᵉ ᵉ

Charlie had been entrusted with the responsibility of getting the cattle station in order and making it pay so that Paddy Callaghan's relations could eventually sell it. Evelyn had never seen anyone work as hard as Charlie and his stockmen. Day after day and week after week they went out mustering while she was left alone on Mount Mulgrave with only Maggie, Albert and Mary, and some of the other locals for company. When Charlie was away Evie prayed that the Mitchell River warriors would not come to steal supplies or take revenge on her for atrocities other white people had committed against them.

Despite her prayers, one day a group of men from the Mitchell River tribe appeared at the station. Alert to their arrival Maggie walked out to meet the approaching men, who were brandishing spears tipped with broken glass. Inside, a terrified Albert and Evie listened quietly. As an Aborigine outside his territory Albert was in greater danger than Evie.

Aware that the boss and his stockmen were away mustering cattle, the tribesmen asked Maggie where the Missus and Albert were.

Even though the men were her distant kinsmen Maggie knew that they would spear her if she refused to answer. She told the men that the 'white Missus' was planting vegetables down by the river with Albert. To get to the vegetable garden the men had to pass the station store and Maggie knew that if they went down there, it was likely they would break in, take the sugar and treacle they loved and return to their camp with as much as they could

Evelyn at Mount Mulgrave with two young Aboriginal children.

carry. As long as they went to the store she would have time to warn Evie to hide.

Some of the Mitchell River men set off in single file towards the vegetable garden, but two of the most ferocious-looking padded up to the veranda intending to go into the house. It was impossible to scream a warning or they would all be speared.

While Maggie was talking to the men, Evelyn and Albert slipped into Evie's bedroom, Albert clutching a gun he had picked up. Although she could not understand what they were saying outside, it was clear from the men's threatening stance and the way they brandished their spears that they were looking for trouble. How she wished Charlie was there.

Evelyn's heart beat wildly as she heard the two Aborigines make their way into the house, spears in hand. She knew she had only seconds to find a hiding place or she could be dead.

Without a word Albert disappeared under the bed like a frightened dog in a thunderstorm and the long quilt hid him from sight. Evelyn thought quickly, then knelt down also and slid out of view as well.

Hardly daring to breathe, she heard the men in the living room. She watched terrified from under the bed as the barbed point of one of the men's spears pushed aside the curtain separating the bedroom from the living room and its owner peered around the room.

After what seemed like an eternity the two men retreated and the curtain fell back. Evelyn wanted to scream but held it in, remaining stiff as a corpse, far too scared to move. She stayed like this, praying she would not sneeze. The room was silent, suggesting the men had gone, but Evelyn did not come out until she heard Maggie say, 'All right now, Missus, him gone now.'[17]

Still shaking with fear, Evelyn crawled out from her hiding place followed by Albert, who with trembling hands attempted to brush the dust off his trousers. Evelyn clung to Maggie, shedding tears of relief.

❧ ❧ ❧

In 1914 World War I broke out. Rupert and Tim Evans, Evelyn's brothers, enlisted as did three of her brothers in England. Not to be outdone, Charlie went to the Cairns recruiting station and volunteered but was turned down on medical grounds. He had continuing problems with his hip and lower back dating back to a fall from a horse while he was working on his first station job in 1904. He was also told that producing food was vital for the war effort, which was a great relief to Evelyn.

During what was known as the Great War, station life went on much as it always had, except that Evelyn and the others did whatever they could to help the war effort. Evelyn taught the Aboriginal women how to knit scarves and socks, and they made huge quantities of beef extract to send to military hospitals overseas. In the second year of the war Evelyn sent dozens of jars of this nutritious 'beef tea' to Australian Army hospitals at Rouen and on the Somme. According to letters she received, it was much appreciated by wounded Anzacs who could not eat solid food.

She also made fruitcakes, using plenty of butter, eggs and dried fruit, which the Red Cross sent out to soldiers at the front. The Aboriginal kitchen hands thought cake making was great fun and never tired of beating the eggs. Evelyn added plenty of treacle to keep the fruitcakes moist. The Red Cross wrote to Evelyn and asked her to add glycerine and plenty of rum, so they would arrive in one piece.

Letters from England were depressing. Evelyn's home town of Ilford had been bombed by the Germans in an attempt to destroy the big Kodak factory that had been built there. Fortunately, Evelyn's parents were safe, but her mother's letters were full of news about young men Evelyn had known and who had been killed at the front in France or at Gallipoli.

Evelyn's brother Tim was one of the Anzacs who landed at Gallipoli in 1915. Evelyn was in Sydney with Charlie who was trying to enlist there when she heard that Tim would be arriving home on the hospital ship *Ballarat*.

Tim had apparently lain unconscious on the battlefield where he fell after a shell had burst over his trench. Five days later when a truce was called to bury the dead, Tim was found still alive.

Shell-shocked and a long time recovering his memory, Tim was sent from Sydney by train to a hospital in Brisbane. Eventually, Evelyn and Charlie arranged for him to be nursed back to health with them at Mount Mulgrave.

≈ ≈ ≈

The Big Wet of January and February 1917 was a very bad one, hot and humid, with a lot of Gulf fever (malaria). Evelyn came down with another bad attack and once again it caused her to lose a much-wanted baby. Although depressed, Evelyn had a strong and stable character and the motivation to get better. For Charlie's sake she picked up the pieces and started again in the hope that one day she would be able to bear a child.

But things were starting to look up for Charlie and Evelyn. By living modestly and working very hard they had saved enough money to fulfil their dream of buying their own land for the time when they would leave Mount Mulgrave. They decided that dairy farming would be the coming thing and they purchased fifty hectares of partly cleared land at Malanda on the Atherton Tableland and then bought another lot filled with gigantic trees, some of which had to be felled to make room for cows.

Mount Mulgrave was finally to be put to auction, and the O'Briens, Pat Callaghan's relatives, were grateful for everything Charlie had done to improve the station. They gave him some racehorses which he had bred and raced successfully, as well as twenty heifers from the station herd to start the Maunsells off with stock for their own new farm.

Leaving Charlie to finish business at Mount Mulgrave, once again Evelyn became a pioneer. She set off to the Atherton Tableland with their cattle and Charlie's beloved racehorses, accompanied by faithful Albert and his wife, Mary. They had insisted on leaving Mount Mulgrave and coming with Evelyn to help her to get the place into some sort of order. From the railway at Malanda they all rode in an open cart out to the property, sitting on top of their suitcases and small items of furniture. It proved to be a bumpy, uncomfortable journey.

On either side of the track Evie could see a tangled forest of huge cedars, silky oaks, rosewood and pine trees. She was relieved to find that, even when the days were hot, the nights were fairly cool. Often clouds hung so low over the mountains that one could walk through them, like mist on Scottish or English moors.

The southern part of the tableland was year-round far wetter than the open forest country around Mount Mulgrave. It seemed to be raining all the time in those pioneering days at Malanda and finding dry firewood was a problem. Evelyn made them all raincoats out of unbleached calico, waterproofed with lampblack and raw linseed oil. In spite of the constant rain, she appreciated the tableland because the climate was mild and more like that of England. She did most of the cooking in the open over a cast-iron camp oven, which she had never used before. She soon got used to it, and even managed to make bread, though some of it was hard as any stone.

There being no lovely homestead, once again Evelyn lived in a corrugated iron shed, this time much smaller than the one at Mount Mulgrave. The shed would remain 'home' until Alby Halfpapp, a pioneer settler and carpenter on the Atherton Tableland, at last built them a cottage and outhouses from black-bean timber. Then they could settle down to enjoy life on the edge of a wonderful rainforest.

With no shops nearby, Evelyn still had to plan ahead for all her purchases. Rations were brought in by bullock wagon and, as usual, some of the flour had weevils in it. But the sugar was no longer in one damp, sticky mass as it often had been out at Mount Mulgrave.

One morning, before Charlie had yet joined them at Malanda, Evelyn awoke to find all the heifers gone. If they could not be located, it would mean a huge financial loss, just as they were starting out on their own. There were no fences to keep the cattle in and the tracks through the scrub led in all directions. Even though the rain poured down, it was crucial to start searching for the herd immediately.

Evelyn knew she could not ask Albert and Mary to go separately to search for the heifers. Being from Wide Bay and the Coleman River they were afraid of what the Atherton Tableland Aborigines might do to them. So Albert and Mary set off searching for the cattle together while Evelyn went alone to adjoining farms asking if anyone had seen the missing herd.

Eventually Evelyn found the heifers and brought them home, but she resolved they *must* erect fences. She had a crosscut saw, maul and wedges, but the trees were new to her and she had no way of knowing what the best timber to use was. When she saw a fencing contractor fixing a bridge she asked for his advice. Armed with some local knowledge she located logs which Albert and Mary sawed into lengths and they all split into posts. They worked with extreme caution because venomous red-bellied black snakes were everywhere. It was back-breaking work but eventually they got the fences up.

Not long afterwards, Charlie and Finlay joined them, bringing more horses from Mount Mulgrave.

Finlay and some of the other Aboriginal hands from Mount Mulgrave decided to stay on at Malanda rather than return to Mount Mulgrave. They found the noisier and densely populated area diverting — and rich in game.

Before going into town on Saturday nights Finlay would often ask Evelyn, 'Missus, you want fowl for dinner tomorrow?'

Innocently Evelyn thought that Finlay was being given the chicken by kind friends in Malanda. So she thanked him and they had several nice Sunday lunches of roast chicken before she realised that Finlay was raiding the neighbour's hen house.

'Finlay, where are you getting these hens?' Evelyn demanded.

He looked genuinely surprised.

'Doesn't matter, does it Missus?' he asked.[18]

After that Evelyn refused all Finlay's kind offers of chicken for dinner.

They were just about settled into their new wooden cottage at Malanda when Charlie received a letter offering him the position of general manager of the huge cattle runs of Wrotham Park and its three outstations, Gamboola, Highbury and Drumduff. Cattle and horses were in Charlie's blood far more than dairy farming and Evelyn recognised this. The Maunsells put a manager onto the Atherton property and went back to the hot, steamy Cape York Peninsula.

Wrotham Park, one of Queensland's largest cattle stations, now owned by the Australian Agricultural Company, lies 300 kilometres west of Cairns. Its 596,000 hectares of rich red soil in a good season today carry up to 35,000 head of cattle.[19] When the Maunsells arrived to manage it, Wrotham Park was a property of cleared land bisected by a broad winding river, which meant it was rarely affected by drought, and running 55,000 head of cattle.

At long last Evelyn was the mistress of a large station homestead complete with all amenities, the sort of home she had dreamed of having when she first came north to live in a tin shack on Mount Mulgrave Station.

Tranquil Wrotham, in the county of Kent, had been where Wrotham Park's founder, A.C. Grant, had been born. He had started his Queensland property as a holding station for beef cattle to be sold at top prices to the European and Chinese miners panning for gold along the Palmer River.

While Mount Mulgrave had remained in the hands of Paddy Callaghan, who had started it in 1874 at the height of the gold rush,

Wrotham Park had had many owner-investors. There had always been friendly relations between the two adjoining properties and joint musters were often held.

At the time Charlie Maunsell was invited to take it over, Wrotham Park and its outstations were owned by Tom Purcell, one of those cattle barons who, like Paddy Callaghan, could scarcely read and write but had a knack of predicting cattle prices, assessing risks and forecasting weather conditions.

Purcell was a good boss to work for. Under Charlie's skilful management, Wrotham Park set records and turned off about 3000 bullocks a year. Evelyn went back to her former job of running the station store and under her capable management they never ran short of food or work clothes. Charlie worked hard with the stock while Purcell remained in Brisbane and organised the sale of the beef cattle, eventually becoming immensely wealthy.

Evelyn was paid the piffling sum of two pounds a week to run the store, which carried enough supplies to service the entire district. Every quarter, Evelyn ordered dozens of shirts, trousers, and elastic-sided boots in different sizes, as well as plenty of blankets and everything else that men in the bush needed. Once more she ordered brooms, flour, jams, raisins, tomato ketchup, tobacco and clay pipes by the dozen for Wrotham Park and the outlying districts.

Wrotham Park Station was only about six miles from the Walsh Telegraph Office and the homestead was connected to it by telephone. The Maunsells had their own private line strung from tree to tree out through Gamboola and Highbury to Drumduff, nearly 160 kilometres away. With a large (by today's standards) 'mobile phone' Charlie could connect to the line anywhere he pleased so the head stations and the outstations were always in contact.

Before long, old Aboriginal friends and staff from Mount Mulgrave Station arrived looking for work at Wrotham Park. The first to arrive were Billy God-help-us, his wife, Kitty, and their children, who had walked forty kilometres across country to announce they would only work for Charlie.

Evelyn and Charlie Maunsell (on the right) with a group outside Wrotham Park homestead.

'Other feller boss no good,' said Billy, whose son was now old enough to go out mustering cattle.[20] So father *and* son signed on at Wrotham Park in order to work with Charlie.

Next to arrive were Maggie, her husband and their young son Robin. Evelyn was especially pleased to see Maggie whom she would never forget had saved her life by sending the threatening Aborigines down to the river when they had come to kill her. Evie and Maggie hugged each other joyfully.

Wrotham Park already had its own workers — Topsy, Dinah and Jessie — helping in the kitchen and in the vegetable garden. Work had to be rearranged to keep them all occupied or, as Evelyn knew, grievances could surface and they might fight among themselves. Evelyn kept Mary and Albert, who had also come with the Maunsells, on household duties, put Maggie in charge of the garden and told Kitty to help with the washing. They soon had a good vegetable garden, watered by hand from buckets carried from a creek by Maggie and other Aboriginal staff.

While relations between the Maunsells and their staff were good, the coming years would prove to be unhappy for many station Aborigines as government policies were implemented to round up Aborigines and send them to Palm Island Reserve. In 1919, the flu epidemic which swept the world hit the Cape York Aboriginal population particularly hard. Evelyn and Charlie were extremely concerned about the fifty or so Aborigines reliant on Wrotham Park, and wrote to the Minister for Health asking for medical supplies for them. In reply they received a large box of medicines, equipment and instructions, which they set about following immediately.

Slowly but surely the flu began taking its toll. As the Aboriginal stockmen and their relatives became ill they were brought to the homestead to be nursed. At one point Evie had more than thirty patients in the house. Using a combination of medicine, feeding and judicious periods in the sun (which Evie thought the best treatment), none of their patients died, unlike on neighbouring properties which had death rates amongst their Aborigines of more than fifty per cent. When they were well enough Evie sent her patients on walkabout so they could use their own bush remedies and build up their strength.

℮℮ ℮℮ ℮℮

Towards the end of 1920 Charlie wrote to Tom Purcell to say he would be resigning early in 1921 because he wanted to take Evie home to visit her family and he wanted to see his own family property in Ireland.

Purcell refused to accept the resignation and suggested Charlie take twelve months' holiday on full pay and find a suitable person to take over as manager while he was away. The Maunsells persuaded Jack Hamill, head stockman and an extremely responsible man, to act as manager.

Charlie and Evelyn were due to sail for Europe in March 1921. Jack Hamill and the rest of the staff organised a 'surprise leaving party', any trip overseas in those days being a once-in-a-lifetime event to be celebrated in style.

On the night of the party, Evelyn and Charlie were out taking a walk. As they returned, the homestead seemed to be unusually brightly lit. They went inside and found that all the lights and lanterns had been put into service. The staff and stockmen had gathered in the dining room, which was decorated with coloured streamers. The table was groaning under the weight of plates of savouries and cakes and a selection of bottles of wine and spirits which, Evelyn noted, the mailman must have been smuggling in for weeks.

Jack Hamill read a testimonial signed by twenty-two of the staff of the four stations. 'We, the undersigned . . . wish you both a safe journey to the homeland and a safe return back to us all at Wrotham Park, and hand you this presentation.'[21] The gift was £75, a large sum for those days. As some of the station hands received only about £2 a week wages it represented a very generous gift indeed.

At the right moment Jimmy Ah Say, the Chinese cook, gave the Aborigines who remained on the station a signal to leave their own supper and to come inside the homestead. They gathered in the fernery and sang a song of farewell before inviting the Maunsells to their camp to attend a special moonlight corroboree. The men had painted their bodies and wore white feathers in their hair; the women beat time on their thighs with their hands, their eyes gleaming in the light of the fire. The rhythm of their chants and the tapping of the music sticks filled the air. Evelyn was touched to be witnessing the unique, mysterious ceremony, a sign of affection and loyalty from her Aboriginal friends. She was determined to bring back special gifts for them all — musical instruments she felt would be ideal.

Evelyn and Charlie spent two days in Sydney visiting Charlie's family, as well as the Halls at Thornleigh, and five Maunsell aunts, who were delighted to learn of the planned visit home and to County Limerick to see Ballybrood, the Maunsell family home. Each aunt took Evie aside and whispered how nice it would be if Charlie and she were to have a son to continue the family line and suggested that perhaps Ireland might work its magic on her.

The sea voyage to England was long and far from pleasant. Charlie and Evie both needed the ship's doctor in the Indian Ocean when ten days' rough weather brought on a flare-up of the malarial fever from which they both suffered intermittently.

In the Red Sea their ship passed through a sandstorm so thick the land became invisible and the deckhands were forced to sweep sand from the decks. The banks of the Suez Canal were lined with British soldiers in uniform who called longingly out to the ship bound for England, 'Tell [King] George we want to go home.'[22]

Evelyn and Charlie left the ship at Toulon in the south of France and took a train across the country. When they crossed the English Channel, Evelyn recalled how she had made that crossing as a young girl, a paid companion to an elderly widow, and could hardly believe how much her life had changed since that fateful voyage.

After landing at Dover, they took the boat train to Victoria Station, marvelling at how green the countryside looked. From Victoria Station they drove down the Mall, past Buckingham Palace to Liverpool Street Station, and took the train to rural Ilford.

They were disappointed to find no one on the station to greet them. Then old Jock, the ticket collector, recognised Evie and told her that her father had met every single train from London from morning to night and had only just returned home. There were no cabs to be had so they decided to walk and paid the only porter to help Charlie wheel their luggage on a trolley.

When they reached Evelyn's childhood home, the porter tipped all the luggage on the front drive, leaving Charlie to guard it. Evie rang the front door bell and hammered with her fists on the door, so excited was she at the thought of seeing her family again after so many years. Evie's mother opened the door and burst into tears and then her sister arrived. They cried, laughed and hugged each other and were so excited that they forgot all about poor Charlie sitting on the suitcases.

Evie's letters had described Charlie as a typical Australian bushman, tall, sunburned and at home in the saddle, but ill at ease in cities. So her family had expected him to be awkward, a little uncouth and unsociable. Discovering their Irish-Australian son-in-law was a handsome, quietly spoken gentleman with perfect manners was a pleasant surprise for Alderman and Mrs Evans.

Evie felt good to be living in a solid, handsome brick house again. The house had not changed; it was just as she had remembered it with bow windows on the ground floor, the wide curved staircase, and bedrooms and bathrooms upstairs. That tin-roofed shed on Mount Mulgrave, with its concrete floor and holes in the shutters to shoot threatening Aborigines, seemed a long, long way away.

After a happy time at Ilford they stayed with one of Evelyn's brothers in Wiltshire. He drove them around Bath and Bristol and to the beautiful villages of the Cotswolds area, with their mellow stone houses and walled gardens full of hollyhocks and herbaceous borders.

Their next step was to take the boat from Liverpool to Dublin. In 1921 there was still a great deal of unrest in Dublin, following the Troubles and the War of Independence. Roads and railways had been damaged in fighting between the Irish Republican Army and British troops. At the port of Dublin their luggage was searched on arrival by customs officers looking for guns.

Charlie hired a taxi-cab and they paid the driver's hotel expenses to drive them to Limerick. One night on the main road to Killarney they saw the door of a cottage fly open and an old man and his wife come running out, scattering pigs and fowl in all directions. 'Stop, stop!' they shouted. 'The bridge was blown up.'[23]

Had the couple not warned the Maunsells, they would have fallen ten metres into the river. Their driver managed to find an alternative route to the charming town of Limerick. They stayed at the Royal George Hotel, which had bags piled round the windows and doorways in case of shooting or bombs thrown by the patriots. The Sinn Fein, Eamon de Valera and his followers wanted an independent Ireland with its own parliament. They felt Michael Collins had sold them short signing the treaty with the British Government which meant that Eire had to acknowledge the British king. This act would cost Collins his life.

Their driver took them to Ballybrood, where the Maunsells had lived for 400 years, now standing deserted except for a farm manager occupying the servants' quarters. Ballybrood was built in Georgian style from imported stone. It had a long drive, a handsome front door, and a large stable yard behind the house with quarters for the servants. Ivy had run wild and covered most of the walls, clogging the gutters.

Evelyn was fascinated to see the house, especially the drawing room which contained beautiful old furniture covered with striped silk. It wasn't hard to imagine the house in the days when the Maunsells had entertained the cream of Anglo-Irish society.

The estate of Ballybrood still had nearly 200 hectares of arable land, which was rented out to tenant farmers. Ireland was desperately poor and their meagre rents were just enough to pay the rates and the farm manager's salary. Charlie, heir to the mortgaged property, had never had a penny from the place and nor had his father.

The bailiff-caretaker, whose name was Breen, showed Charlie the estate's books, and invited them to a very modest meal. Clearly, with the Troubles raging in Ireland and the Sinn Fein burning down country houses, selling Ballybrood was out of the question.[24]

The trip to Ireland was like a second honeymoon for the Maunsells, as Charlie had no cares or work to occupy him. And Evelyn would never forget the green of the fields of southern Ireland and the romantic appeal of Ballybrood. After they returned to stay with her parents at Ilford, Evelyn discovered to her delight that what Charlie's aunts had whispered *had* come true. The magic of Ballybrood had made her pregnant.

In October it was time for them to leave. They decided to take a ship that went via Canada and the United States. Their voyage from Liverpool to Quebec in the SS *Minnedosa* was a rough one. Evelyn, pregnant and worried about the baby, stayed in their cabin resting most of the time. Charlie, who enjoyed the rough seas, often ventured onto the deck. By the time the St Lawrence River was in sight, the weather was calm and Evelyn was able to join Charlie to gaze at the approaching Quebec shores lined with beautiful maple trees in autumnal shades.

They visited Montreal and New York as well as Niagara Falls, then travelled by train across the prairies and over the Rockies, eventually arriving at Vancouver. There they boarded a ship bound for Sydney. Though the Pacific crossing was smooth, Evelyn consulted the ship's doctor, anxious that nothing should go wrong after her previous miscarriages.

On their way north from Sydney, they stopped off at Brisbane to see Tom Purcell, by now in his seventies and very wealthy indeed. Purcell had bad news: he was planning to sell his interest in Wrotham Park. Charlie was taken by surprise at Purcell's announcement and wondered about his and Evelyn's future.

They arrived in Cairns in the first months of 1922 and Evelyn went straight into St Anthony's nursing home. Charlie returned to Wrotham Park to relieve Jack Hamill as manager. The staff were puzzled that Evelyn was not with him but Charlie, probably scared of yet another miscarriage, said not one word about the pregnancy, promising she would return soon. The staff were consumed with curiosity, but did not like to ask too many questions.

He handed out the presents he and Evelyn had brought back in their shipping trunks. They had purchased accordions and mouth-organs for the Aboriginal men, a gramophone and records for the staff, a new white suit for Albert, and fishing lines for Maggie and the other Aboriginal women.

On 8 May 1922 Ron Maunsell was born in the nursing home in Cairns — a perfectly healthy and sturdy baby. One of the first things Evelyn did was wire the good news to Charlie's aunts. Charlie came to Cairns to see his infant son and take Evelyn back to Wrotham Park.

Everyone was surprised to see Evelyn arrive holding a newborn baby wrapped in a shawl. Charlie had still not told anyone about her pregnancy. The staff were delighted and made a great fuss. Evelyn had never been so happy.

⚜ ⚜ ⚜

As he had warned, Tom Purcell eventually sold Wrotham Park for a very good profit. By 1925 Charlie had had enough of working for the new owners and resigned. He and Evie now had their young son's future to safeguard and their dairy farm at Malanda to build up.

Leaving Wrotham Park was hard. They had become fond of their many staff, who were now like family. Charlie and Evie felt they could not leave behind faithful old Albert and Mary — or Kitty's

COURTESY RON MAUNSELL

Charlie, Evelyn and Ron Maunsell on the Atherton Tableland.

daughter Josie — so the three staff came with them. It was a sad day for Evelyn when she left Dick and Maggie and the other faithful friends she had known since Mount Mulgrave days.

Jack Hamill, who had done a fine job as surrogate manager, also asked for his final cheque the day they departed and rode away from the homestead with them.

The Maunsells subsequently spent nearly twenty years on the Atherton Tableland carving out their home and farm from the scrub and watching young Ron grow up tall and strong like his father. Evelyn loved the crisp air and cool nights, the green grass and clear running creeks on the tableland. She worked hard but no harder than all the other women dairy-farming in the area. Cows always had to be milked, the separating done, the cream cans made ready for collecting early in the morning, and the butter churned and sent away by rail.

Dr Jarvis Nye from Atherton believed that these pioneering women worked far too hard and often kept them in hospital longer than necessary because he knew that as soon as they were home with a new baby or recovered from an illness or injury the women would go straight back to work milking cows — as Evelyn did.[25]

Albert and Mary, in spite of their attachment to Evelyn, could not take the cold and wet of the tableland and asked Charlie to arrange for their return to Cooktown, where Albert wanted to spend his old age. Josie also left to return to her Mitchell River people.

Once their son Ron went to boarding school, Charlie arranged for a teenaged boy from an orphanage to come to the farm to help. Evelyn mothered the abandoned Tony, who had been left on the steps of a Townsville orphanage, and helped him manage his wage as well as earn some additional money.

By October 1939 young Australians were enlisting in another world war. Ron signed up to the Royal Australian Air Force (RAAF) as soon as he was old enough. On his last day on the farm he helped his father with the afternoon milking as usual and in the evening they went into Malanda for his send-off party. It was pouring rain the night they farewelled Ron and the following morning he departed. Evelyn felt as if 'the bottom had fallen out of the world'.[26]

As soon as he was of age, Tony, too, left to enlist. Evelyn and Charlie were now working the farm on their own. Ron had told his parents that when the war was over he did not want to continue dairy farming and preferred beef cattle. When the opportunity arose, Evelyn and Charlie sold the property and retired for a while to a much smaller farm on the outskirts of Brisbane. By now Charlie was sixty and Evelyn was fifty-six, and the long hours of milking had become too much.

After his discharge Ron worked at sinking dams for a while and then went into a partnership with his parents. They bought Rio sheep station, close to Longreach in central Queensland.

Once again they experienced the pitfalls of the pioneering life. The house was basic and the laundry block was only four posts with a few sheets of galvanised iron over the top, a bench with two round tubs and a copper boiler set on an open wood fire. Winters can be freezing in Longreach, and Evelyn did the washing in two thick overcoats.

Charlie and Evelyn spent a year living there with Ron. During that time Rio Station was hit by a plague of black rats which gnawed away busily through the bottom of doors to get to food. It was horrendous, with rats everywhere. There was little the Maunsells could do but wait until the thousands of rats moved on, heading north for the Gulf of Carpentaria.

Evelyn had been longing for grandchildren and she and Charlie were happy when on 17 April 1954, Ron married Joan Meekin. Now with Rio in good hands, the Maunsells retired to Brisbane for the second time, where Evelyn worked very hard for the Country Women's Association (CWA). She was very fond of her daughter-in-law and thrilled by the arrival of three lovely granddaughters: Joanne, Margaret and Barbara.

Evie was very proud, too, when in 1968 Ron, who was extremely popular locally, was elected as a Federal senator. He remained in that position until 1981. Ron Maunsell would eventually sell his outback property of Rio to a neighbouring station owner, retire to Buderim and then move north to Cairns to live with one of his daughters.

Charlie Maunsell died in May 1970 aged eighty-seven; Evelyn died seven years later. One of the last things Charlie said to Evelyn was that he had never realised until he visited her home what a sacrifice she had made leaving a life of comfort behind to go with him to Mount Mulgrave.

Evelyn was able to reassure Charlie that it had not been a sacrifice for her. She had enjoyed pioneering the outback and sharing his life, tough as it had been. He had been the only man for her; and their long and happy marriage, and their handsome, successful son had rewarded them for a life of struggle.

Catherine 'Katie'
Langloh Parker
1856 – 1940

Myrtle Rose
White
1888 – 1961

ON THE DESERT FRINGE

'The outback is a cruel place,' wrote Jeannie Gunn to Jock McLennan, a former Elsey stockman, on hearing of the death of 'the Fizzer', the intrepid postman who had drowned crossing a river in the Never-Never.[1] Catherine Parker and Myrtle White would also experience the cruelty and pain of the bush, including flood, drought and red dust. Both of these determined, resourceful women had a gift for writing and both followed their husbands into some of the harshest regions on the planet.

Born during a sandstorm near Broken Hill, Myrtle Rose Kennewell nearly died when her tiny nostrils became blocked by flying sand. Her mother had been seven months pregnant and travelling by covered wagon in the Broken Hill area when she went into labour prematurely, miles from a doctor. Frantic with worry, Myrtle's father pitched their tent, placed his wife inside and drove hell for leather to try and find someone to deliver the child. Alone in the tent the labour continued until Myrtle was born. Swirling sand coated the baby and almost suffocated her before Myrtle's father returned with a woman who unblocked Myrtle's air passages and cut the umbilical cord.[2]

Katie Field was born over three decades before Myrtle. Her birth was supervised by her maternal grandmother at the Newland family home at Encounter Bay, South Australia. Martha Newland and Katie's grandfather, the Reverend W. R. Newland, would take a special interest in the education of their grandchildren, as they had their own children. They saw that Katie was a clever little girl and intended for her to learn Latin, Greek and French.

The Reverend and Mrs Newland were cultured people, well-travelled classicists in love with ancient Greece. They were determined that their granddaughters would not suffer by living in the outback when the family moved there around 1859, after Katie's father became interested in land opening up around the Murray and Darling Rivers. At Marra Station, the five young Fields — two boys and three girls — and their later siblings were tutored by their well-schooled mother and their classically educated father who exposed them to Greek myths and legends.

Katie's father, Henry Field, had come out from England as a young man in 1837 and run a pastoral property with his brother at Yankalilla, supplying meat to whalers at Encounter Bay. He and Sophy Newland, Katie's mother, were married in 1849. After his brother's death in 1860, Henry farmed around Encounter Bay until the move to Marra Station.

Once at Marra the children maintained contact with their grandparents, accompanying their mother on several visits back, including the one she made for the birth of Rosa Emily (Rosina) in 1860.

At Marra Station the girls, Jane, Katie and Henrietta, were cared for by an Aboriginal nursemaid named Miola. At bedtime she introduced the girls to the myths and legends of the Yuwaalaraay (Euahlayi) people, one of the largest Aboriginal linguistic groups in northern New South Wales. Miola related the ancient Aboriginal legends of Byamee, the sacred being or 'All Father' of her ancestors, as well as tales of Yuwaalaraay ancestral spirits like Yubbah the Carpet Snake, Ooboon the Blue-tongued Lizard, and Mouyi the White Cockatoo.

On hot summer afternoons at Marra Station while baby Rosina rested with her mother, Miola would take twelve-year-old Jane, six-year-old Katie and four-year-old Henrietta for a paddle in the Darling River. One fateful afternoon Miola and Jane swam to the middle of the river leaving the two younger girls in the shallows. A current seized Katie and Henrietta and swept them out of their depth. Both little girls screamed for help and thrashed about in terror. Miola and Jane swam over to save them. Miola dragged Katie to the bank thereby saving her life. Jane tried to save little Henrietta but Henrietta clung to her in terror and dragged Jane down.

Alone on the beach with Katie and unable to see either Jane or Henrietta, Miola ran to find Henry Field who was working close by. They returned to see Henrietta's corpse floating by the river bank but no sign of Jane. All hands were mustered to drag the river and finally it gave up Jane's body.[3] Clever, pretty little Jane had been the apple of her father's eye and he never forgot her. Katie, the second daughter, suddenly became the eldest but always felt that her sisters' deaths were her fault; had Miola not saved her she could have saved them instead.

In 1871 Sophy Field learned she was pregnant with her eighth child. As she was now in her mid-forties, doctors feared the birth could have complications. At this time Katie's two elder brothers were at school in Adelaide and perhaps the family decided it was time to rest from running a property. Henry Field left Marra Station in the hands of his brother-in-law and took a six-year lease on a house called The Lodge in Adelaide.

In the 1870s birthing practices were hazardous and maternal mortality rates very high. Katie took over the running of the house while her mother was in labour. After giving birth to a son named Edward on 11 April 1872, Sophy became weaker with puerperal (childbed) fever. As her temperature soared it became apparent the doctors could not save her and she died an agonising death.

Katie turned sixteen three days later. She was then in her final year at Miss Senner's School for Young Ladies in Palm Place (later part of St Peter's College, Adelaide, which her brothers had attended). She engaged a housekeeper to run the house and a nanny for Edward and, after they came out of a period of mourning, acted as hostess for her father.

Following Sophy Field's death, Katie's father decided to leave The Lodge and move to Glenelg. Although she wrote nothing down about their introduction, perhaps it was at one of her father's functions that she met tall, broad-shouldered Langloh Parker, a dashing grazier just as successful as her adored father. Langloh Parker was much older than herself, with the confidence and charisma of a successful man who has travelled the world. In fact, he was in many respects very similar to Henry Field. Both were tall, athletic, distinguished-looking men, and their careers had followed the same path in the wool boom. Both had gambled by borrowing large sums from the banks to buy stock — gambles which, due to seasons of good rainfall, had paid off handsomely with large wool cheques and stations sold for profits.

Katie, by now a very attractive young woman, seemed far more mature than her sixteen years. She knew her father was thinking of remarrying — to Mary Servante, a woman in her early forties, whom they both felt would make an excellent mother for baby Edward. Henry Field did not object when Langloh Parker, twice Katie's age, started sending flowers and paying his respects to Katie.

The highly eligible Langloh Parker was reckoned to be an extremely 'good catch'. A brilliant horseman, winner of many amateur steeplechases, he was charming, considerate and believed to be very rich. Langloh seemed fascinated by Katie. They went out riding together, suitably chaperoned, as Katie loved horses and riding as much as Langloh did. Katie was flattered by Langloh's attentions, enjoyed his company, and was the envy of her former classmates when she accepted a proposal of marriage from this charismatic, handsome, urbane man who had resisted marriage for so long. In her journal written later in life, Katie claimed Langloh had virtually 'plucked her from the schoolroom'. Today psychologists might deduce that Katie was marrying a father substitute.

Katie Field and Langloh Parker were married on 12 January 1875 at St Peter's Anglican Church, Glenelg, then a small fishing village. The bride was eighteen and the groom was thirty-five. She was taken everywhere by her proud husband, keen to show off his attractive, amusing young wife to friends and relations at balls and parties. They made a handsome couple. Langloh's investments were doing well and Katie was deeply in love. Since she was a superb rider, happiest on horseback, Katie was pleased to accompany her husband on brief trips to the outback, but the couple spent most of their time in the city — in Adelaide, Melbourne and Sydney.

In 1879 Langloh was planning to take his wife on her first trip to Britain and Europe when his business partner, Colonel Ward, announced he wanted to sell out. He asked Langloh to buy him out of the properties they owned.

The banks were loath to lend Langloh any more money, so reluctantly he had to borrow at eight per cent interest from the tight-fisted cattle baron Jim Tyson, to take control of all his isolated grazing properties. The largest of Langloh's properties was Bangate Station situated north-west of Walgett on the New South Wales–Queensland border.

In those days few educated women were prepared to endure the isolation, hardships and deprivation of bush life, especially if they had young children. Langloh told Katie he would live on Bangate Station, 800 kilometres from Sydney, and run the other properties from there, and gave her the choice of staying in Sydney or braving the outback with him.

Katie could not bear the thought of staying in Sydney without her husband, and insisted she would accompany him. Langloh was delighted but warned her she would be surrounded by rough boundary riders, stockmen and drovers; it was an almost exclusively male world. Knowing of Sophy Field's death in childbirth, Langloh insisted that, since there was no doctor close to Bangate, if Katie became pregnant she must spend the period of her confinement in Sydney. He did not mince his words when he told Katie:

> The bushman, out and out, will be terrified of you, and
> will think I'm a blamed ass to take you out there . . .
> However he may object to your being there, he'll do his
> level best for you when you are there!'[4]

Langloh also warned Katie that, without the diversions of Sydney, she might be bored in the outback. Furthermore, she would be

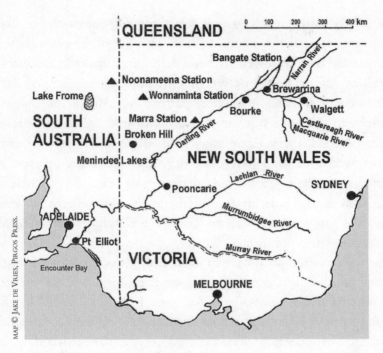

surrounded by hundreds of Aborigines. His words amazed Katie, who replied that she wasn't in the least afraid of Aborigines. She had played with Aboriginal children at Marra Station and been saved by an Aboriginal girl.

Katie told Langloh that while he was away she would spend her time riding and keeping a journal 'to remind me of things in my old age'.[5] In that journal Katie described lavish farewell parties and festivities to mark their departure. At one dinner given by Langloh's male friends she was presented with a pair of silver entree dishes — a token of their admiration that she had *chosen* to accompany her husband to the outback.

The vast Bangate sheep station was situated on the Narran River (Narran being a Yuwaalaraay word for 'winding'), a tributary of the upper Darling. The region had been explored by Sir Thomas Mitchell in 1846, who spotted its potential as sheep country. The Parkers' journey there was arduous and took almost a week by train, coach and buggy.

The journey started in Sydney. The Parkers went by narrow-gauge railway across Emu Plains and up the steep slopes of the Blue

Mountains, with the Nepean River lying far below them 'like a silvery carpet snake'.[6] Then came a bumpy, rattling journey by coach to Bourke, followed by several hundred more kilometres in the jolting station buggy drawn by four horses.

They stayed in bush inns whose patrons were 'in various stages of intoxication'.[7] Those not already dead drunk leered at her, and Langloh would hurry Katie away from them and into the private parlour which, more often than not, had a cracked mirror and armchairs draped in crocheted antimacassars stained with hair oil. Such bush inns, Katie dryly noted, nearly always boasted grand names like The Imperial or The Royal Hotel, whatever the socialist allegiances of the publican.

They ate dinners of greasy mutton and boiled potatoes followed by suet pudding, or jam roly-poly, or fried eggs and bacon from wild pigs. After one particularly vile meal, Langloh joked that when travelling through the outback you had to 'be prepared to eat a dead horse, and you generally are, so invigorating is the bush air'.[8]

Soon they were passing through black soil plains, which turned into sandy soil with grey-green saltbush and spinifex. Katie found the plains had a strange beauty of their own — with drooping, silvery-grey myall and coolibah trees bearing pink flowers hidden among their grey leaves under intensely blue skies. At first Katherine loved these skies. But the long years of drought which ate up their money meant that in time she would grow to hate them.

Beyond Lightning Ridge they passed through groves of casuarinas whose branches sang in the wind. It reminded Katie of the surging of the sea at beloved Glenelg, where her father had bought his house. Katie would later write that the Aborigines claimed the noise was the wailing of boys who had died before they could take part in initiation ceremonies designed to turn them into men.[9]

Bangate Station comprised 90,000 hectares of grazing land, some freehold and some leasehold, with a frontage of forty-seven kilometres along the winding Narran River, a tributary of the Darling, the river of Katie's bush childhood. The Narran flooded after rains and in drought seasons became a series of muddy waterholes. The sheep station itself resembled a small village with wooden huts and outbuildings, a station store, a saddlery and a blacksmith's shop.

The climate was a harsh one, varying from blazing heat in summer to freezing cold in winter. Katie's journal ignores the lack of sanitation and running water, nor does it mention the isolation. To Katie none of this mattered. When she arrived in 1879, she found Bangate delightful and spent her time riding with Langloh or on her own.

She soon discovered that the Aborigines who lived on Bangate and its surrounding lands were called the Noongahburrah, a branch of the Yuwaalaraay-speaking tribes whose hunting territories had stretched as far as Marra Station. Katie wrote of employing three part-Aboriginal girls as maids. One of them was an orphan whom Katie wanted to take under her wing, but she did not think it right for her to grow up alone at Bangate and was delighted when another Noongahburrah mother agreed to let Katie train her daughter to become a maid.

Katie Parker started what she called her 'bush book' long before Jeannie Gunn had published *We of the Never-Never*. In a strange co-incidence Katie wrote of Langloh by his Aboriginal name 'the Matah' ('senior man' in the Yuwaalaraay language) in the same way Jeannie called Aeneas Gunn, 'the Maluka', the term used by Yangman Aborigines. The Noongahburrah called Katherine 'the Innerah' (mistress), a term of respect.

Katie's writings show her determined to see the best side of outback life, and she wrote whole chapters about the beauty of the trees, wild flowers and birds. *Australian Legendary Tales* was published in 1896 by Mrs K. Langloh Parker, using her husband's name, just as Jeannie Gunn published as Mrs Aeneas Gunn. *My Bush Book* ends in 1901, the year Jeannie Gunn married and arrived at Elsey Station, and over a decade before the younger Myrtle White went to isolated Noonameena Station.

๛ ๛ ๛

Katie was not long at Bangate before she returned to town briefly and there had an accident. She did not tell much about this in her journal except to say that the fall broke one wrist and cracked a few ribs. She also suffered unspecified pelvic damage which would make it impossible for her to have children.

After her accident, horse riding, formerly Katie's passion, was beyond her and she was frequently in pain from bones that had been broken and not set very well. But as always, she was dogged and determined. When she returned to Bangate she set about developing new interests, in particular 'domestic skills'. Learning to cook became increasingly important, as a series of drunk, incompetent or worn-out cooks and 'married couples' came and went from the station.

Another blossoming skill was gardening. Fearing that she would be miserable and alone on the property, a city friend sent her a gardening encyclopaedia. With the aid of a series of either opinionated or incapable gardeners, Katie managed to produce fruit and vegetables deemed exotic at a time when most people in colonial Australia lived on cabbage and beans and scurvy was endemic in the outback.

She grew Jerusalem and globe artichokes, squash of various types, kohlrabi, salsify, okra, endive, eggplants, chillies, capsicums and sweet potatoes. In summer, there were watermelons and rockmelons, passionfruit, mulberries, grapes, figs and oranges; and mandarins in winter. She also grew pomegranates on learning that the rind was excellent for summer dysentery, or Barcoo fever, as it was known. Apple trees, however, resolutely refused to fruit in spite of all her efforts.

Katie's gardens had to withstand not only the vagaries of uncertain weather, but of human nature as well. The employment of one pigtailed Chinese gardener with psychiatric problems was terminated when he ran amok with a knife and nearly killed one of the Aboriginal house girls. Another gardener tore out all Katie's precious carnations and replaced them with cabbages while she was busy nursing a sick stockman. This made her so furious she refused to speak to him again and he soon also departed. In time, floods would mean the ruin of the precious flower gardens and vegetable beds Katie had worked so hard to establish.

Bangate Station.

Katie's accident meant that she could no longer participate in the musters that she had enjoyed when she first came to Bangate. But there were other sides of pastoral life that she voluntarily avoided. 'I get no amusement out of sheep,' she wrote in her journal. 'Shearing can be cruel, and smelly it certainly is.'[10]

The outback life still brought her pleasure. She took an interest in the native plants around her, troubling to learn the botanical names of many, and she was a keen observer of the bird life at Bangate. In the summer, she was careful to leave out dishes of water and birdseed on the verandas for the birds. She had a horror of birds kept in cages and wanted to see them free and happy. She fed oatmeal to the ring-necked doves and the butcher birds, and the top-knot pigeons, with their neat little heads, pink toes and pink flush on each side of their plump breasts. She watched entranced as birds came to splash in the water dishes — cheeky yellow-headed mynahs and raucous kookaburras. She even had a pet black swan she named Diogenes, which swam in a tub and which she thought something of a philosopher. Diogenes had been brought to her by a Noongahburrah man when it was wounded and became so tame it ate from her hand.

๕ ๕ ๕

With a good complement of staff and no children to occupy her, Katie was able to spend time listening and learning from the Noongahburrah. She described the Noongahburrah as:

> a very fine tribe both as to physique and intelligence . . .
> plenty of fish in their creek, plenty of game — kangaroo,
> bustards, emu, duck . . . and in good seasons, quantities
> of grain from luxuriant grasses on their creek banks . . .
> abundant eggs of swans, emu, duck, water hens . . . and
> native fruits.[11]

Like her contemporary Daisy Bates, who also observed Aborigines at first hand and wrote about them, Katie Parker started off by learning some of the Yuwaalaraay language in order to compile vocabularies of the commonly used words of the Noongahburrah.

She found the Noongahburrah women fascinating. She respected their complex law system and their tribal government by elders, and was always very polite to them. In return they respected her. As she gained their trust, the women and the elders of the tribe went on walks with her to show her places and objects that were sacred to them — things they would not have revealed to any other European, male or female.

At various times the women and the elders gave her painted digging sticks, *nulla nullas* or war clubs, throwing boomerangs and incised shields painted with ochres and pipeclay. She used these as decoration on the wooden walls of the long verandas.

On one occasion she was presented with a *nulla nulla* by one Aboriginal woman for the express purpose of murdering 'the mortgagor' (presumably James Tyson). The woman had heard how if the mortgagor foreclosed, the Parkers would be forced to leave. When Tyson visited the property, the woman called Katie away from a conversation with him and pushed the *nulla nulla* onto her to 'gib him one crack longa head'. The woman reassured Katie it had 'bin kill plenty black peller'. Katie was further touched that the woman was prepared to do the deed herself if Katie was too squeamish, and to face the magistrate, to whom she would explain that the man was taking things that 'belongin' my Missus'.[12]

In addition to speaking their language, Katie took great interest in Aboriginal myths and legends, at a time when few Australians were interested and most thought the Aborigines would soon die out.

Using various Aboriginal friends as interpreters to help her with Yuwaalaraay words she did not know, Katie wrote down their stories in her notebooks, translating as literally as possible to retain the Noongahburrah view. She would often invert an object and verb, just as is done in Yuwaalaraay, giving her sentences a curious flow, but otherwise she wrote in clear English which made the books she would publish popular with readers.[13]

She described how:

> During the eleven years which I practically devoted to
> the study of their folklore . . . [they revealed] how all
> their natural world is divided into totemic families . . . I
> shall never forget my rambles through the Bush with a
> retinue of natives. I learnt that every distinctive bit of
> nature — say, a heap of white stones, the red mistletoe,
> the gnarled dark excrescences on the trees . . . each had its
> legend.[14]

Katie also tried to help the Aboriginal children with the eye afflictions they so often suffered. On her arrival at Bangate, she had been distressed to find:

> . . . every second person seemed to have sore eyes . . . I
> seemed to be always issuing eye lotion according to a
> prescription given me by an old squatter doctor in
> Melbourne . . . [Some] had swelling blight — 'bungey
> eye', colloquially called — from a fly sting which the
> blacks used to cure by pressing on hot budtha twigs and
> the whites with the blue-bag.[15]

She taught the Noongahburrah children to bathe the affected eye with salt water and made her staff do the same whenever their eyes became infected. She was also careful to wash her own eyes frequently and in this way avoided getting ophthalmia.

Now that she was living in the outback, Katie bitterly regretted she had no nursing experience. She wrote how among her 'amateur ministrations' were:

> attending to the fleshy part of a hand nearly blown off by
> a bursting gun. The flesh had to be cleaned, disinfected
> and patched up. Then a broken arm had to be set . . . a
> baby to be helped into the world prematurely owing to a
> buggy accident . . . a man practically drowned swimming
> in the river in floodtime, to be resuscitated.[16]

To their many visitors who called socially, or the bush folk who came looking for assistance, Katie and Langloh Parker appeared wealthy and successful. They had a vast property, a handsome homestead, Aboriginal maids in uniform, and the services of cooks, gardeners and married couples to help them.

Like many bush people of the era, whenever the Parkers entertained they did so lavishly. Guests arrived from all over and were housed in the huge homestead. There were dancing and amateur theatricals with programs designed by Katie. These were the golden days of Bangate and photograph albums recorded the fun — musical evenings with Katie and other guests playing the piano, sing-songs, and amateur theatricals on the veranda. To amuse the guests on one occasion she organised a competition to see which man could make the tastiest damper and the ladies acted as judges.

But the drought was taking its toll. Lack of rain was turning the land into a fissured mass of red dust. Normally an excellent source of water, the river was drying up until it consisted of a chain of muddy waterholes in which scrawny half-starved sheep and cattle bogged down and had to be dug out before they died of thirst or starvation.

By 1887 after a number of bad seasons the Parkers were struggling financially. Although the district had seen improvements, such as the new bridge across the Narran River, some of the infrastructure had cost landowners dearly. The rabbit-proof fence Langloh had been forced to erect cost 'enough to buy a snug freehold in more civilised parts', mused Katie.[17] As the expenses mounted, Langloh, already in debt to James Tyson for the original purchase, sought to take out a second mortgage from Dalgety and Company. Dalgety's sent an inspector to write a report on the situation at Bangate. He found Langloh Parker was running it well but needed still more water tanks. Langloh had already built five large tanks, but this was considered inadequate for a station carrying 96,000 sheep and 4600 head of cattle. And by the next year the number of sheep had risen to 138,000.[18]

Despite their financial difficulties, the Parkers continued to help their less well-off neighbours. Katie described one dreadful day in the relentless heat when she was putting up a neighbour and her two children. One of the children developed a raging fever, which no amount of bathing or fanning could cool. Used to the deaths of so many children in the bush, Katie and the mother agonised over whether to incur great expense and have the possibly drunk doctor called for or take the feverish child into town. Katie observed that they were almost as poor as their neighbours, but she nevertheless consulted Langloh.

'Poor little devil. Doctor of course,' declared Langloh. 'What's a few more pounds to an overdraft?' So he rode off in the morning and brought the doctor back late in the afternoon. Thankfully the child recovered but that wasn't always the case. Just a few weeks before, a woman had appeared at the homestead looking for a place to bury her treasured daughter who had suddenly died. Reluctant to bury her 'among the deadbeats' in the cemetery alongside the pub, she had noticed the well cared-for graveyard at Bangate where her little Janie might be given 'a thought now and agen', as the woman and her husband made their way about the outback looking for work. The Parkers let them bury their child at Bangate.[19]

The drought continued over seven long years, and it proved impossible for the Parkers to meet the mortgage repayments. In 1890, in spite of Langloh Parker's hard work and Katie's stringent economies, most of their sheep and cattle had died and Tyson foreclosed on his mortgage. Dalgety's repossessed the property, keeping Langloh on as manager. It was dispiriting and a great financial loss, but the Parkers still had a small nearby property, Grawin South, to call their own.

OFF TO THE SANDHILLS

In many respects Myrtle Kennewell had a happier childhood than Katie Parker, although she had no loving nursemaid and no loving grandmother to encourage her studies.

Myrtle was raised amid the rough and tumble of a large family of ten siblings in the Barossa Valley. This meant money was always short in the Kennewell household, although there was always plenty of love and laughter. As the eldest, Myrtle had to become the practical daughter who cared for younger siblings.

By the age of sixteen the family had moved to Williamstown, near Adelaide. Myrtle left school and was sent away to help her Aunt Elizabeth who owned the Packsaddle Hotel, north-west of the Darling River. Here she would meet the man she would marry and follow to the outback.

Cornelius White was a muscular, good-looking but shy young man of whom her aunt spoke highly.

Con White had left his parents' home near the Murray River at age eleven to go and live with a guardian at the local

COURTESY AUSTRALIAN NATIONAL LIBRARY.

Myrtle Rose White as a young girl.

Mechanics Institute. At fourteen he felt the call to adventure too strong to ignore, and he left the security of town and the labour of school books for a life in the open air. He headed towards Queensland and soon found work droving cattle. He loved outback life and was offered a job as a stockman and then some years later promoted to manager of a large cattle station, something very unusual for a young man still in his early twenties.[20]

Used to spending most of his time in the company of men, Con was shy and awkward with women, had no gift for small talk and few social skills. However, he found warm-hearted Myrtle, with her relaxed sense of humour, easy to talk to. Con was no drinker but started haunting the Packsaddle Hotel hoping he might get a chance to talk to the owner's pretty niece. Myrtle found him attractive and the two of them took long walks together in the afternoons when she was free.

The friendship blossomed. Soon Con confided to Myrtle that his ambition was to own a cattle property, but obtaining the necessary capital was a problem. Myrtle reminded him how Sir Sidney Kidman had started out with only a few shillings and had become Australia's wealthiest pastoralist.

The year was 1906, only five years after Federation, Australia was still a pioneering society and cattlemen were the aristocracy of the bush. But those who worked the land hardly lived like lords. There were few of the tinned food products that enliven meals in the outback today, and none of the frozen products available today. Before refrigeration the diet was limited; fruit and vegetables withered in the heat. Most bushmen lived off corned beef, damper with treacle and black tea, their only vegetable being 'fat hen' or wild pigweed.

When Myrtle left Packsaddle to return to her family, Con returned to droving, writing to her when he could. When Myrtle did not receive her weekly letter she worried that Con might have had a riding accident and so wrote to her aunt at Packsaddle asking for news. She was distressed to learn that Con had collapsed with pain to his heart and been sent to hospital. Doctors had warned him that he must eat a more balanced diet or he would die of heart disease.

Myrtle decided to take a job as a domestic servant at a nearby property, and and went about seeing (as far as she could) that Con ate a healthy diet and recovered. Since there was no dole or sickness benefit, Con had to return to work as soon as possible. He had always loved horses and managed to find a job driving a horse-drawn cab. He worked hard, saved up, bought his own horse and carriage and was granted a cab driver's licence.

Con wanted to have money in the bank before he asked Myrtle to marry him. Although he owned very little apart from his horse and carriage, he promised Myrtle that as soon as he was well enough he would go back on the land as a cattle station manager and earn a good salary. They could live in the manager's house, save hard and fulfil his dream of buying a property.

For Myrtle money did not matter. They could get married and she would continue to work as a cook. She urged Con to take things slowly, aware that his health would take some time to recover fully before they could return to the outback.

On 19 October 1910 Miss Myrtle Kennewell and Mr Cornelius White were married quietly at St Peter's Church, Broken Hill. Con continued to work as a cabbie. A year after they married Myrtle gave birth to a little girl whom they named Doris.

Con applied for several station manager's jobs without success, and in 1914, when Australia went to war, volunteered for army service. When he was examined by an army doctor he was rejected on health grounds, which upset him badly.

Con's knowledge of beef cattle was profound and he had a reputation as a very hard worker. In time he received an offer of a station manager's job. His prospective employer was a man Con had worked with years ago and whom Myrtle referred to in her memoirs as JDD.

Con and Myrtle talked things over. Noonameena (Lake Elder Station) in South Australia[21] was in a very remote area but the job was a highly responsible one. Having been offered the inducement of free bores by the Government of South Australia, JDD had taken out pastoral leases on seven vast cattle runs in the north-east of the state, near the Broken Hill region where Myrtle had nearly died at birth. Con accepted JDD's offer, sold his horse-drawn cab and in 1915 he, Myrtle and little Doris prepared for the move to sandhill country. The whole area was a virtual desert of sandy plains and dunes. In summer, temperatures hovered around 50 to 60 degrees Celsius. One of Australia's driest and harshest places, the annual rainfall was less than 100 millimetres per year. Few Europeans had ever lived there. In fact, it was so dry Myrtle noted that Aborigines rarely roamed in the area. Previously it had been impossible to raise any cattle or crops at all. Only the deep, government-funded bores made the area viable for farming.

In effect, Con, now the manager of seven remote cattle runs, had become part of an ill-fated experimental project to raise beef cattle in sandhill country. In wartime, fired by patriotism, Con saw this as an important job with the added benefit of a free house for the manager. Besides, getting the job was a boost to his ego. He regarded it as an exciting challenge.

By now Australian troops were fighting at Gallipoli and in northern France. To feed the army vast quantities of corned beef were needed. The Whites planned to work hard, live frugally, save money and reckoned that their savings would mean that once the war was over they could buy and stock a cattle run of their own. Although Myrtle was reluctant to leave the city with all its diversions, for Con's sake she was prepared to 'give it a go'.

Con left for Noonameena before Myrtle to inspect all the cattle properties, meet his jackaroos and stockmen and make the living quarters as comfortable as possible. They had made plans for Myrtle and Doris to travel to an old homestead at the outstation called Mirrabooka until a proper homestead could be built. 'I'll be in fairly often, and JDD tells me there is a very capable couple at Mirrabooka,' Con promised.[22]

Broken Hill would be their nearest town. A bitumen road from Broken Hill to Mirrabooka, where goods were stored, petered out before Mirrabooka and was replaced by sand.

Myrtle learned that Noonameena was regularly reached by camel track through eighty kilometres of sandhills. All goods and foodstuffs arrived at the homestead by camel train. Indeed, camels would become Myrtle's lifeline. Although it was 1915, there was no telephone and Myrtle would spend years without access to a phone or radio.

Six weeks after Con departed, Myrtle and four-year-old Doris bundled into JDD's big open-topped touring car for a day-long journey to Mirrabooka. What she saw as they drove along were acres of reddish sand blown into furrowed patterns by the wind, contrasting with the deep blue of the sky. Towards the end of the day, the car became stuck in sand, still a few kilometres short of Mirrabooka. Seemingly undaunted JDD jumped out of the car to begin the march on foot to the station. Tired and disappointed, there was nothing Myrtle or Doris could do but follow. Stumbling through sand they reached a lake which had formed after rains: another delay as they detoured around it. With shins bruised and skin torn the trio finally reached the four-roomed cottage in the dark.

They were met by Mrs Smithers, a surly, elderly housekeeper who clearly disliked having another woman around. The 'Boss' was out on the property and not expected back for a week. The grumpy housekeeper provided them with something to eat and Myrtle retired to a sleepless night.

The next morning as JDD was leaving, he informed Myrtle that the housekeeper and her husband had handed in their notice and would be off in a fortnight. Myrtle would be alone in the house with only a young child for company, surrounded by 12,000 square kilometres of sand and silvery-grey mulga. There was no inside toilet, only a large latrine pit to the rear of the homestead surrounded by a few flapping bits of hessian. The bathroom, which Myrtle conceded was a modern affair, was blocked off with a door only about a metre tall. There was no refrigerator or cool cellar. All butter, milk and meat had to be kept cool in a hessian-lined Koolgardie safe. Mail was collected by camel once a fortnight. There was no telephone and as far as Myrtle knew no other woman living within miles.

However, to Myrtle's surprise, a man arrived that morning looking for the housekeeper to attend his wife who had gone into labour two months early. Declaring she could not possibly go, Mrs Smithers ordered Myrtle to attend. Myrtle remembered back to Doris's difficult birth. The doctors had given Doris one chance in a thousand of surviving. What chance would this woman have with only inexperienced Myrtle attending the birth?

It was a tense journey back to the man's home as he wondered how his wife was faring and regretted the fact that he had missed JDD and his car by only two hours. When they finally arrived they

The Noonameena homestead under construction.

were met by the man's three terrified children. Myrtle felt justifiably nervous. She entered the house and found her patient. When she met the woman's relieved eyes, all fear disappeared and she set to with commonsense. It was a long night, and in the end the baby died. But the mother survived. From the moment she had known another woman would be there to help, the mother had seemed to rally.

Myrtle and Doris stayed with the woman for two weeks after the birth and came to appreciate all the personal touches the woman had made to her humble earthen-floored shack in the outback. Whatever was to hand had been converted into something charming and useful — packing cases into gaily covered furniture, goat-skins tanned by the woman herself into floor covers, and everywhere flowers brought in by the children. Myrtle felt ashamed that she had had any reservations about her own more comfortable home.

She returned to Mirrabooka to take up her duties running the house somewhat buoyed by the experience. Once Mrs Smithers and her husband left, she decided to take on the job of cooking for fourteen men herself. With Con often away and the men quartered in their own area, it was a lonely life, but Myrtle thought of the determination and fortitude of the 'Little Mother' she had stayed with and cheered herself up.

Con and the men spent much of their time working the cattle at the main run at Noonameena and building a new homestead there. On one occasion Myrtle accompanied JDD on a trip with cattle-buyers out to Noonameena. The sand was so soft that JDD's custom-built touring car sometimes sank up to its axles in sand but having been fitted with special large tyres it managed the trip. Myrtle faced almost perpendicular descents down the sandhills with her heart in her throat.

She was horrified by her first sight of Noonameena. Its vastness and the inaccessibility of its 'treeless waste' disturbed her.[23] But the work on her new home was well under way, and a few months later the house was ready enough to move into.

Myrtle, who loathed sand, was now surrounded by acres and acres of the stuff. Sandstorms were frequent. For days on end red sand, fine as dust, hung in the air, making them all cough and splutter. Day after day the wind blew clouds of sand over everything — food, furniture, curtains, bed linen, books. On waking in the morning the only clean place in the whole house would be where they had lain their heads on the pillows. Myrtle hated it but was determined to stick it out, for Con's sake.

She described the red soil as 'stretching away and away and away'. The view was always the same — red sandhills with patches of greenish-grey mulga and occasional splashes of a more vivid shade of green from bullock bushes which provided fodder for the cattle, the leopard trees with their mottled grey trunks, and the greenish-grey saltbush.[24] The area had its own wild beauty but, used to the lush green of the Barossa Valley where she had grown up, Myrtle found the aridity depressing.

Their bore water tasted disgusting, so finding unsalted drinking water, as well as fresh and nutritious food, was a constant problem. Housekeeping was exhausting in the torrid heat. Hot water had to be run off each morning from the taps so that the water supply would be cool enough to drink later. Myrtle had 'an endless job' filling earthenware coolers with water and, on the rare occasions when they had some, with milk.

Myrtle craved fresh vegetables but whenever she ordered a case from the station agent, they were withered or rotten by the time they arrived.

Replacing household items was also a problem. Even a lost pair of scissors could be a disaster with no possibility of buying another unless an Afghan pedlar arrived with a camel train.

Once it was finished, Noonameena homestead was more comfortable than Mirrabooka. It had cement floors, a dining room, office, pantry, guest-rooms, bathroom and separate men's quarters and kitchen. A flour store was built up on piles to allow circulation and other stores were kept in a large underground cellar. Myrtle ordered carpets, wallpaper and curtains. Once the materials arrived by camel train and the wicker baskets and bales were unloaded, she got busy, sewed curtains and papered over large cracks in the plastering. To create an illusion of coolness, she ordered a moss green carpet for the bedroom. She had chosen curtains patterned with roses, the sort of tea roses her mother had grown at home in the Barossa, determined their bedroom would be a refuge from the sandhills and mulga that surrounded them.

As unpaid store manager, her job was to place bulk orders for everything needed to feed and clothe the men. She did the orders twice a year. Supplies came out from the agent at Broken Hill by bullock dray or by camel and took over a week to arrive.

The station relied on its own supply of meat. They killed a beast or two each month and lived on fresh beef for two days and salt beef

A camel team would bring supplies to Noonameena from Broken Hill.

for the next twenty-nine. In the fierce heat, with no refrigeration or ice house, keeping things fresh was a nightmare. As Myrtle wrote, 'Butter was a hope of the future and a thing of the past.'[25] It was too hot even for jellies to set.

Still craving fresh green salads and juicy tomatoes, fresh apples or peaches, Myrtle tried growing them. But, no matter how hard they tried, vegetables and fruit proved impossible to grow, watered only by the salty bore water. To prevent scurvy Myrtle dosed them all with cod liver oil and lime juice if she could get it.

When the Whites arrived at Noonameena they were true European pioneers, farming country that had never been fenced or farmed before. JDD had been attracted to take the land up by the sinking of bores but also the nutritious grasses that grew after the rains. But the rains had stopped just as he took possession and, by the time the Whites settled in, there were only a few drops falling each month.

In a good season, Noonameena and its outstations could carry about 5000 head of beef cattle. But over the seven years the Whites stayed, the land degraded considerably. The hoofs of so many thousands of cattle caused the sand to 'dreft' around the waterholes, cutting the natural 'skin' of the land's surface. When finally the drought ended and it rained, mobs of cattle would bog down in quicksands that developed around the waterholes.[26]

Little Doris thrived in the harsh surroundings. She was thrilled with the beloved pony she acquired, as well as a cattle dog pup she named Bluey and from whom she was inseparable. A tomboy, Doris loved the freedom of outback life. Mounted on her pony she seemed fearless and the station hands taught the little girl to crack a stock whip and round up cattle. By the time she turned eight, Doris was out mustering cattle with the station hands.

Riding around on her pony one day Doris found a human skeleton, which Myrtle presumed was that of an Aborigine. Myrtle rarely encountered tribal Aborigines in the area; presumably even they considered food too hard to find in this arid wilderness.

A year later Doris found more skeletons. She rode out with Con to see them and he reckoned they were of two stockmen who had died of thirst in the sandhills. They had, it seemed, been taking a short cut across country and had lost their way. With only one water bag between them, it appeared they had died a slow and miserable death.

Doris was a healthy active child, and did not seem to mind that she had no playmates of her own age. With the help of textbooks sent out by camel train from a library at Broken Hill, Myrtle did her best to educate Doris. She read the books with her daughter who proved to be a quick learner.

≈ ≈ ≈

Even though Myrtle and Doris had now settled into the Noonameena homestead, Myrtle saw little of Con. His duties ranged from as far afield as the Lake Frome basin to Milparinka in the north-west of New South Wales. As well as the stock, Con had to manage a large number of men. Some of the stockmen were reliable, others drunkards and troublemakers. Con had to deal with fist fights and accidents in which stockmen were gored or fell off their horses and broke arms and legs.

In the days before refrigeration, butter and milk were cooled in a Koolgardie safe. Water dripped down hessian or cloth into a tray.

Whenever she could, Doris tagged along with the men so Myrtle sought refuge in the mundane routine of housekeeping — Monday washing day; Tuesday ironing with flat irons heated on the stove which had to be stoked with firewood; Wednesday sewing and mending; Thursday baking; and Friday 'turning out' rooms, moving the furniture, sweeping and polishing.

Not only was the heat stifling in summer but the mosquitoes were voracious. There were no flyscreens, only citronella to keep the pesky creatures at bay. When the family tried sleeping out in the front garden believing it would be cooler, they were kept awake by not only the droning mosquitoes but the howling of dingoes.

But the wind and sand were Myrtle's firm enemies. She described the silence that heralded the coming of a cyclonic storm. The wind would drop and then the fierce storm would sweep through the depressions between the sandhills, the house taking the full brunt of the clouds of stinging, whirling sand:

> Timber creaks and strains, roof-iron begins to lift and flap, and widow-sashes rattle and shake . . . Meanwhile, the dust thickens and deepens . . . until one stifles and feels that all hope is lost . . . If you can take it with a Christian spirit, thankfully, uncomplainingly, you are the salt of the earth. Personally I never could.[27]

As at Katie Parker's Bangate, domestic staff came and went. Some of the married couples were unsatisfactory; some drank to excess; one couple deliberately scorched Doris's best dress out of spite. In fact, most of the domestic staff Myrtle employed to help her cook for the station hands proved more trouble than they were worth,

COURTESY REDLANDS SHIRE MUSEUM, QUEENSLAND.
PHOTO © JAKE DE VRIES, PIRGOS PRESS

A wood-burning stove (with no temperature controls) of a type popular just before World War I.

and Myrtle would frequently take on cooking for the men herself, as she had done at Mirrabooka.

During her first year at Noonameena, Myrtle became pregnant again. Having no telephone and no doctor to call anyway, it was necessary to go to the city to give birth. On the appointed day the skies opened with rain so the journey had to be delayed. For two more days they waited until the skies cleared. Con, Myrtle, Doris and a maid set out in the station buggy. They made good progress to begin with and eventually changed horses, sending the old team that had pulled the buggy back with a stockman. But not much further on the first of a series of problems arose. The reins of the leading horse became unbuckled and slipped from Con's hands. Without his guidance, the lead horse began to turn in ever decreasing circles, until it seemed certain the pole yoked between horse and buggy would break. Myrtle was ever grateful that it held, as Con jumped down and placated the leader. It would have been a forlorn place to have been stranded.

Back on track, they soon reached what had previously been a dry lake they would have crossed comfortably. Now it was a stretch of oozing mud. They had no alternative but to go round it.

To help ease the load for the poor horses struggling along the heavy ground at the lake's edge, Myrtle, Doris and the maid climbed down and walked. Eventually the horses were too tired to move. They rested a bit and set off again. The next hitch was a thunderstorm which wet them through and turned their route into another lake. They continued on painfully slowly, and just before darkness met up with the change of horses Con had arranged to come from a depot.

But luck was against them again. The horses were changed, and as they proceeded the new leader seemed to go forward erratically. Con realised the horse had a form of sandy blight or blindness. The poor old previous leader had to be harnessed up again.

Late that night, six kilometres short of their destination, they finally stopped when the horses sank deep into some soggy ground and the pole that had held out so splendidly before broke. There was nothing for it but to make camp. A boy accompanying them was sent off to get a tent and blankets from the depot.

And so pregnant Myrtle cooked a meal on the camp fire, boiled the billy and settled down for a night on branches cut from buck bushes. A new buggy arrived the next day with fresh horses and they reached the place where a car was expected to take Myrtle on to Adelaide for the birth of her second child.

Hardly were they out of the buggy than a cyclone hit the town and they had to wait three days for it to blow over. In the meantime the car still had not arrived, so the party set out again in the buggy. Finally, after another two days on the road, they met the car.

In comparison with the awful journey, the birth was uneventful. Proud Myrtle returned to Noonameena with a five-week-old baby boy whom they named Alan. He was chubby and good-natured with cornflower-blue eyes and Myrtle adored him. She also took back with her a young girl of seventeen to help with Doris and Alan and decided to have the stock and station agent look for another married couple. The prospect of caring for her family, as well as cooking for the men without the labour-saving devices we now take for granted, was daunting.

The couple located by the agents arrived. They claimed they had been in service with Dame Nellie Melba at her home in Victoria, luxurious Coombe Cottage, not really a cottage but a mansion, surrounded by green lawns and a swimming pool. The wife took one look at the red sand around Noonameena and in the house and decided she'd been totally misled. She told Myrtle that when she had been employed by Madame Melba, all she had had to do was to cook vegetables and wash up — light cleaning duties only!

The couple also had a child, who unfortunately arrived with a raging temperature. Whatever the illness was, everyone at the station came down with it except baby Alan and Myrtle. Their start was not a good one. Instead of getting help, Myrtle now had three extra people to cook for. They had come so far there was nothing for it but to give the couple a try. Myrtle may have wished she sent them packing in view of what happened next. Hoping to cash in on the bounty for dingo hides, inexperienced Cecil the husband laid baits around the wood heap without tying the dogs up. Poor Bluey, Doris's beloved dog, was killed along with all the other station dogs.

Next Myrtle employed two single girls, in the vain hope they would be company for each other. Unfortunately the two girls loathed each other. Bertha, the elder, was a hard worker but had a sharp tongue. Ruth was an unstable girl who was teased unmercifully by Bertha over her fondness for a good-looking station hand.

One morning Bertha taunted her colleague, saying that one of the station hands had boasted to his co-workers that he had had sex with Ruth. Ruth turned white and then red with rage. As luck would have it, when Ruth was in the boning room cutting up the meat for the next meal, in walked that particular station hand for his breakfast. Enraged to think that he had been discussing her like that, Ruth picked up the boning knife and slashed the handsome stockman across the face. The knife was razor sharp, and almost removed the man's nose and carved a deep gash in his chin.

The injured man was brought to Myrtle, bleeding copiously. She did her best for him but had no anaesthetic or morphine to ease the pain. Ruth departed on the next mail run from the station, along with Bertha.

Although she provided first aid to injured stockmen, Myrtle found it hard when her children had accidents. She could not bring herself to insert a needle and stitch up her beloved daughter when she fell and gashed her neck on the metal roof of the homestead's cellar. She took a deep breath and disinfected Doris's wound. She held both sides of the wound together by applying sticking plaster, and prayed it would heal without becoming infected. Eventually Doris's wound did heal but forever after her shoulder had a long red scar.

❧ ❧ ❧

The addition of 'Miss Seventeen' (as Myrtle called her), the girl who returned to Noonameena with Myrtle after Alan's birth, livened things up for the stockmen. Miss Seventeen played the young men off against each other but seemed to prefer one station hand above the rest. Tim was a tall, bronzed, broad-shouldered young man with deep blue eyes, and the two of them spent their evenings on long walks amid the sandhills. It seemed wedding bells were in the air. Then suddenly Miss Seventeen seemed to lose interest in him.

Fortunately for Tim a new housemaid arrived. Myrtle called her 'Miss Dimple' because she was all smiles, sweeping lashes and long blonde hair. Before long, Tim and Miss Dimple were spending a lot of time together. Both of them asked to take leave at the same time and when they returned Tim started to fix up a tent which he pitched behind the homestead. Miss Dimple demurely sewed cushion covers and bedspreads. Eventually their secret leaked out. They had been married by special licence and would only be staying at Noonameena for another six months, as they were saving hard to buy a place of their own. To Myrtle it seemed that the only permanent residents of Noonameena were the White family.

❧ ❧ ❧

While Doris had been a relatively easy baby, Alan seemed to have a constant problem with his tonsils or stomach. On one occasion he went into convulsions, his tiny body alternately rigid or gyrating in spasms. For days Myrtle kept sponging and fanning him in an effort to bring his temperature down. It was too hot to take a feverish baby on the many days' journey to a doctor.

To make it worse she had influenza herself and was shivering and shaking with fever. She was also pregnant again. Alan's convulsions grew worse and worse and Myrtle feared her baby son would die. Little Miss Seventeen was so terrified that she fainted — which was not much help to Myrtle. For days Alan suffered in a feverish state. Finally a cooler change came through and Myrtle decided to embark on the long trip by car over sandhills and risk a rise to searing heat to reach the nearest doctor.

Con and Myrtle had spent some of their savings on a Ford car they named Henrietta, which Myrtle described as 'a 1914 buckboard, hoodless and comfortless.'[28] Once they had a car, what they most needed was a road through to the depot. Helped by the station hands Con had bravely attempted to pack down a graded track through the dips in the sandhills. Despite the hard work the

Sandbogged cars in the sandhill country of north-eastern South Australia often had to be hauled out like this.

road was not very successful. Now, in desperation, Alan, Con and the very pregnant Myrtle set out in the car on the half-made road, accompanied by some station hands on horses for the first forty kilometres.

Then the worst happened: the Ford bogged down in soft sand. Four men tried to push and two horses tried to pull Henrietta out of the sand. They placed baulks of timber under the wheels. But the car was heavy, loaded up with a tuckerbox full of food and two days' supply of drinking water in metal canteens. It remained stuck fast.

The midday heat was terrible and little Alan suffered as the temperature soared. Myrtle was beside herself, as she tried to cool her baby boy. She sat under a mulga, desperate for shade from the blazing sun, fanning Alan's burning body with wet cloths. She watched as the men and horses slowly progressed, until they reached the last and biggest sandhill which blocked their path to the better stretches of road.

As Con revved the engine two of the horses panicked and fell. For a dreadful moment it looked as if their flailing hoofs might kill one of the stockmen. But the men kept calm and soothed the horses. Finally they were over the sandhill and safely on the other side.

All the while, Alan's temperature was so high Myrtle feared he would be dead by the time they reached a doctor. Still driving by evening, the party was held up again by a sandstorm. Finally they reached the depot where they spent the night. Next day after covering twenty kilometres, Henrietta became stuck in a creekbed. Pushing and pulling, they could not move the car. Myrtle knew that the only passing traffic on this road was the fortnightly mail lorry or an occasional private car.

'My son will die,' she thought as Alan's fever mounted. She cradled him on her lap in the shade of a big gum tree, the only shade around, and offered up a silent prayer for a lorry or car to pass by.

Her prayer was answered. The mail truck with sixteen passengers came into view. It stopped and took Myrtle and Alan in the cab. Poor Con had to walk back to the depot in terrible heat.

The trip still took Myrtle another fourteen hours and Alan was barely alive when they reached Broken Hill.[29] Declaring it a miracle that Alan had survived, the doctor warned Myrtle that he would most likely suffer convulsions again. He prescribed a long period of convalescence in a cooler climate. How on earth could she manage that? The doctor sat Myrtle down and suggested she rent a room in a private house by the sea until her third child was born.

Myrtle took his advice in part. After her baby was delivered, she set up a home in Broken Hill, where a doctor was on hand, as were other amenities of civilisation. Myrtle would always be convinced that her period of worry over Alan caused her third baby, Garry, to be a nervous and highly strung little boy. Suffering reflux, Garry was unable to keep food down, and a stressful and anxious time ensued for Myrtle. She stayed on in the city for nine months after Garry was born, but ironically began to think about safety in the sandhills again as the children came down with measles, whooping cough and chickenpox. Con was eager for Myrtle to return, and after hiring two new girls to help her back at Noonameena the family rejoined him.

ℓℓ ℓℓ ℓℓ

It was apparent to Myrtle that Con was wearing himself out, working seven days a week at the expense of his health and his family. By this time JDD had sold Noonameena (Lake Elder Station) to Sidney Kidman. Myrtle felt that Kidman's company was taking advantage of her husband's good nature and resented the fact that they underpaid and overworked him.

Operating a station on the desert fringes was tough. Even when the seasons were passable and the market good, Con was at the mercy of sometimes inexperienced stockmen to get the herds to market. As well as plagues of dingoes, there were rabbits.

The constant battle with sand continued. In 1920 a severe drought began to take its toll. When the main bore which watered the cattle silted up, pressure was placed on swamp waters. Diversions from the bore were not enough. Myrtle watched weakened cattle struggle to find water, pausing at the foot of sandhills with heads hanging waiting to gather strength, the crows hovering overhead then swooping down on sick and dying animals and pecking out their eyes. Soon hundreds of cattle were dead. The drought dragged on for a year, with heartbreaking promises of rain as clouds formed only to fade away.

When rain finally did come it surprised everyone. It rained in torrents, flooding the homestead at Noonameena to a depth of seven centimetres. With the flooding came scorpions, spiders, snakes and disease. The steamy heat and the flies gave the children Barcoo fever, making them vomit.

But the rain also brought life back to the sandhills. Around the bore, the flowers burst into colour — bluebells and wild geraniums blossomed and a convolvulus put out pink flowers. As the swamps refilled, the birdlife returned. The station seemed in as good a state as ever.

After seven years at Noonameena, Con decided it was the right time to leave. As if in answer to a prayer, the newly installed telephone tinkled with the offer of management of Mordern and Wonnaminta stations in far western New South Wales. But the Whites had to make their decision quickly — they would need to be there in three days' time.

After three frantic days packing, the family left Noonameena, driving Henrietta the Ford along behind a neighbour's borrowed Dodge tourer, hoping to reach Mordern, some 240 kilometres east as the crow flies, that day. Shortly before dusk the lights of the Ford fused, leaving them in darkness. They continued to drive on in the wake of the Dodge, guided only by the light fanning out beyond the car's black bulk.

Suddenly there was a crash and a jolt, as the Ford driven by Con slewed and rolled into a ditch. The others in the Dodge piled out to see what had happened. They were thankful Con was safe but dismayed to see the Ford damaged. By now the younger children were tired, hungry, cold and fretful.

The men decided to take the family on in the Dodge to a bush pub on the Tibooburra mail road, only a few kilometres away. Con would spend the night by the wreck and be on the job at daylight and save precious time.

Arriving at the pub, they settled in but not for long, as the jolting and extreme fatigue had brought on one of Alan's gastric attacks. The castor oil bottle, Myrtle's 'trusty friend', which usually helped settle Alan's stomach, was in the stranded Ford. The night was a terrible one. No one slept.

By mid-afternoon they were off again and finally reached Wonnaminta. In bygone days Wonnaminta had employed between eighty and ninety men and three maids. Myrtle thought the collection of old buildings she confronted was more like a small village than a farm. The big old house now had a ghostly haunted feel, its rooms bare of furniture and the wallpaper peeling away in festoons.

However, it was to Mordern, another twenty kilometres away, they were heading so they pressed on. They reached Mordern homestead in darkness, tired and hungry. The house was chilly and damp, and Myrtle was appalled to find one main bedroom with only one bed to hold all five of the family. The manager Con was replacing lived at Mordern, helped by a married couple, but the housekeeper had not even lit a fire in welcome, let alone made the beds. Indeed, she proved so unwelcoming that a housemaid Myrtle had brought with her and come to rely on left within the first fortnight.

There was one improvement in Myrtle's new home and that was the presence of trees, but just as at Noonameena she saw Con only rarely, when he called in from some far corner of the properties. The married couple soon departed, having first raided the vegetable garden, and Myrtle took to cooking, cleaning and establishing a new garden. She grimly observed:

Domestic help remained a never-ending problem —
either because we didn't have it or because we did. One
short week in the bush was sufficient for the first cook
and housemaid we acquired. They came out on one mail
and departed homeward on the next, and I took up the
daily round again . . . I dreamed of a few days in bed as
one might dream of Paradise.[30]

Soon she became overtired and ill. The doctor at Wilcannia was
consulted by phone and prescribed two weeks in bed. Capable little
Doris had to take over as head cook, housekeeper and bottle washer
for twelve hungry people, as indeed she did the next time Myrtle
was sick and was forced to go to hospital.[31]

But there was little rest for Myrtle. She had been in hospital for
more than two weeks when she was finally able to hobble from her
bed to make a telephone call to Mordern. There, she discovered,
everyone but Doris had been confined to bed with flu. Immediately
she organised someone to take her home the next day.

ll ll ll

After three years at Mordern, the Whites were beginning to feel
unhappy. Promised rises in salary had not been honoured and the
dream of owning their own land was fading. Con decided to make
the break with Kidman's company, and announced it just as Kidman
was touring his properties in the area. Kidman was not about to let
such a hard worker go, and made more promises of money. Much
to Myrtle's regret Con changed his mind.

Kidman also suggested Myrtle might go 'south' to Adelaide for a
break. There was sense in this suggestion as the boys had continued
to be plagued with sicknesses such as tonsilitis that required
expensive long trips to hospital there. So the family travelled to
Adelaide where they bought a house for Myrtle and the children to
live in.

It was a lonely existence for Myrtle in Adelaide, and despite
Kidman's assurances to Con, the money he had offered never
materialised. Con and Myrtle revived the plan to buy their own

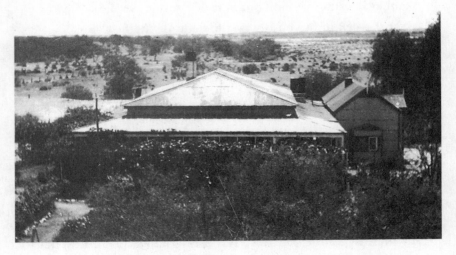

The manager's homestead at Wonnaminta Station, New South Wales, circa 1930.

land, but with the Depression just beginning, the Adelaide house was now worth only a fraction of what they had paid for it.

In something of a reverse, doctors were also now advising Myrtle to take Garry to a warmer climate, and when Con suggested she come back to the outback Myrtle agreed. She let the 'White Elephant', as she called the Adelaide home, and returned this time to Wonnaminta, where Con and the other men had moved the manager's residence.

Reviving the gardens and putting the buildings back into order were Myrtle's first priorities. The children took up their correspondence courses and Con returned to mustering, shearing and the daily grind of station life. Myrtle rued the fact that the Depression and what turned out to be cuts to Con's salary meant the boys could not go to boarding school and participate in the education and sporting activities available there. But they made the most of what they had to hand, with cricket matches between station teams and others in the district, or golf games on improvised station courses.

Out of all the worry and anxiety came one thing — Myrtle's book titled *No Roads Go By*, based on her journal. The book found a publisher and received wide acclaim when it appeared in 1932.

It drew attention to the difficulties of women with sick children in the outback. Through a chance meeting with the Reverend John Flynn, who was on a bush tour, and a talk about her difficulties to some businessmen, she was able to help Flynn raise money for his Australian Inland Mission Aerial Medical Service based at Cloncurry.

Flynn would travel around Australia with a copy of *No Roads Go By* in his suitcase. He found it helped fundraising for his Flying Doctor Service to read from the chapter about Myrtle's terrible journey with Alan over the sandhills to hospital.

John Flynn's work would continue and the Flying Doctor Service would grow to employ, through the assistance of public donations and government grants, radio transmitters, aeroplanes, pilots and doctors to bring what John Flynn called 'a mantle of safety' to outback families.

Myrtle was delighted she had been able to help raise funds to relieve the lot of outback women like herself. But the Whites' financial situation was not improving.

In 1937 the Depression began to ease. Myrtle described that year as one of:

> . . . much portent . . . Prosperity was steadily returning —
> but not for us. At the beginning of the depression one
> hundred and fifty pounds a year had been cut from the
> Boss's [Con's] salary, a further one hundred pounds
> followed a little later. We expected to share in the lean
> years, but, having done so, also expected to share in the fat
> — which we didn't. The cuts in the Boss's salary — much
> more than fifty per cent — were never restored . . .[32]

Another property had been added to Con's management with no addition to his salary. Sidney Kidman, who, despite letting Con down on occasions, had valued his management, died in 1935. Con finally understood Kidman's promises would never be fulfilled. The 'White Elephant' in Adelaide was still worth less than the money they had paid for it many years earlier, and too often their tenants were late in rental payments. Con was now fifty-five, Myrtle forty-nine. The dream of owning their own land was at an end.

During the year Con was struck down with flu which turned into bronchial pneumonia, but he continued to work hard. He had not taken more than six weeks' sick leave in twenty-two years. To his surprise he received a letter from the board of directors asking for his resignation. Despite having eventually received a substantial bonus, Myrtle was disgusted by Con's treatment. She wrote bitterly:

> 'Owing to ill health and advancing years' the Boss was deemed incapable of doing his job; yet on his departure the Powers that Be found it necessary to allot that same job, or jobs, to not one man, but three . . . in addition, the car that had played such a sinister part in our lives was replaced by a *new* one without loss of time . . . [33]

A BITTER-SWEET END

Similar feelings of frustration and depression experienced by the Whites were felt by Katie and Langloh Parker when Langloh was bankrupted. Langloh had stayed on as manager at Bangate working for Dalgety's for a short time, but there were differences of opinion. Eventually the Parkers held a final auction sale and moved to the neighbouring and much smaller run called Grawin South, which they had purchased some time before. Here they lived in a humble bush dwelling with a bark roof and ant-bed floor. It cannot have been easy for Katie but she bore it far better than Langloh. He was now sixty, felt his life had been a failure and became immensely depressed.

Katie, however, had her writing to fall back on. She worked to collate and refine the Aboriginal stories she had collected, and sent a manuscript copy to the publisher David Nutt in London. The manuscript was accepted and Katie's first book appeared in 1896 with an introduction by the noted anthropologist Andrew Lang. Sales of *Australian Legendary Tales* were strong enough to warrant a second edition in 1897, and a second collection of stories, *More Australian Legendary Tales*, in 1898.

While Katie continued to write about the bush and her Aboriginal friends in contributions to journals and newspapers, Langloh could not shake off his depression. Hoping a change of environment might cheer him, the Parkers went to stay with Katie's brother George Field on his station in western Queensland. But the drought continued there and Langloh found little relief.

Katie and Langloh moved into rented rooms in Sydney. Early in 1903, Langloh suffered pain in his stomach and could not eat. He was eventually diagnosed with cancer of the stomach. Katie, now forty-seven, nursed him through six months of terrible suffering before he died.

Katie still had a small income from Grawin South where the seasons were now better and in 1904, two years after Langloh's death, she decided to take a trip to England. It was a chance to see where her ancestors had come from, a place she had always wanted to visit.

On board ship, published authoress Mrs Langloh Parker, by now quite a celebrity, met a tall, quiet bachelor lawyer who was fond of books. His name was Randolph Percy Stow and they saw London together. Perhaps Percy fell in love with Katie's warmth, energy and quick wit. Katie knew he could never replace Langloh, who had been the love of her life, but she was older now. She craved different things from when she was eighteen, and she and Randolph had so many interests in common. Neither of them had children to worry about, so when Stow proposed they get married in London and surprise their relatives with a *fait accompli* Katie accepted.

They married quietly amid the splendour of St Margaret's, Westminster, and returned to South Australia to live at Glenelg, where Katie and her family had lived before her marriage to Langloh.

Their lives were agreeable. Both she and Percy loved books and art and led an interesting life, entertaining writers and artists and travelling overseas every year. The Stows were close friends of Hans Heysen and his wife and owned a marvellous collection of Heysen's paintings.

In 1905 Katie revised and enlarged some chapters from her children's book on Aboriginal legends and republished them as an adult book in London under the title *The Euahlayi Tribe: A Study of Aboriginal Life in Australia*. This book also included twelve chapters that were originally part of the *My Bush Book* manuscript, as well as a long and detailed introduction by Andrew Lang.

Katie corresponded with ethnologists all around the world and in 1930 wrote another book *Woggheeguy: Australian Aboriginal Legends*, published by Preece of Adelaide. It was beautifully illustrated by her friend Nora Heysen, daughter of Hans and the first woman ever to win an Archibald Prize. (This book has now become a valuable collector's item.)

Katie died at her home, No. 5, Kent Street, Glenelg, in March 1940, and was buried in St Jude's Anglican cemetery. *Australian Legendary Tales* continued to be read overseas and was republished after her death in both American and Russian editions. *The Euahlayi Tribe* was recently placed on the internet as part of the Gutenberg Project for disseminating important books internationally.

ESCAPE FROM THE SAND

After selling the 'White Elephant' the Whites had just enough money to buy an old rambling guesthouse at Aldgate in the Adelaide Hills. Doris had already set herself up in an employment agency catering for the needs of people on the land. She left her business to help Myrtle run the guesthouse. Then she met Jim Chambers, a man who loved horses and the outback as much as she did. They became engaged and after marrying, Jim and Doris returned to the outback — eventually in 1948 to manage Wonnaminta.

With the guesthouse to run, Myrtle was kept busy cooking, cleaning and trying to make time to write between domestic chores. When World War II broke out in 1939, both White boys were old enough to enlist, which meant another heartache for Myrtle. But she was nevertheless proud of them.

In the second year of the war tragedy struck. Con died of a massive heart attack. She soldiered on alone at the guesthouse but there was another bitter blow in store: Garry's plane was declared missing on a flight over Malaya. Devastated by the news, Myrtle refused to admit Garry could be dead. She attended spiritualist meetings and had her belief that Garry would eventually return bolstered by mediums.

'There is no death,' she wrote at the end of her second book, published in 1955, thinking, as always, of Garry lost somewhere over Malaya.[34] Sadly the dead were dead and would never return.

Author Myrtle Rose White, as pictured on the jacket of No Roads Go By.

At the end of the war, Alan was demobilised and returned to his favourite way of life — like his father he was happiest on the land.

Gradually Australians recovered from the effects of World War II. Publishing and paper supplies became easier to obtain. Myrtle's best-selling book *No Roads Go By* was republished in 1952 and became popular with a younger crop of readers.

In 1954 a special edition of *No Roads Go By*, illustrated by Elizabeth Durack, was published in Britain where it also proved very popular. The book showed British people what the outback was really like. It brought Myrtle a swag of letters from English wives and mothers who admired her courage in raising children under great difficulties. She donated some of her royalties to the Flying Doctor Service in memory of her old friend John Flynn, who had died three years previously, his ashes interred under a cairn of stones in the shadow of Mount Gillen, near Alice Springs.

In those days Myrtle wrote her books by typing them slowly using two fingers on an old Corona portable.[35] She typed and retyped her manuscripts, making carbon copies and undertaking all the corrections slowly and laboriously.

The wonder is that she managed to complete *No Roads Go By*. She had written it while running a large homestead, ordering all the supplies, caring for three children and a husband, supervising meals for station hands and battling sand in a home which lacked any of the labour-saving conveniences that women take for granted today.

The title *No Roads Go By* was a quotation from a poem by Banjo Paterson. The book's grim humour and its account of the gritty realities of outback life, so different from *We of the Never-Never*, touched a chord in the heart of the public. It was praised by the *Times Literary Supplement* and the *Times Literary Review.* Myrtle was asked to write another book and produced a novel the following year titled *For Those That Love.*

In the Adelaide Hills, while answering letters from readers, Myrtle continued to run her guesthouse efficiently. She would tap away at her latest book in what little spare time was left. Her style was humorous and unpretentious.

As a thank you for years of patient work for her family, Myrtle was taken to India on holiday by Doris and Jim Chambers. Myrtle insisted on visiting an orphanage near Bombay to which she donated some of her royalties from *No Roads Go By.*

In her later years Myrtle enjoyed attending meetings of the Fellowship of Australian Writers, met fellow authors, such as Kylie Tennant, and visited art exhibitions with Miles Franklin and her artist friend Pixie O'Harris.[36] Myrtle's final book was *From That Day to This.*

In July 1961, when Myrtle was seventy-two and visiting Alan who was running the vast Lalla Rookh Station in the outback near Port Hedland, she complained of feeling tired and retired to bed early. That night she died in her sleep. After cremation, half her ashes were interred in her husband's grave, the other half taken to Wonnaminta.

ENDNOTES

CHAPTER 1: FARMING FRESH FIELDS

1   Two accounts of the life of Georgiana Molloy and the Bussell family can be found in Hasluck, Alexandria, *Georgiana Molloy: Portrait with Background*, Oxford University Press, Melbourne, 1955; and Lines, William J., *All Consuming Passion: Origins, Modernity and the Australian Life of Georgiana Molloy*, Allen & Unwin, Sydney, 1994. The more recent Lines book frequently adopts a different view from Hasluck's, especially regarding Aboriginal and colonial relations.

2   *The Australian Dictionary of Biography*, Vol. 2, 1788–1850, Melbourne University Press, Melbourne, 1967, relates that Captain John Molloy was named after his foster father, Captain A.J.P. Molloy, a penniless sea captain dismissed from the British Navy for cowardice in 1795. The registration of John Molloy's death in October 1867 at Busselton Court House gives his birthdate as 5 September 1780. In an article entitled 'Links with the Past', published by Horace Stirling in the Perth *Sunday Times* of 22 May 1921, the author records that John Molloy's fees at Harrow and Oxford were paid by an unknown benefactor. Stirling records, too, that on reaching his majority Jack Molloy was handed a sum of money by lawyers acting for the Duke of York to buy himself a commission as an officer in the army or navy.

Captain Molloy's regiment was widely known as the 'Green Jackets' because, instead of wearing red jackets, like the rest of the British Army, they camouflaged themselves in dark green.

3   For details about the Swan River Association, see Battye, J.S., *Western Australia*, Clarendon Press, Oxford, 1924; Uren, Malcolm, *Land Looking West: The Story of Governor Stirling in Western Australia*, Oxford University Press, London, 1948; the James Stirling papers, Battye Library, State Library of Western Australia, Perth; and Cameron, J., 'Information Distortion in Colonial Promotion: The Case of the Swan River Colony', *Australian Geographical Studies*, Vol. 12, No. 1, 1974. See also *ADB*, Vol. 2, *op. cit.* entries on Thomas Peel and on Solomon Levey.

4   Ogle, Nathaniel, *The Colony of Western Australia. A Manual for Emigrants*, James Fraser Publishers, London, 1839, the unfortunate Ogle being another of the Swan River settlers.

5   Bussell Family Papers, Battye Library, State Library of Western Australia, Perth.

6   Letter from Georgiana Molloy to Helen Story, 25 January 1830, Battye Library, Perth.

7   Friend, Mary Anne, Journal, 1834, cited in de Vries-Evans, Susanna, *Pioneer Women, Pioneer Land*, Angus & Robertson, Sydney, 1987, pp. 243–51. Captain and Mrs Matthew Friend, who had been interested in receiving a land grant, took their ship to Tasmania and were given a land grant there instead. Mary Anne's story was related in *Another Two Years at Sea* by Jane Roberts & M.A. Friend, London, n.d.; see also *ADB*, Vol. 1, *op. cit.*, pp. 417–18.

8   Georgiana Molloy to Helen Story, 1 October 1833, Battye Library, Perth.

9   The duties of a Government resident magistrate were listed in a decree from Lieutenant Governor Stirling dated 21 March 1831, cited in Hasluck, *op. cit.* appendix D.

10   Captain Molloy named various points on his land at Augusta, WA, after a different title of Frederick, Duke of York, such as Point Frederick, York Street, Duke's Head and Osnaburg, the duke being also Duke of Osnaburg.

11   Georgiana Molloy to Maggie Dunlop, 12 January 1833, Battye Library, Perth.

12   Fanny Bussell to Mrs Frances Bussell, 21 April 1833, Bussell Family Papers, *op. cit.*

13   *Ibid.*

14   Bessie Bussell to Fanny Bussell, 5 November 1833, Bussell Family Papers, *op. cit.*

15   In fact Georgiana was wrong. The Bibbulmun used broken glass for *tipping* their spears to make them far more deadly, as glass splinters had terrible effects on wounds.

16   Georgiana Molloy to Helen Story, 8 December 1834, Battye Library, Perth.

17   Georgiana Molloy to Mrs Kennedy, 29 May 1833, Cumbria Record Office, Carlisle, and Georgiana Molloy to Elizabeth Besley, 13 November 1833, Battye Library, Perth.

18   Georgiana Molloy to Helen Story, 8 December 1834, Battye Library, Perth.

19   Bussell, Bessie, Journal, Bussell Family Papers, *op. cit.*

20   Bussell, Bessie, to Capel Carter, 13 September 1835, Bussell Family Papers, *op. cit.*

21   Bussell, Bessie, Journal, Bussell Family Papers, *op. cit.*

22   *Ibid.*

23   *Ibid.* See Hasluck, *op. cit.*, pp. 164–5. Lines, *op. cit.*, who is far more sympathetic to the Bussells, does not mention the noisy corroborees at Windelup. On p. 299 he details the story of the Vasse settlers and the gradual extinction of the Wardandi whom Lines refers to simply as 'Nyungar'. AITSIS Library states that 'Nyungar' is a generic word and the clan around Augusta and the Vasse were Wardandi-Bibbulmun.

24   Georgiana Molloy to Helen Story, 8 December 1834, Battye Library, Perth.

25   Georgiana Molloy to Captain Mangles, 25 January 1838, Battye Library, Perth.

26   The fine was so small that in spite of the efforts of the Exeter Hall reformist movement, who wanted native people treated as British subjects with the full rights of any subject of the British Crown, settlers continued to murder members of the Wardandi-Bibbulmun. The end result was that by 1907 the largest group of Aborigines in Western Australia had died out, either murdered by settlers or dead from imported diseases such as measles, mumps and syphilis, or from alcohol addiction. The death of the last member of the Bibbulmun was recorded by Daisy Bates, who had made an anthropological study of various Bibbulmun groups and their language. In 1907 Daisy described burying Joobaitch, the last of the Bibbulmun. She recorded in her memoirs that when Captain Stirling arrived at Swan River in 1829, he estimated over 1500 Bibbulmun roamed the country from Perth to the Vasse.

27   Georgiana Molloy to Captain James Mangles, 31 January 1840, Battye Library, Perth.

28   In the 1830s, decades before the great Hungarian scientist Ignaz Semmelweiss made his important discovery that puerperal or childbed fever could be prevented using antiseptic methods, infection was frequently passed to the mother from the unwashed

hands and blood-stained clothing of the doctor or midwife. These discoveries came too late to help Georgiana and many women like her.

29   Georgiana Molloy to Captain Mangles, June 1840, Battye Library, Perth.

30   The account of John Ramsden Wollaston's stay with the Molloys is contained in Wollaston's *Picton Journal*, Paterson Brokenshaw, Perth, 1948.

31   Wollaston, *Picton Journal, op. cit.*, pp. 34–6 and 161.

32   Georgiana Molloy to Captain Mangles, n.d., Battye Library, Perth.

33   Cited by Hasluck, *op. cit.*, pp. 177, 479.

34   See Moyal, Ann, *A Bright and Savage Land: Scientists in Colonial Australia*, William Collins, Sydney, 1986, p. 109. Unauthorised appropriation of women's work continued for decades. Professor Radcliffe-Brown plagiarised Daisy Bates' unpublished study and never even returned her original when she requested it. It was published in Bates' own name after her death as *The Native Tribes of Western Australia*. Note also Professor Edgeworth-David's appropriation without permission of the scientific research of Georgiana King. These were not the only cases. Women were banned from membership of most scientific organisations, including London's prestigious Royal Geographical Society which, in the 1870s, turned down applications for membership from Gertrude Bell the archaeologist, and Mary Kingsley the explorer of Africa, only admitting them in the 1880s with reluctance.

CHAPTER 2: THE MOTHER OF THE NORTH-WEST

1   Nancy E. Withnell Taylor's biography of her grandparents, *A Saga of the North West: 'YEERA-MUK-A-DOO'*, Hesperian Press, 2002, provided material for this chapter. Nancy E. Withnell Taylor was the daughter of the late Horace Withnell, one of Emma and John Withnell's twin boys. Information on Emma Withnell comes also from *ADB*, Vol. 6. *op. cit.* Emma's life has also been briefly related by Eve Pownall in *Mary of Maranoa: Tales of Australian Pioneer Women*, F.H. Johnstone, Sydney, 1959. Emma is also mentioned by J.S. Battye & M.J. Fox in *The History of the North-west of Australia*, Jones, Perth, 1915.

2   As well as Emma Withnell, their illustrious descendants would include the famous mining entrepreneur Langley 'Lang' George Hancock.

3   Cited in Taylor, *op. cit.*, p.12.

4   Later the entire area with Roebourne, Cossack and Port Hedland as its main ports would become known as the Pilbara. Nickol Bay was named by Francis Gregory.

5   There is no record as to how many days the Withnells had to remain on the island before the *Sea Ripple* could be refloated.

6   It was usual in Emma Withnell's day for a ship to sound one gunshot on arrival and a second one on landing.

7   The chair is today in the Roebourne Museum.

8   Withnell family records, cited by Taylor, *op. cit.*

9   It must have taken the Withnells years to increase their stock to an economically viable flock by breeding alone. It is likely that they purchased additional sheep, perhaps with some financial assistance from Emma's father, George Hancock.

10   Cited in Taylor, *op. cit.* and Pownall, *op.cit.*

11   Sholl, R.J., Journal 1886, Manuscripts Department, Battye Library, Perth.

12   Vaccinations against smallpox had begun after Edward Jenner developed his cowpox vaccine in 1796.

13   Taylor, *op. cit.*, p. 123.

14 Nancy E. Withnell Taylor describes the friendship between the Withnells and the Ngarluma. Emma's son John would write a book about the Aboriginal tribes of the north-west of Western Australia and provide Daisy Bates with information for *The Native Tribes of Western Australia*, National Library of Australia, Canberra, 1985 (published posthumously).

15 Emma Withnell renamed Sherlock Station, Brooklyn, but from records it appears that Sherlock Station remained the more widely used name.

16 Figures from Taylor, *op. cit.*, p. 230.

17 *Ibid.*, p. 236.

CHAPTER 3: MOTHERING SEVEN LITTLE AUSTRALIANS AT ALICE SPRINGS

1 Information about life at the telegraph station has been derived largely from the memoirs of Atlanta's eldest daughter, Doris Bradshaw (Blackwell), who provided a lively account of an intelligent girl growing up in the outback in *Alice on the Line* (Doris Blackwell and Douglas Lockwood, Rigby, Adelaide, 1965). Using extracts from her father's diary, Doris presented a rather more vivid portrait of him than of Atlanta. Additional information about life at the Alice Springs Telegraph Station is contained in Francis Gillen's collected letters to Professor Baldwin Spencer, *My Dear Spencer: The Letters of F.J. Gillen to Baldwin Spencer*, eds. Mulvaney J., Morphy, H. & Petch, A., Hyland House, Melbourne, 1997; Brown, Shirley, *Alec, A Living History of the Telegraph Station*, Alice Springs, 2002; and Thomas Bradshaw's photographs on display at the old telegraph station, Alice Springs.

The original Alice Spring rises in a waterhole in the normally dry riverbed of the Todd River, named after Alice Todd. The telegraph route through 'Alice Spring' was discovered by Scottish-born explorer John Ross, the second man to cross the Australian centre after John McDouall Stuart. After the telegraph station and post office were moved to Stuart (renamed Alice Springs), the buildings at the old telegraph station housed children removed from Aboriginal mothers. It was then known as the Half-Castes Home.

Interestingly, John Ross was the great-grandfather of Alec Ross, a part-Aboriginal man who works as a guide at the old telegraph station who was removed from his mother when he was sick. 'That's why I was taken from my mother and "removed" to the Alice Springs Telegraph Station. If I hadn't been taken away I'd never have enjoyed the life I live today. I understand why they took us away and gave us good meals to get me back into good health again . . . because my mother lived like her people did centuries earlier — a rough kind of life, surrounded by dogs — out in the bush with nothing,' Brown, *op. cit.*

2 Thomas Bradshaw seems to have been a distant relative of Aeneas Gunn's cousin Joseph Bradshaw, a pioneer of the Kimberleys. Joseph Bradshaw has gone down in history because, when searching for new grazing lands for his cattle, he discovered the mysterious and elegant cave paintings of the Kimberley region known by Aboriginal people today as Gwion-Gwion. A dispute now rages over whether they were painted by Aborigines who have lost this particular technique (so different from other Aboriginal art) or were painted by people from elsewhere, possibly South-east Asia, or, as researcher and author Graham Walsh believes, by a people who predated Aborigines in that area.

3 Stationmaster Stapleton was speared to death by Aborigines at Barrow Creek Telegraph Station, and the future Superintendent Ernest Flint was also speared and left

for dead but later recovered. The death of Stapleton led to a massacre of the local Aborigines by white troops and native police, who on occasions took a very active part in neck-chaining and killing rival Aboriginal tribes.

4   The old Ghan steam train, known as the 'Red Rattler', ran from Adelaide to Oodnadatta; the new Ghan, in 2004 linked to Darwin, does not pass through Oodnadatta. However, the old part of the line is almost as bumpy as the line Atlanta travelled on. The new line between Alice Springs and Darwin is considerably smoother and fulfils the hopes of the pioneers that one day the Australian continent would be traversed by a train.

5   See Hill, Ernestine, *The Territory: A Sprawling Saga of Australia's Tropic North*, Angus & Robertson, Sydney, (1951) 1981, p. 212 for a description.

6   Blackwell & Lockwood, *op. cit.*, p. 38.

7   *Ibid.*, p. 35.

8   See Brown, Shirley, *Alice Springs, Past and Present*, Brown Publishing, Alice Springs, 1993, p. 6.

9   Ownership of the Hermannsburg Mission was handed to the Aboriginal people in 1982.

10   Information about Constable Willshire in Strehlow, T.G.H., *Journey to Horseshoe Bend*, 1969.

11   Spencer and Gillen's *The Native Tribes of Central Australia* influenced contemporary anthropological theory, although some of the authors' social Darwinian assertions about the fossilised society and childlike character of the Arrernte arouse great controversy today. Despite some of his conclusions, Francis Gillen is deemed an important figure in the history of anthropology. Gillen made wax dictaphone recordings of the Arrernte (also known as the Arunta or Aranda) and was allowed to take photographs of secret initiation ceremonies. His diary was published by the South Australian Museum, Adelaide, in 1968; the museum holds the original, along with an important collection of Gillen's photographs of Arrernte ceremonies. Thomas Bradshaw's photographs of his family life and of the local Arrernte are owned by the Northern Territory Department of Primary Industry, Planning and Environment, Arid Research Centre, Alice Springs.

12   According to Stuart Traynor, Senior Interpretive Officer for NT Department of Primary Industry, Planning and Environment, the remaining glass-plate negatives of Thomas Bradshaw's are housed in a safe in the department's office at Alice Springs and a display of prints at the telegraph station. The originals cannot be seen but there is an album of high-quality prints in the department's library. Some glass-plate originals were destroyed by mistake when the Bradshaw family lived in Adelaide.

13   *Naragu* (or namesake relationship), where one person is named after another, is common in Aboriginal society. This seems to have occurred with Tryphena (who appears as Tryff in Thomas Bradshaw's photograph album). She was named after Mrs Tryphena Benstead, wife of Bill Benstead, a pioneer pastoralist who had raised her.

     Information about Amelia Pavey from telephone interviews with Rosalie Kunoth-Monks, Amelia's granddaughter, 12 and 18 July 2004, and from NT Primary Industry, Planning and Environment department library, Alice Springs. Jack Pavey appears in the library records as Amelia's father. Kunoth-Monks confirmed that Jack Pavey was Amelia's father and that Amelia was angry and distressed that he had abandoned her. She had no idea what became of Pavey in later life. Kunoth-Monks also said that the 'Bradshaws were wonderful people who taught Amelia never to hate anyone on the basis of colour'. Kunoth-Monks was the star of Charles Chauvel's film *Jedda*. She lives in Alice Springs.

14   Blackwell & Lockwood, *ibid.*, p. 57.

15   *Ibid.*, p. 97.

16   The grave is still there.

17   Shepherd, Shirley, The Role of White Women in Central Australia Until 1911, unpublished manuscript, Peter Spillett Library, Northern Territory. Details of Arrernte women's food gathering from *The Native Tribes of Central Australia, op. cit.*, which is still a major source of information about the Arrernte and their traditional practices.

18   Blackwell & Lockwood, *op. cit.*, p. 67.

19   *Ibid.*

20   *Ibid.*, p. 100.

21   *Ibid.*, p. 68.

22   The Strehlows returned to Germany for two years to educate their children but come back to Hermannsburg. Their son T.G.H. (Ted) Strehlow would become a famous anthropologist and linguist and a founding member of the Australian Institute of Aboriginal Studies. He would be given some of the most sacred *tjuringa* (ceremonial carvings) of the Arrernte by the elders and many of these are now stored in the Strehlow Research Centre at Alice Springs.

23   Blackwell & Lockwood, *op. cit.*, p. 108.

24   In her memoir Doris does not elaborate on her mother's gynaecological problems but it appears Atlanta could have had one of several complications — from a prolapsed womb to acute vaginitis, a common enough problem among women in hot climates before the discovery of antibiotics in the 1940s.

25   Blackwell & Lockwood, *op. cit.*, p. 108.

26   *Ibid.*, p. 101.

27   *Ibid.*, p. 200.

28   *Ibid.*, p. 201.

29   *Ibid.*, p. 203.

30   Personal communication, Graeme Shaughnessy, Strehlow Research Centre, Alice Springs.

31   Brown, *op. cit.*

CHAPTER 4: THE STORY BEHIND *WE OF THE NEVER-NEVER*

1   For a description of life in the Northern Terriroty and information about the Bradshaws and Aeneas Gunn, see Hill, Ernestine, *The Territory: A Saga of Australia's Tropical North*, Angus & Robertson, 1951 (and subsequent editions), in particular pp. 245–54. Sources for Jeannie Gunn's story are Gunn, Mrs A., *We of the Never-Never*, Hutchinson of Australia Melbourne, (1908) 1982; Gunn, Mrs A., *The Little Black Princess*, A. Moring, London, 1905, reprinted by Angus & Robertson, Sydney, 1982; Gunn Papers 1841–1912, National Library of Australia, Canberra; Nesdale, Ira, *The Little Missus*, Lynton Publications, Blackwood, SA, 1977; *ADB*, Vol. 9, Melbourne University Press, Melbourne, 1983; Linklater, H.T., *Echoes of the Elsey Saga: Research of Pioneers of the Northern Territory in the Epochal Days of the Elsey Station*, self-published, 1980; and Willing, Tim & Keneally, Kevin, *Under a Regent Moon*, Department of Conservation and Land Management, Western Australia, 2002. Also Broadbent, David, 'The Elsey Myth Revealed', *The Age*, 12 May 1979.

2   The *ADB* and Nesdale, *op. cit.*, differ on this point.

3   See Hill, *op. cit.*, pp. 169–70.

4   Jeannie Gunn to Bob Gunn, Gunn Papers, National Library of Australia, Canberra.

5   For the story of Mary Jane (Guy) Bradshaw, see James, Barbara, *No Man's Land: Women of the Northern Territory*, Collins, Sydney, 1989.

6   This reason is mentioned by Jeannie Gunn on p. 4 of the illustrated edition of *We of the Never-Never*, a deluxe edition published by Angus & Robertson in 1987.

7   This aspect of station life is not mentioned in *We of the Never-Never*. The practice of Aboriginal women being used as 'stockmen's gins' occurred on many pastoral stations. It was referred to with indignation by other female authors such as Jessie Litchfield and Katherine Susannah Prichard. Letters held in the John Oxley Library, Brisbane, dated 1910 and addressed to several Protectors of Aborigines by an anonymous writer to complain about the practice of keeping 'stud gins' for the boss's exclusive use, while 'stockmen's gins' were passed from hand to hand.

8   For the following quotes, see *We of the Never-Never, op. cit.*, chapter 2.

9   *Ibid.*, chapter 3.

10   Preludes to *We of the Never-Never*, 1908 edition and others.

11   The following quotes, *We of the Never-Never, op. cit.*, chapter 4.

12   *Ibid.*, chapter 5.

13   For the following quotes, see *We of the Never-Never, op. cit.*, chapter 6.

14   See examples cited in Nesdale, *op. cit.*, and Hill, *op. cit.*

15   Aeneas Gunn to Bob Gunn, February 1902, Gunn Papers, *op. cit.*

16   For the following quotes, see *We of the Never-Never, op. cit.*, chapter 7.

17   For the following quotes, see *ibid.*, chapter 9.

18   For the following quotes, *ibid.*, chapter 10.

19   For the following quotes, *ibid.*, chapter 11.

20   *Ibid.*, chapter 12.

21   The Fizzer drowned trying to cross Cummings Creek. He was buried there and in 1911 reburied at the Elsey Memorial Cemetery about twenty kilometres south of Mataranka.

22   Jeannie learned that Dolly's (Bett-Bett's) father was Lewis Cummings, a Glaswegian employed by the Overland Telegraph Line, who had left the Roper River camp and gone to work in Adelaide and of his later marriage. For almost half a century, possibly to shield Dolly and other stockmen who had also fathered children, Jeannie kept silent, mentioning only Dolly's mother Katie Wooloomool in a newspaper article in *The Age* in 1955.

23   *The Little Black Princess, op. cit.*, p. 156.

24   That Dolly did indeed choose to stay with the Gunns is indicated in a recording made when Dolly was in her nineties as part of a series of oral history recordings about Darwin. A transcript of the interview is in the archives of the Northern Territory in Darwin (NTRS 226). Due to Dolly's advanced age, the interview is rather rambling but the recording is very clear. See also Frizell, Helen, 'Whatever Happened to the People of the Never-Never?', *Sydney Morning Herald*, 3 January 1982; and Linklater, *op. cit.*

25   Gunn, Mrs A., 'Australia's Little Bett-Bett is Now a Grandmother', *The Age,* 15 January 1955.

26   Gunn, A., *Northern Territory Times*, 21 October 1902, cited in Nesdale, *op. cit.*, p. 67.

27   Gunn, A., letter to *Northern Territory Times*, January 1903, cited in Nesdale *op. cit.*, pp. 66–7 and Hill, *op. cit.*, p. 248. Goggle Eye's death is described in chapter 12 of *The Little Black Princess*.

28   *We of the Never-Never, op. cit.*, p. 126.

29   *Ibid.*, p. 177.

30   *Ibid.*, p. 139.

31   For the following quotes, *ibid.*, chapter 16.

32   This was a fairly usual attitude at that time. During World War I, for example, some Anzac soldiers in Egypt and in France (mainly bushmen from Victoria) told their

officers they did not want to be nursed by women; they preferred to be nursed by male orderlies. See the story of Sister Alice Kitchen, in de Vries, Susanna, *Heroic Australian Women in War,* HarperCollins, Pymble, 2004.

33   *We of the Never-Never, op. cit.,* p. 103.

34   Aeneas Gunn to Bob Gunn, 9 October 1902, Gunn Papers, *op. cit.*

35   Jeannie Gunn to Bob and Nellie Gunn, 7 November 1902, Gunn Papers, *op. cit.*

36   *We of the Never-Never, op. cit.,* p. 235.

37   Jeannie Gunn to Nellie Gunn, December 1902, Gunn Papers, *op. cit.*

38   Jeannie Gunn to Bob Gunn, n.d., Gunn Papers, *op. cit.*

39   *We of the Never-Never, op. cit.,* p. 238.

40   Jeannie Gunn's notes and letters to her family and those to the family of her husband are with her personal papers in the Manuscripts Section of the National Library of Australia, Canberra.

41   *We of the Never-Never, op. cit.,* p. 185. These words and many other unrelated passages have been removed from abridged Angus & Robertson editions.

42   See Willing & Kenneally, *op. cit.*

43   See Broadbent, David, 'The Elsey Myth Revealed', *The Age,* 12 May 1979, reporting on the research of Dr Francesca Merlan among the Mangarrayi. See also Merlan, Francesca, *Big River Country: Stories from Elsey Station,* IAD Press, Alice Springs, 1996, pp. x–xvi; and Yunupingu, Galarrwuy, *Our Land is Our Life: Land Rights Past, Present and Future,* University of Queensland Press, St Lucia, 1997.

44   *We of the Never-Never, op. cit.,* p. 68.

45   *Ibid.,* p. 186.

46   *Ibid.,* pp. 185–6.

47   Jock McLennan to Jeannie Gunn, n.d., Gunn Papers, *op. cit.*

48   Jeannie Gunn to Jock McLennan, n.d., Gunn Papers, *op. cit.*

49   McAleer, A.J., 'The Diggers' Heroine of Monbulk', introduction to *My Boys: A Book of Remembrance,* by Mrs Aeneas Gunn, Monbulk RSL, Monbulk, Victoria, 2000.

50   Mrs M. Berry, reminiscences of Mrs Gunn, cited in McAleer, *ibid.*

51   McAleer, *ibid.*

52   Transcript of Dolly Bonson's recorded interview, Northern Territory Archives, Darwin (NTRS 226); also Frizell, *op. cit.;* and Linklater, *op. cit.* Linklater's uncle had known Jeannie at the Elsey.

53   There are no extant letters detailing any contact between Mrs Gunn and Lewis Cummings, or referring to transactions with Dolly's Aunt Judy or her mother. Jeannie mentions in her 1955 article (*op. cit.*) that Dolly had written to her in 1925 saying her mother was with the tribes around old Elsey homestead.

54   Frizell, *op. cit.*

55   According to Jeannie, Dolly told Linklater that she was born in 1892, which would make her fifteen.

56   Gunn, Mrs A., Australia's Little 'Bett-Bett is Now a Grandmother', *op. cit.*

57   In her 1955 article in the Melbourne *Age,* Jeannie gave some of the details of Dolly's early and later life, stating that Dolly was by then a grandmother. She also refers to the 'white strain' in Dolly which allowed the tribe to give her up and encouraged Europeans to protect her. Copy in State Library of Victoria

58   Alfred Derham, letter, cited in Nesdale, p. 160.

59   In 1995, management of Elsey pastoral activities was taken up by Max and Mabel Gorringe. The property is today considered one of the best Aboriginal-managed ones in Australia.

Chapter 5: An English Rose in the Outback

1   Evelyn Maunsell's story about her engagement and her Cairns wedding were published in a local Limerick newspaper in July 1921 when she was in Ireland. It was based on a journal she kept. Evelyn made several copies of her journal, and gave one to her brothers Tim and Rupert Evans, another to her young sister Ida, one to another brother and one to her parents. Decades later these accounts were used by the late Hector Holthouse, a Queensland sugar chemist and journalist, as the basis for his book *S'pose I Die*, published by Angus & Robertson in 1973 and still in print. Much of the account of her life in this book also relies on this source.

2   Holthouse, *ibid.*, p. 16.

3   *Ibid.*, p. 32.

4   *S'pose I Die*, based on a copy of Evelyn Maunsell's diary and written in an era before political correctness muzzled a lot of statements about the past, recounts (pp. 88–9) how when a Chinese man came to Mount Mulgrave looking for a job, Mary told Evelyn that the Coleman River people preferred to eat white men because the Chinese were 'too salty'. Evelyn noted that 'old-timers' she spoke to told her, on the contrary, 'cannibal blacks preferred Chinese . . . because the whites were too salty'.

5   See Pike, Glenville, *Queensland Frontier*, Rigby, Adelaide, 1978; and Holthouse, *op. cit.* p. 7, where Evelyn Maunsell alludes to Jimmy Collins' reputation.

6   The non-payment of this money is at the time of writing a matter of dispute between Aboriginal groups and the Queensland Government.

7   Information on Paddy Callaghan (whom Evelyn Maunsell refers to as Pat Callaghan) comes from Pike, *op. cit.*, p. 274.

8   Litchfield, Jessie. *Far-North Memories,* Angus & Robertson, Sydney, 1930, p. 56.

9   Her first order included four tons of flour; a ton of coarse salt and a bag of fine salt; twelve seventy-pound bags of sugar which often arrived in a sticky mass; one bag of brown sugar (for the spiced, salted beef); one case of tea; cases of raisins, currants and sultanas; twenty pounds each of cream of tartar and bicarbonate of soda; two cases of assorted jams; two hundred tins of treacle and golden syrup; six bags of polished rice; three bags of Chinese unpolished rice; one large cask of curry powder; cases of dried apricots, peaches, prunes and apples; a sack each of dried peas, potatoes and onions; a case of Holbrook's dark brown sauce and one of tomato ketchup; bottles of lemon and vanilla essence; hops to brew home-made beer; and Epsom salts (used to cure everything from indigestion to stomach cramps, warts and piles). The order also included two large cases of pipe tobacco, one case each of wooden and clay pipes, and two large cases of matches. See Holthouse, *op. cit.*, pp. 39–40.

10   Holthouse, *op. cit.*, p. 75.

11   This method is not recommended for the treatment of poisonous bites. The pressure immobilisation method followed by prompt medical attention is the recommended treatment today. See Queensland Poisons Information Centre 13 11 26 www.health.qld.gov.au/poisonsinformationcentre

12   Holthouse, *op. cit.*, p. 98.

13   *Ibid.*, p. 100.

14   Evelyn calls it 'beef tea', a term widely used in Evelyn's time but rarely heard today.

15   *Ibid.*, p. 100.

16   *Ibid.*, p. 101.

17   *Ibid.*, p. 115.

18   *Ibid.*, p. 168.

19   Wrotham Park Station is owned by the Australian Agricultural Company and is run by R.M. Williams Holdings. The former Wrotham Park homestead no longer exists but today there are a series of smaller lodges above the river for visitors who wish to experience outback life in comfort.

20   Holthouse, *op. cit.*, p. 176.

21   *Ibid.*, p. 203.

22   *Ibid.*, p. 204.

23   *Ibid.*, p. 206.

24   Evelyn relates that after the partition of Ireland in 1921 and the declaration of the Irish Republic in 1937, Ballybrood (by now crumbling badly) was taken over by the Government of Eire, or Southern Ireland; see Holthouse, *ibid.*, p. 207.

25   Holthouse, *op. cit.*, p. 217.

26   *Ibid.*, p. 221.

CHAPTER 6: ON THE DESERT FRINGE

1   Undated letter, Gunn Papers, National Library of Australia, Canberra.

2   The *ADB*, Vol. 12, *op. cit.*, records in the entry for Myrtle Rose White that her parents' names were Dinah and Mark Kennewell. Information about the life of Myrtle White comes largely from this entry as well as her autobiographical books *No Roads Go By*, Rigby Ltd, Adelaide, (1932) 1962; and *Beyond the Western Rivers*, Angus & Robertson, Sydney, 1955.

3   The deaths of Jane and Henrietta Field were noted in the Adelaide *Advertiser* of 10 February 1862, and mentioned in the introduction to Katie's journal, published in book form by Marcie Muir as *My Bush Book*, Rigby, Adelaide, 1982. Information about the life of Catherine Langloh Parker comes largely from this source.

4   Muir, *ibid.*, p. 46.

5   *Ibid.*, p. 47.

6   *Ibid.*, p. 49.

7   *Ibid.*, p. 58.

8   *Ibid.*, p. 59.

9   *Ibid.*, p. 62.

10   *Ibid.*, p.105.

11   *Ibid.*, p. 147.

12   *Ibid.*, p. 90.

13   The fact that Katie had tried deliberately to create the sentence structures of Yuwaalaraay was pointed out by Henrietta Drake-Brockman in an appendix to the published edition of K. Langloh Parker's *Australian Legendary Tales*, Angus & Robertson, Sydney, 1954, 1955, and other editions.

14   Muir, *op. cit.*, p. 146.

15   *Ibid.*, pp. 115–16.

16   *Ibid.*, pp. 111–12.

17   *Ibid.*, p. 139.

18   Figures taken from the report made by Dalgety's cited in Muir, *ibid.*, pp. 34–6. In 1892 a bore was put down which successfully watered the property. Today Bangate Station is about a quarter of the size it was in Katie and Langloh Parker's day.

19   *Ibid.*, pp. 133 & 138.

20   Myrtle White is very circumspect about her own and her husband's past, living as she did in an era when authors revealed far less than they do today. Myrtle is careful to

refer to family members by aliases in her books; Con is referred to as the 'Boss'; her daughter Doris is 'Little 'un'; son Alan is 'Boy'; and son Garry is 'Little Brother'.

21 Myrtle refers to Lake Elder Station and its depot as Noonameena and Mirrabooka, which style I have followed here.

22 White, *No Roads Go By, op. cit.*, p. 15.

23 *Ibid.*, p. 50.

24 *Ibid.*, pp. 73–4.

25 *Ibid.*, p. 76.

26 See Mary Gilmore in her introduction to *No Roads Go By*, Rigby, Adelaide, 1932, p. 8 where she discusses 'drefting', which also caused sand to bank up against the windows of the homestead.

27 White, *No Roads Go By*, 1962, p. 97.

28 *Ibid.*, p. 134.

29 Myrtle does not say which town she stayed in, referring to it only as 'the city nearest to [the sandhills]', *ibid.*, p. 139. It was presumably Broken Hill.

30 White, *Beyond the Western Rivers, op. cit.*, p. 78.

31 Myrtle does not specify what her illnesses were.

32 White, *Beyond the Western Rivers, op. cit.*, p. 219.

33 *Ibid.*, p. 225.

34 *Ibid.*, p. 229.

35 Her typewriter was bequeathed to the Mortlock Library in Adelaide and her manuscripts are in the Manuscripts Department of the National Library in Canberra.

36 Myrtle White Papers, Manuscripts Department, National Library of Australia, contain references to Myrtle attending an exhibition at the Art Gallery of New South Wales with Miles Franklin as well as meetings of the Fellowship of Australian Writers.

INDEX